SHAKESPEARE'S PHILOSOPHY OF EVIL

SHAKESPEARE'S PHILOSOPHY OF EVIL

By

LLOYD C. SEARS

Dean Emeritus, Harding College
Searcy, Arkansas

THE CHRISTOPHER PUBLISHING HOUSE
NORTH QUINCY, MASS. 02171

PRINTED IN
THE UNITED STATES OF AMERICA

To my wife, Pattie Hathaway Sears,
for whose inspiration through the years
I cannot begin to express my love and appreciation

PREFACE

NO GENERATION has surpassed ours in its sensitivity to injustice, cruelty, and suffering, for we have seen the ruthlessness of power demonstrated in two World Wars and in several lesser aggressions, in the slaughter of countless millions, in the attempted liquidation of races and nations, and in the callous oppression of minorities. Many, with their ideals frustrated or wrecked by the injustices and violence of our times, have turned bitterly against society and have sought refuge in existentialism and other nihilistic philosophies; for, they feel, if there is a good and all-powerful God, surely he would not permit such injustice and suffering as we have seen. Others have sought solace in denying the existence of Evil except as an irrational tradition or a figment of the imagination, for there seems to be no standard of right and wrong, but all values are a matter of personal opinion, and people approve any means that appears to bring their desired ends. Consequently many, frustrated like Hamlet, have given way to pessimism and despair.

But the problems we face are not new; they were common before Plato and Job, and out of them brilliant minds have developed interesting philosophies. But no one has spoken more vividly, more realistically, and with more ultimate faith on the whole problem of Evil than William Shakespeare, not in obscure philosophical terms, but in terms of living tragedy and triumph; and he has treated the subject with a universal perspective that applies to every age. There have been millions of Hamlets, in different situations, to be sure, but with the same basic doubts and frustrations—wondering why people must suffer injustice and wrong, whether there is any standard of right and truth, or whether our concept of the Good is a mere mental mirage, asking what is the source and the destiny of that which we call Evil, and whether we are actually free souls or only blind puppets of circumstance.

To all these questions and others Shakespeare has a clear and deeply touching word to say, and some of his ideas, such as his definition of justice, we are only now beginning to understand. The following chapters will show how emotionally involved Shakespeare was in these most puzzling of all philosophical questions. They will also add significance and meaning to a number of the plays as they reflect the thinking of the world's most penetrating minds on the fundamental problems of humanity.

To Dr. Charles Reid Baskervill of the University of Chicago, who suggested the importance of this study, I cannot adequately express my appreciation. His scholarship and his interest in the beginning of the study were a constant inspiration. He was eager to see it published, but since his death I have thoroughly revised and, I believe, greatly improved the manuscript which he read.

Lloyd Cline Sears
Harding College
Searcy, Arkansas

CONTENTS

Our natures do pursue,
Like rats that ravin down their proper bane
A thirty evil, and when we drink we die.
Measure for Measure I, ii, 132-134

Chapter 1

"THIS HARSH WORLD"—

HAMLET AND PESSIMISM

The Problem and Background

A man's view of the world has always had a profound influence on his way of life, and the most brilliant minds in every age have tried to unveil the mysteries of human conduct, to understand the causes of conflict, suffering, and frustration—the whole problem of Evil.

The conflicting philosophies of Stoics, Epicureans, and Skeptics centered around it, and in the Renaissance it was the absorbing problem of moral philosophy. But no writer of that, or of any age, has reflected so profoundly or felt so deeply as Shakespeare the problem of evil as it affects humanity, and perhaps no one, even through suffering, has arrived at a more satisfactory solution. Three centuries later, he still has a clear and vital message for us and for our age of doubt and pessimism, of new and radical thought—an age in many ways strangely like his own.

To understand this message, however, we must first survey as concisely as possible the philosophical concepts which influenced his thought. It is not to be supposed for a moment that Shakespeare wrote his plays to develop a philosophical idea. On the contrary, he was above all things a supreme dramatic artist, and such philosophy as is interwoven with the action of his plays is always secondary to the exigencies of his art. Nevertheless, one who reads his plays with understanding is constantly amazed at his acquaintance with philosophy, with the penetration of his thought, and with the skill by which the action clarifies or intensifies a philosophical concept.

How widely Shakespeare was read in the philosophies of his time no one can know, but it is fairly certain that he was acquainted with the writings of a number of the leaders in humanistic thought, including Montaigne, Justus Lipsius, Giordano Bruno, Machiavelli, Gelli and others. With Marlowe he may have attended discussions of the "little Academe" of liberal thinkers as he later enjoyed lively debates with the learned Ben Jonson.

But the general patterns of moral philosophy, both ancient and medieval, had in Renaissance times become so widely disseminated through all avenues of thought—poetry, drama, sermons, proverbs, and moral treatises —that they were a common heritage. Aristotle had come down through the Schoolmen, and, as modified by St. Thomas Aquinas and others, had furnished the basic philosophy of the Catholic Church. Neoplatonism had descended not only from St. Augustine, to whom the reformers had turned for spiritual inspiration, but even more directly from Plotinus, Proclus, Boethius, and Dionysius through the great Neoplatonic revival in Italy. Though Stoicism had interwoven itself in a most confusing fashion with Christian and Neoplatonic thought, it had been definitely preserved in Cicero, Seneca, and Virgil, whom Shakespeare could have read in school.

But it is needless here to trace the avenues of philosophic thought to Shakespeare's time. It is sufficient to say that no period had been so keenly alert to every phase of human learning, and that out of the multiplex systems of moral philosophy, ancient and medieval, Grecian, Jewish, and Oriental, the Renaissance was gleaning its treasures, often strangely confused and chaotic, but casting their patterns of light and shade over the art and the reflective thinking of the age. In this period too no mind was keener than Shakespeare's in cutting through the superficial and arriving at essential truth.

Interesting attempts have been made to reconstruct the philosophical patterns behind Shakespeare's work, and valuable studies have been made of the problem of Evil in *Macbeth* and *Othello*. But so far no study has attempted to analyze the problem systematically and relate the material of the other plays to the background of Shakespeare's thought. That he was intensely concerned with the problem is evident from many of the plays. In *Hamlet* the clash of two world views raises profound questions both for his world and for ours.

In *Troilus and Cressida* he gives a most penetrating analysis of the problem which still
troubles our times—the relativity of values
versus a universal standard. In *Measure for
Measure* he suggests a concept of human justice which is new to many even in our twentieth century, and in *King Lear* he ponders the
justice of the universe. In *Macbeth* he explores
the essence of Evil and its ultimate destiny,
and in the last plays he gives final answers to
many of the questions he posed earlier. Though
Shakespeare's answers, penetrating as they
are, will not satisfy every reader, his broad
and sympathetic understanding of the human
problem is profoundly appealing, and the
background material out of which his thinking
apparently grew gives fresh interpretations of
a number of the plays.

Philosophy after Plato had become dominantly moral and practical. The problem of
Evil, which included the whole range of the unpleasant, ugly, or discordant, demanded a
rational explanation, and this explanation in
large measure determined the world view of
each system of philosophy—Platonic, Stoic,
Epicurean, Skeptic, Cynic, and the various
minor groups. Aristotle had distinguished
between Good and Evil as those qualities which
lead either to the attractiveness of an object
or its repulsiveness: "On the one hand are
'the beautiful,' 'the expedient,' and 'the pleasur-
able'; on the other hand, and opposed to these,
are 'the ugly,' 'the hurtful,' and 'the painful.'"[1]

Philosophically there was no essential difference between a toothache and a murder. Both belonged to the painful, or the unpleasant, and both demanded explanation in a world intelligently planned.

Not until Leibniz do we find an elaborate classification of the aspects of evil, but pre-Renaissance philosophy was cognizant of differences. Earlier Greek philosophers, as well as the monistic system of Plotinus, had attempted metaphysical explanations. Metaphysically, they held, suffering and frustration in the universe arose inevitably from the mere finiteness of things, limitation viewed against a background of the limitless. Because the world is finite, there arises the tormenting thirst for the infinite, and the individual is unhappy because he is an individual and not the whole. The world itself is evil merely because it is finite, subject to change and decay.

The aspects of physical and moral evil grew out of the metaphysical. Physical evil was the suffering produced by the cosmic friction. The mutability and flux of things, the discordant and opposing forces in the universe, caused destruction and loss; and since men were placed in a changing world, their wills and plans, even bodies and minds, were subject to the same mutation. They suffered disappointment, misfortune, disease and death, and "the thousand natural shocks that flesh is heir to." Physical evil, then, included all the suffering resulting from the clash of the individual with his physical environment.

Moral evil was associated with the human will. It was thought of as an imperfection, or disease, in which the mind was divided against itself, but in which its ultimate decision possessed all the qualities of a moral act. Moral evil, however, was inextricably involved with the physical, because any decision of the will might conflict with other wills and result in suffering and loss. This accentuated the problem of evil; for what kind of world is this in which such conflict is possible? It was conceivable to imagine with the Stoics a world of perfect harmony, in which no good conflicted with another, but each was supplementary to all the rest, a whole so perfect that he who should be true to his own self could not then be false to any man. But the concept of such an ideal only emphasized the actual, and moral evil took on deeper significance as it was related to the physical.

Arising, moreover, from the consciousness of evil in a world of human conflict was the problem of universal justice. If it could be shown that in all the cosmic friction the righteous flourished and the wicked were brought low, that there was an intelligent and just apportionment of reward to merit, the explanation of evil might be simple. The mind would acquiesce in the justice and order of things. It is this aspect of evil which was so boldly presented by the author of Job, and which indeed runs through so many of the great reflective tragedies. For the concept of evil challenged the foundations of faith in a rational world and questioned the existence of an intelligent God. The early skeptics expressed the difficulty most succinctly in their famous dilemma: If there is a God, he is either powerless to eliminate the evil of the world, or he does not desire to do so. If he is powerless, he is less than God; if he does not desire to eliminate evil, he is more ignoble than men, for even men would abolish evil if they could.

It is unnecessary in this study to trace the attempts of philosophies, Oriental and European, to account for evil in an ordered world. Only certain broad basic attitudes need here be suggested, while more specific concepts will be presented later where necessary. Epicureanism, observing the problem of evil—the suffering, waste, degeneracy, and injustice in the world—and not able to harmonize it with the providence of loving, all-powerful gods, concluded that the world came about by the accidental clash of atoms whirling ceaselessly through an infinite void. After centuries of constant, unintelligent change the world would disintegrate and dissolve into atoms again, to continue whirling endlessly through limitless space. Without a universal order or plan, without a divine providence, evil was merely another unintelligible accident as natural in every way as good. Thus by excluding the gods the Epicureans eliminated evil as a problem.

The skeptics, as their dilemma implies, accepted as one of their two most positive tenets the non-existence of any supernatural power. Hardly more positive, also, was their theory of the uncertainty of all knowledge, or even of existence. To the skeptic there was no certainty in anything, either good or evil. All was a matter of personal opinion with no foundation in reality.

The Stoic, on the other hand, with his pantheistic interpretation of the world, accepted with implicit faith the existence of God. To him God *was* the universe, and his divine providence predetermined each least event. But with this faith the Stoic was hard put to explain the presence of evil and to harmonize suffering and justice. In this extremity he borrowed from the skeptics their argument concerning the uncertainty of things, and with superb confidence announced that there was no evil in the universe except what might be found in the human will, in its resistance to the divine providence implanted in all natural things. All suffering and human conflict were merely the result of change and therefore neither good nor evil. To hold faith in the gods the Stoics in large measure denied the existence of evil.

These great systems of thought are typical of many later philosophies. The existence of evil forced Plutarch, the Zoroastrians, and the later Manichaeans to accept a duality of primal spirits—beneficent and malignant. Plotinus

champions a monistic interpretation of the
world and labors hard but unsuccessfully to
deny the existence of evil except as a metaphysical necessity resulting from the imperfection of matter. With St. Augustine,
Christian thought became fused with Neoplatonic philosophy. To Augustine the basis
of evil was metaphysical, consisting in the
fact that the creation arose from nothingness
and tends to slip back into nothingness again.
With the exception of Pelagius both Christians
and Neoplatonists associated evil with matter,
and as a result the medieval mind became obsessed with the utter depravity of the flesh
and of the material world. The classic of the
Middle Ages in epitomizing this pious disgust
and hatred of the world was *De contempu
mundi, sive De miseria conditionis humane*
of the young Giovanni Lothario de Conti, af-
terward Pope Innocent III. This famous little
book is extant in an English translation by
H. Kerton as early as 1576 under the title *The
Mirror of mans lyfe,* and its somber echoes
were heard from many a pulpit.

The gloomy world-view of the Middle Ages
was relieved slightly by the rise of Scholasti-
cism with its revival of Aristotle. By cham-
pioning the goodness of all Being, the absolute freedom of the will, the the supremacy
of Eternal Law, out of which grew Reason and
Natural Law, St. Thomas Aquinas prepared the
way for the Humanists with their ideal of the
perfectibility of man. Others like Duns Scotus

and William Ockham, by taking issue with Aquinas's doctrine of Reason and Natural Law and by placing all concepts of moral good and evil in the divine will, or the divine fiat, unintentionally laid the foundation for the growth of skepticism in the Renaissance. For, argued the skeptical, if the reason is of no value in determining good or evil, if there is no certainty in the report of our senses, how can we be certain of any values? How can we know that God has willed or that he even exists?

In the brilliant awakening of the Renaissance with its insatiable thirst for knowledge, the growth of skepticism brought penetrating doubts and questionings. Through the maze and conflict of ideas, however, emerged two broad outlines of reflective thought, two world-views.

The optimistic faith of the Humanists in the perfectibility of man, the freedom of the will, the glory of the present, is in sharp contrast with a revived pessimism of the Middle Ages. Glowing through the Humanistic thought is the superb faith of Stoicism, the influence of Aquinas, and the fine idealism of the Platonists. Darkening the pessimistic gloom are the various philosophies of disillusionment from the Pyrrhonists' keen skepticism, the Cynics' bitter hate, the Platonists' disgust at the world, through Plutarch, Pliny, Innocent III, to the deepening cloud of Calvinism with its revival of the darker aspects of Augustinism.

The Clash of Two World-Views

Hamlet may truly be said to mark the beginning of Shakespeare's reflective study of the problem of evil. In his earlier plays, to be sure, a sense of evil strikes discord into the harmony of things, but usually with staccato notes, sharp, clear, but immediately silent, or with plaintive minors without depth and harshness. At the news of Gloucester's murder in *Richard III* Queen Elizabeth exclaims, "All-seeing Heaven, what a world is this!"[2] The honest Falconbridge, as he finds the body of the lovely child Arthur, is dismayed at the sudden revelation of the wickedness of the world and the uncertainty of life:

> I am amazed, methinks: and lose my way
> Among the thorns and dangers of this world.[3]

In striking contrast with this honest emotion and the violent grief of Constance, the young Dauphin cries, in the sentimental tone of a dilettante in human sorrow:

There's nothing in this world can make me joy:
Life is as tedious as a twice-told tale
Vexing the dull ear of a drowsy man;
And bitter shame hath spoiled the sweet world's
   taste,
That it yield's nought but shame and bitter-
   ness.[4]

In one of the finest passages before *Hamlet* which pictures the evils of the world, we find this same note of shallowness and insincerity. The dethroned Richard II entertains himself in prison by turning his cell into an imaginary world, peopled with discontented thoughts at strife with one another and themselves.

> Thus play I in one person many people,
> And none contented: sometimes am I king;
> Then treasons make me wish myself a beggar,
> And so I am: then crushing penury
> Persuades me I was better when a king;
> Then I am king'd again: and by and by
> Think that I am unking'd by Bolingbroke,
> And straight am nothing: but whate'er I be,
> Nor I nor any man that but man is
> With nothing shall be pleased, till he be eased
> With being nothing.[5]

The passage is a penetrating analysis of one phase of "this all-hating world," the eternal frustration of human desire. Ambitions are thwarted by physical impossibilities, the joy of power defeated by treasons, lowliness made miserable by penury, and even divinest hopes nullified by fears and doubts. It is the inevitable penalty of finitude, the metaphysical source from which all other evils flow. It is the price of being, that must be paid by "any man that but man is," and from which there is no relief except "with being nothing." The curse of the finite is that Will ever exceeds the Power. Even in love the monstrosity, as Troil-

us laments, is that "the will is infinite and the
execution confined, that the desire is boundless
and the act a slave to limit."[6]

The profundity of the truth underlying
Richard's meditation is not destroyed, but
even accentuated, by the childish fancy of the
king, who seems only to skim the surface of
his thought, unaware of the depths beneath.
For him, and indeed in all the plays before
Hamlet, the sense of evil is attached concretely
to individual things, his overthrow by Bolingbroke, his desire to escape his prison, his fear
of poverty; but in *Hamlet* the sense of evil,
growing out of concrete suffering, rises above
it into pure philosophic reflection, a probing
into universal truth.

To arrive at the point of view which *Hamlet*
assumes toward the problem of evil, we must
first understand the optimistic philosophy
which it so profoundly questions. St. Augustine had acclaimed the dignity of man before
the fall and the possibility of his future glory.
Man was not made as a stone, which has only
being, nor even like animals, which have
growth and feeling, but man possesses Reason by which he may know God. Though he is
but little lower than angels, because he is the
Son of God, and because of the glory to which
he can attain, he may become "hayle-fellow"
with the angels and even superior to them.
Yet, this dignity is not because of his worth,
but through the pure grace of God.[7]

With the coming of the Renaissance, how-

ever, the new and intense interest in pagan
philosophies, which were untroubled by the
theological abstractions of faith and grace,
turned the attention of thinkers more and more
away from the absolutism of God to the dignity
of man and the possibilities of human perfection. Man's place as the center of the universe gains prominence over his fall. La
Primaudaye writes:

> When I direct my flight . . . vnto the
> heauens, and with the wings of contempla-
> tion behold their wonderfull greatness,
> their terrible motions . . .   the lively
> brightness, rare beautie, and incomparable
> force of the sun and moone . . . the infinite
> number of goodlie stars . . . and from this
> excellent and constant order of all these
> things, as one rauished and amased, when
> I withdraw my spirite lower into the ele-
> mentarie region, to admire and wonder at
> the spreading of the earth amidst the wa-
> ters . . . when I admire the diuersitie of
> times and seasons, the continual spring of
> fountains, the certaine course of riuers
> and generally, so maine wonderful works
> vnder the cope of heauen, I cannot maruell
> enough at the excellencie of Man for
> whom all things were created. . . .[8]

La Primaudaye condemns Pliny, Homer,
Theocritus, and others for their pessimistic
view of the imbecility and miseries of man,
but at the same time he believes the Stoics

overstated man's excellence in ascribing to
him natural graces which, by the quickness
of his own understanding, might bring him to
perfection. To La Primaudaye the grace of God
was also necessary; but, this once granted,
then "by philosophie we are taught that perfection, which concerneth all the actions and
dealings of man. . . ."[9]

Giovanni Battista Gelli attributes the glory
and excellence of man to his perfect freedom of
will and to his reason. His reason, which is
divine, permits him to know his own excellence and exalts him above all other creatures,
even the incorruptible heavens; for though the
heavens are glorious and the sun out of his
"inexhaustible Storehouse gives light to all
the rest of the celestial Luminaries," yet he
knows not his own excellence and use. Man,
however, by means of his God-like reason and
the freedom of his will, may attain to perfection:

If he lift up his face toward the Heavens
whence he came, and like an inquisitive
Philosopher considers the Beauty of the
celestial Bodies, the wonderful harmony of
Nature, the agreeable vicissitudes of Sea-
sons, and the like, he will soon change himself from a terrestial to a heavenly Crea-
ture, and if despising all the allurements
and obstacles he finds from his body, he
seriously applies his thoughts to the con-
templation of divine Things, he shall almost make himself a God.[10]

Gelli is too much a Platonist to believe that this absolute perfection can be fully attained until the soul is free from the encumbrance of the flesh, but it is, nevertheless, within the power of any man to attain ultimately "a perfection that is hardly to be imagined."[11]

This new hymn to the dignity and perfection of Man, so different in its exultant optimism from the gloom of original sin and predestination, rose triumphantly and filled the Renaissance mind with visions of hitherto undreamed-of achievement. Man, the microcosm, or "little world," contained within himself all the perfection of the universe, even that of a minor god;

> Man is the little world, (so we him call).
> The world the little god, God the Great All.[12]

But among all those to catch the new strain no one sang with bolder, clearer tones than Marlowe. In Faustus, though human effort is conventionally misguided and comes to naught, we have the longing to carry achievement to the utmost limits of the mind of man, by tiring the brain to "get a deity"; and when Faustus is struck with admiration at the glory of the heavens, even Mephistopheles bears witness to the greater dignity of man:

But think'st thou heaven is such a glorious
    thing?
I tell thee, Faustus, it is not half so fair
As thou, or any man that breathes on earth.[13]

It is *Tamburlaine*, however, inadequate as it is in grasping the problem of evil and amoral in its attitude toward cruelty and wrong, that gives us Marlowe's finest philosophy of human greatness. Coming up from the sheepfolds, the young brigand thinks it the part of men to affect "thoughts coequal with the clouds." With "divine ambition puff'd" he feels himself an equal of the gods. It is within his power, inspired by love and beauty, to achieve perfection. For Jove himself once masked in shepherd's weeds,

> And by those steps that he hath
> scal'd the heavens,
> May we become immortal like the gods.[14]

Whether many Humanists shared this extreme philosophy of human greatness, which Marlowe himself could not satisfactorily reconcile with the mystery of death and the fact of inhumanity and cruelty, it is impossible to say. But the significant fact is the tendency in all this new philosophy to exalt the natural virtues, the dignity of man, and the supreme value and possibilities of human life.

Against this bright optimism the reaction of *Hamlet* comes with an impression of bitter disillusionment, like an awakening from idealistic dreams to some hideous reality. The play as a whole contains the elements of both optimism and pessimism, for Hamlet's awakened doubts and cynicism are silhouetted against the brighter background of humanistic idealism. Hamlet has been reared in the philosophy of the time. To him the world had seemed a goodly frame, the brave o'er-hanging firmament a majestical roof fretted with golden fire, and man the perfection of creation. None of the eulogies of men surpasses the admiration of Hamlet:

> What a piece of work is man! how noble
> in reason! how infinite in faculty! in form
> and moving how express and admirable!
> in action how like an angel! in apprehen-
> sion how like a god! the beauty of the
> world! the paragon of animals![15]

The young prince himself has followed the ideals of his philosophy. He is the embodiment of the Humanist's concept of the perfect gentleman: he is the courtier, soldier, scholar, "eye, tongue, sword."

> The glass of fashion and the mould of form,
> The observ'd of all observers. . . .[16]

He is an ardent lover, a dutiful and loving son, a frank and sincere friend. For him the world has had no thorns, and his philosophy of optimism was the natural and normal thing. But when the play begins, a radical change has already started in the thinking of the Prince, which is to deepen by degrees from mere violent grief, through cynicism and doubt, to a settled faith in the futility of life and a hatred of the world.

Just at present we need not be so much concerned about the psychological causes of this change. They have been well attributed by Professor Bradley[17] to emotional shock, and similarly by Miss Cambell[18] to violent grief. That this was the origin and commencement there can be no doubt. Hamlet had to learn the other side of life, or shall we say, life as a whole? He had to experience the evil, as well as the good. But the consciousness of evil grows inevitably out of pain. It was without doubt the sudden and untimely death of Hamlet's father, breaking his idealistic concept of human worth with an acute and vivid sense of the fraility of life, that set in order his whole train of thinking. No doubt, it was also the immediate infidelity of his mother which shattered his faith in the purity of love and revealed to him the hollowness of vows and the strength of fleshly appetite. Out of this consciousness of evil known grew suspicions he could not stifle of worse things yet unseen, and hard upon this came the revelation of his uncle's guilt, confirming his inmost fears and opening to the vision of his tortured soul the bewildering depths of human depravity. And added to all the rest he must bear the unexplained desertion and seeming treachery of the only being whose love might still have lightened the gloom.

Yet it was not so much the sudden loss but the manner of the loss that increased a hundredfold the intensity of his pain: his father murdered, and by a brother's hand, a deed that bore the "primal eldest curse"; a mother idealized in his father's love, turning to incest and beastly lust with the murderer of her husband while harboring, as he supposed, the guilty knowledge of his crime. So Hamlet stood alone, forsaken or separated from those he loved by a dark abysm of crime bitterer than the separation of death.

It is a repetition of the age-old tragedy of Job, but with two important differences. First, the tragic situation in *Hamlet* is far more basic and intense. Job suffered the loss of wealth and the respect of friends, the loss of children who were apparently upright and honorable, physical pain, and finally discouragement from his wife through her love and sympathy for him. But the tragedy of *Hamlet* is the anguish of a sensitive soul over the depth of moral corruption and callous cruelty in those whom he had most honored and loved. In the second place, Hamlet possesses little of the simple patience and humility of Job, and centuries of earnest question and answer also divide their points of view. But fundamentally the situations are alike; each is a soul in pain seeking to solve the riddle of the painful earth.

Far from being simple and easy to understand, however, Hamlet's personality is extremely complex and, superficially at least, so contradictory that he finds it impossible at times to understand himself. He upbraids himself bitterly for being a "dull and muddy-mettled rascal," a villain, a coward, who would not resent a "lie i' the throat, As deep as to the lungs."

The play gives ample evidence of Hamlet's perfection as a courtier and scholar, and though the action involves no war, we have abundant evidence of his ability as a soldier. He is certainly not indecisive, as he is sometimes protrayed; nor is he a weakling too delicately reared to act; nor is he a coward. Instead he reacts instantly when the Ghost motions him to follow, and he resists all efforts to stop him: "By heaven, I'll make a ghost of him that lets me." When Polonius cries out behind the arras, Hamlet's sword is as quick as thought.

He perceives at once the deception of Rosencrans and Guildenstern, and the break with his old friends is decisive and complete. He even looks forward with keen delight to matching wits with them on the voyage. He tells his mother.

> There's letters sealed, and my two school-
>   fellows,
> Whom I will trust as I trust adders fanged,
> They bear the mandate. They must sweep my
>   way,
> And marshall me to knavery. Let it work,
> For 'tis the sport to have the engineer
> Hoist with his own petar. And 't shall go hard
> But I will delve one yard below their mines
> And blow them at the moon: Oh, 'tis most sweet
> When in one line two crafts directly meet.[19]

Quick and decisive also was his change of

the King's commission, for "Ere I could make a prologue to my brains, They had begun the play." When the pirates attack there is no hesitation. Fearless of danger, Hamlet leads the counterattack and alone leaps aboard their ship.

His challenge of Laertes at Ophelia's grave is sudden as a flash of lightning, and his entering the duel in spite of "auguries" is an act of courage and decision. Throughout the play, in fact, Hamlet's personality dominates the action. He has a strength that makes the other characters seem like puppets around him. His intelligence, his wit, his blistering satire and cynicism against spies and "waterflies", his integrity in contast with the sham and hypocrisy of the court, and his ability to act with decision and soundness of judgment give him a force of character that leads us to agree with Fortinbras, that "had he been put on" he would "have proved most royally." Even at the moment of death his concern is for the welfare of the kingdom and he gives his dying voice to Fortinbras.

Neither was Hamlet too "conscientious"— either consciously or subconsciously, as has been suggested—or too delicate to carry out his father's command. In fact he feels prompted to his revenge by both "Heaven and Hell." When he sends his old friends intentionally to their deaths, he says,

They are not near my conscience. Their defeat
Does by their own insinuation grow.

'Tis dangerous when the baser nature comes
Between the pass and fell incens'd points
Of mighty opposites.[20]

Though he expresses a natural "repentance"
at the mistake of killing the snooping Polonius, he considers it a necessary part of his
commission, for

Heaven hath pleased it so
To punish me with this, and this with me,
That I must be their scourage and minister.[21]

And of the King he feels he would even be
guilty himself if he failed to execute justice
upon him:

. . . is 't not perfect conscience,
To quit him with this arm? And is 't not to be
damned
To let this canker of our nature come
In further evil?[22]

Though Hamlet is naturally courteous with
all who are sincere, he speaks with shocking
contempt of the father of the girl he loves as
he lugs "the guts into the neighbor room," and
tells the King that Polonius is "At supper . . .
Not where he eats, but where he is eaten. A
certain convocation of politic worms are e'en
at him . . . you shall nose him as you go up
the stairs into the lobby." And as the attendants rush out, he calls, "He will stay till you
come!"[23]
When he learns from Laertes of the treachery
of the King and the poisoned sword and cup,

there is no "delicacy" with which he drives the "venom" to its "work," and forces the poisoned cup down the throat of the "incestuous, murderours damned Dane." When the right moment comes, Hamlet can act with terrifying swiftness and with brutal callousness and disregard for the feelings of others—qualities which may be essential to the soldier in times of crisis.

But as Coleridge pointed out long ago, Hamlet does have one quality which might prevent impetuous action, or perhaps any action at all: He is a thinker. Shakespeare is certainly aware of the tendency of the scholar to think through and around any course of action, and both Hamlet and Troilus consider it a handicap. Hamlet asks why any one would "grunt and sweat under a weary life," when he "might his quietus make With a bare bodkin,"

> But that the dread of something after death,
> That undiscovered country from whose bourn
> No traveler returns, puzzles the will,
> And makes him rather bear those ills we have
> Than fly to others that we know not of?
> Thus conscience does make cowards of us all,
> And thus the native hue of resolution
> Is sicklied o'er with the pale cast of thought
> And enterprises of great pitch and moment
> With this regard their currents turn awry
> And lose the name of action.[24]

Hamlet is using the terms "conscience" and "regard" in the sense of intense thought. When he sees the soldiers of Fortinbras marching to battle for a little piece of ground

> Which is not tomb enough and continent
> To hide the slain,[25]

he upbraids himself again for his own lack of action:

> Now whether it be
> Bestial oblivion, or some craven scruple
> Of thinking too precisely on the event—
> A thought which, quartered, hath but one part
>   wisdom
> And ever three parts coward—I do not know
> Why yet I live to say "This thing's to do,"
> Sith I have cause and will and strength and
>   means
> To do 't.[26]

Troilus also is contemptuous of those who allow reason to interfere with action.

> Manhood and honor
> Should have hare hearts, would they but fat
>   their thoughts
> With this crammed reason. Reason and respect
> Make livers pale and lustihood deject.[27]

Though Shakespeare knows the scholar is not always a man of action, in Hamlet he balances the qualities of the thinker with a quickness of perception and an intensity of emotion that lead him to act with intelligence. Much has been made of his failure to kill the King as he prays. He is overjoyed by the success of his *Mousetrap* and the King's sud-

den revelation of his guilt. Now there is nothing to restrain him. He "could drink hot
blood, And do such bitter business as the day
Would quake to look on," but when he stands
behind the King with his sword drawn ready
to strike, he suddenly stops. Is it here that the
scholar, the hesitant thinker emerges filling
him with a fear of action? Is it not rather the
far more terrible rage of the soldier who with
difficulty restrains himself from striking the
man in prayer that he may wreak the more
horrible vengeance which the King so justly
deserves?

Though Hamlet condemns himself for in-
action, he is even more fearful that the intensity of his emotions may become uncon-
trollable. He is afraid that, like Nero, he might
even kill his own mother, and his rage at
Ophelia's lie and the "bravery" of Laertes'
grief drives him to the verge of madness.
He values Horatio especially because, unlike
himself, he is not "passion's slave."

We are not here concerned, however, either
with the complexity of Hamlet's mind or with
his suffering, no matter how intense and mad-
dening it may have been. For philosophy suffering is but a symptom, and the thing of
moment is the cause behind it, and the conscious reaction to it—one's explanation of the
world in relation to the fact of suffering and
evil.

Yet it is Hamlet's very intensity of emotion,
his capacity to feel so extremely his father's

murder, his mother's guilt, Ophelia's deception—all the hypocrisy and sham of the court
—that plunges him into such unbearable
bitterness. A Horatio might have accepted all
this as the way of the world and gone quietly
about his own affairs. But Hamlet has idealized
his mother and father, and his love for Ophelia. Suddenly his faith in all that is beautiful
and holy and good is swept away.

His first and immediate reaction, then, to the
evil so unexpectedly revealed is a profound
change from an optimistic to a pessimistic
view of the world. The light went out and left
the world in darkness. It is the natural reaction of a consistent mind, as true today as in
Hamlet's time. Face to face with the stupendous fact of death, sudden, unmerited, deso-
lating, and with the overpowering realization
of evil, of the deepest depravity even in those
whom he had honored and loved, his mind
could find no consistency except in pessimism.
Faith in the justice of the world, the goodness
of human nature, and its capacity for perfection could not be reconciled with blood-red
fact that cried louder than the voice of faith.
Only in a world in some way fundamentally
bad could such manifest evil exist.

It is not strange, therefore, that Shakespeare
represents Hamlet's mind, divided by the irreconcilable antinomy of good and evil, as
seeking its logical and emotional unity in
pessimism. Other minds had been driven to the
same conclusion; it was the prevailing view

of religious thought. From Augustine through Innocent III the tendency had grown to regard the world as hopelessly corrupt and irredeemably lost. Thomas Beard, in his *Theatre of Gods iudgements* voices the religious pessimism of his age. As one is grieved, he says, to see a garden of exquisite flowers "withered and scorched by the violence of some outraged tempest," so one is grieved at seeing the "disorders and hurliburlies" that "disfigure the face of the whole world," men not restrained by any bridle,

> running fiercely into all filthinesse and mischiefe. . . . all which evils are so common and so vsuall at this time amongst men, that the World seemeth truely to bee nothing else but an ocean full of hidious monsters, or a thicke forrest full of theeues and robbers, or some horrible wildernesse wherein the inhabitants of the earth, being sauage and vnnatural, void of sense and reason, are transformed into bruite beasts. . . .[28]

Spenser gives poetic voice to the same gloomy view. His belief that the world was growing daily worse and worse was based not only upon the prevailing corruption, but upon the cosmic shift in the planets which had thrown it so out of balance that the longer it endured the more evil it would become.[29]

> Me seemes the world is runne quite out of square,

From the first point of his appointed sourse,
And being once amisse grows daily worse and
　　worse.[30]

Similarly old Thenot in the *Shepheardes Calender* asks,

Must not the world wend in his commun course
From good to badd, and from badde to worse,
And from worse into that is worst of all,
And then returne to his former fall?[31]

Examples of this gloomy world-view could be
multiplied by the scores. It is not here intended
to imply that Shakespeare was influenced
either by Spenser or by Beard in the pessimism
that colors *Hamlet* and the following plays; it
is only intended to suggest a strong current of
gloom opposing the optimism of the Humanists and growing constantly stronger. Indeed,
the pessimism of *Hamlet*, as we shall see, has
quite a different flavor from this pious and
religious doom of a wicked world. It is far more
basic, penetrating, questioning. But after all
is said, pessimism of whatever brand or degree
is intrinsically related and has fundamentally
the same origin—an emotional or logical reaction to the phenomenon of evil; and it relates
the particular wrong to the universe as a whole.
The crime or injustice becomes an essential
part of the world in which it occurs.

So in Hamlet the consciousness of evil
throws its dark shadow over the whole world.
The ways of men and their customs and ideals

suddenly become stale and unprofitable; the
beauty in life vanishes and leaves only the
hideous and the coarse.

How weary, stale, flat, and unprofitable;
Seem to me all the uses of this world!
Fie on 't! O fie! 't is an unweeded garden,
That grows to seed; things rank and gross in
　nature
Possess it merely.[32]

Through the struggle in Hamlet's mind to retain its unity, even its sanity, this "goodly
frame," the earth, becomes a "sterile promon-
tory"; the "majestical roof fretted with golden
fire" changes to a "foul and pestilent congre-
gation of vapours"; and man in his pride and
glory seems nothing but a "quintessence of
dust." The world has become a prison, and
Denmark one of the worst confines, wards, and
dungeons. The values of life have vanished,
leaving in their place only a sense of its utter
futility and loathsomeness, besides which the
eternal sleep of death is "a consummation
devoutly to be wish'd."

Corruption Mining All Within

When we turn to a more careful analysis of
Hamlet's indictment of the world, we find a repetition of the age-old charges of human depravity, inhumanity and suffering, universal
injustice, the vanity and worthlessness of
human effort, the certainty of death and eternal
oblivion, and a doubt of any compensation be-

yond the grave. Time worn as these fears and questionings are, they nevertheless spring with perennial vigor and freshness in the mind of Hamlet.

This is due partly to the universal and fundamental interest in the problems involved which demand some solution in every thinking mind, but perhaps it is due even more to the technique of the play. In the first place, the mind of Hamlet is not the dispassionate and imperturbable mind of the Stoic, who takes the rewards and buffets of fortune with equal thanks, nor has it been dulled with long community with the world. On the contrary it is alert, penetrating, piercing through the surface of custom and convention to the truth of things, and revealing the truth in all its gruesomeness with an intensity of passion and a bitter cynicism that carries conviction.

In the second place, except for brief intervals, all attention is centered upon him; he holds the spotlight from first to last; his thinking dominates the play. Around him move the currents of ordinary life, feasting and drinking, affairs of state and war, intrigue, the hollow vanity of the court. These serve as background for his thought. Through and through the body of the world his intellect flashes, laying bare its sordidness and sham, its corruption and vanity, but Hamlet walks alone and apart. He is at odds with life because it is earth-centered and belongs to time, while he is bound to death and belongs to eternity. He is like a questioning spirit

from another world weighing the worth of this
and finding it but vanity.

The first element in this vanity of life is the
corruption hidden beneath its surface and min-
ing all within. Outwardly the face of things
is smooth; the court adjusts itself to the change
of kings and moves forward in its customary
way. There is a momentary observance of
"obsequious sorrow," but it is only superficial
show, "With one Auspicious and one Drooping
eye."[33] It is a part of the "uses of this world,"
and Hamlet is stung to the quick with its hypocrisy. The uncle becomes the loving, kindly
father, seeking with smiles to win the favor of
his "son"; the Queen becomes the twice-solici-
tous mother; and life again is filled with gaiety
and laughter. But it is the nature of corruption
that it works below the surface, and Hamlet
learns that in Denmark a villain may smile
and smile, and underneath the smiles hide murder, and that even religion itself is but a cloak
for vice. As Polonius expresses it in a momentary flash of self-searching, and unintentional
irony,

> with devotion's visage
> And pious action we do suger o'er
> The devil himself.[34]

The depravity of his mother was most difficult to understand. He could find no excuse for
her unnatural revolt except an impulse born in
hell. Outwardly her loyalty to the king was
firm, for

> she would hang on him,
> As if increase of appetite had grown
> By what it fed upon.[35]

But inwardly her seeming-virtuous will was
corrupt beneath the level of the beast "that
wants discourse of reason." Hamlet tried in
vain to fathom the causes of her change. No one
with eyes and natural sense could so have
erred; it could not have been love, for at her
age the heyday in the blood was tame and
waited upon judgment.

> Sense, sure, you have,
> Else could you not have motion; but sure, that
>   sense
> Is apoplex'd for madness would not err,
> Nor sense to ecstasy was ne'er so thrall'd,
> But it reserv'd some quantity of choice,
> To serve in such a difference. What devil was 't
> That thus hath cousen'd you at hoodman-
>   blind?
> Eyes without feeling, feeling without sight,
> Ears without hands or eyes, smelling sans all,
> Or but a sickly part of one true sense
> Could not so mope.[36]

It was a viciousness of nature that acted
against all reason, sense, and judgment. But it
was only one instance of the universal depravity of our race, where to be honest is to be
one man picked out of ten thousand, and where,
if every man had his desert, none would escape whipping.

Hamlet's mind recoiled at the indescribable

beastliness of sensual appetite. Love, as revealed by the life of the court and the infidelity
of his own mother, was degraded to the foulness
of lust, and beauty was a pander to transform
"honesty," or virtue, to a bawd. So ingrained
was evil that there was no way to redeem the
nature of man from its corruption; for not even
heaven-infused virtue could "so innoculate our
old stock but we shall relish of it." A nunnery
was the only sanctuary to guard the purity of
the girl he loved, for even marriage reeked of
lust and smelled of the primal hereditary sin.
No more marriages should be allowed. They
served only for the breeding of sinners, and
why should corruption be propagated when
even the honest were better never born? In the
anguish of his soul Hamlet denounced the baseness of all human flesh:

> I am myself indifferent honest, but yet
> I could accuse me of such things that it were
> better my mother had not borne me. I am
> proud, revengeful, ambitious, with more
> offences at my back than I have thoughts
> to put them in, imagination to give them
> shape, or time to act them in. What should
> such fellows as I do crawling between heav-
> en and earth? We are arrant knaves all....[37]

In this torture scene with Ophelia it is the
idealism of the old Hamlet and the intensity of
his love upsurging again within his soul, suddenly confronted and shattered by the present
stark negation of his mind, his loss of faith in

love, his realization of Ophelia's deception,
that drives him almost beyond the bounds of
sanity. The old Hamlet cries, "I loved you once,"
but the Hamlet who has found by bitter experience that love is only lust answers back,
"I never loved you." The struggle between love
and cynicism, faith and negation, wrings his
inmost soul and breaks out in vitriolic denunciation of human corruption and the breeding of
sinners.

In his revulsion at the impurity of love and
hereditary corruption, Hamlet's tone is akin
to the gloomiest note of the old religious pessimism. The Manichaeans had forbidden marriage, or at least birth, because it continued the
corruption of the human race. The Montanists
and other heretical sects held similar views,
and there was even a strong feeling in the
orthodox church that it was better for men
never to be born. St. Augustine cries,

> I am an unhappy man, even a sorry man
> borne of woman, shortlived, full fraught
> with many miseries; even a man that is
> like vnto vanitie, matched with witlesse
> beastes, and already become like vnto
> them . . . . Agayne, what am I? A darke
> dungeon, wretched earth, a child of wrath,
> a vessel meete for dishonor, begotten with
> vncleannes, liuing in misery, and dying in
> distresse. . . . I am a vessell of dung, a
> coffin of rottonnesse, full of loathsome-
> ness and stinch, blind, poore, naked, sub-
> ject to exceedyng many necessities . . .

mortall, and miserable: whose dayes passe away as a shade, whose life glanceth away as a shadow by Moone light, growyng as a flower vpon a tree, and fadyng out of hand agayne, now florishing and by and by withering agayne.[38]

Such complaints at the miseries of men were common in religious thought. Stephen Gosson's *"Speculum Humanum,"* first printed in Kerton's *Mirror of mans lyfe,* turns into wretched verse the same philosophy:

O what is man? or whereof might he vaunt?
From earth and aire and ashes first he came
....
A drie and withered reede, that wanteth sap,
Whose rotten roote is reft even at a clap;
....
A lame and lothsome limping-legged wight,
That daily doth God's frowne and furie feel;
A crooked cripple, voide of all delight,
That haleth after him an haulting heele,
....
A wretch of wrath, a sop in sorrow sowst,
A brused brake with billows all bedowst;
A filthie cloth, a stinking clod of clay;
A sack of sinne that shall be swallowed aye.[39]

Fundamental in Augustine's thought, as in Gosson's, is the idea that all the miseries of man come from the fact that he is "born of woman," "begotten in uncleanness," from a "rotten roote" bringing his evils with him into the world.

Innocent III is even more brutal in denouncing the vileness of human life.

> Truelye man is made of earthe, conceyved in sinne, and borne to payne. Hee doeth commit in this lyfe, wicked and shrewde turnes which bee not lawful. . . . Through his wicknesse hee shall become food to ye fire, meat for worms, and a lumpe of putrifaction loathsome to behold.[40]

The Pope dwells again and again with disgusting coarseness upon the uncleanness of physical birth. "Man is made of dust, of clay, of ashes: he is conceiued in the wanton desire of fleshly luste, in the heat of carnall appetyte, in the foul delight of leacherye, and which is worse, in the spotte of sinne."[41] Any fleshly tie, even of marriage, is unclean in the cardinal's immaculate theology.

> For who knoweth not yt carnall knowledge (although it be in marriage) cannot be had wt out ye motion of the flesh, without the heat of carnall desire, and without ye foul delight of wanton lust. Whereby the seedes conceiued are adulterate, defiled, & corrupte.[42]

Hamlet's mind, in its bitterness against life, has sunk almost to the level of the good Pope's; it is overwhelmed with the uncleanness of love

and the whole process of life. His thought connects gruesomely the breeding of maggots in
dead dogs with human conception in the woman he had loved. Men have become for him little
better than miserable worms "crawling between heaven and earth."

Yet unlike the Pope's, Hamlet's thought is
not so much obsessed with the foulness of sex
as with the insignificance and vileness of men
in their arrogance and pride. He has something
of the spirit of Montaigne:

> Presumption is our naturall and origi-
> nall infirmitie. Of all creatures man is the
> most miserable and fraile, and therewith-
> all the proudest and disdainfullest. Who
> perceiveth and seeth himselfe placed here,
> amidst the filth and mire of the world, fast
> tied and nailed to the worst, most senseless,
> and drooping part of the world, in the vilest
> corner of the house, and farthest from
> heavens coape, with those creatures, that
> are the worst of the three conditions; and
> yet dareth imaginarily place himselfe
> above the circle of the Mone, and reduce
> heaven under his feet.[43]

Even closer to Hamlet's thought is Montaigne's denunciation of the futility of human
rage. With all his ambitions and revengeful
pride, man is but a mere insect on the face of
the earth.

> This many-headed, divers-armed, and
> furiously-raging monster, is man: wretched

weake and miserable man; whom if you
consider well, what is he, but a crawling,
and evermoving Antsneast?[44]

Hamlet's cynicism is Montaigne's heightened
by the bitterness of passion and embracing not
only the insignificance but the depravity of
men.

The Whips and Scorns of Time

Out of this basic corruption of man's nature
arises the second aspect of evil, which fills
the mind of Hamlet with a sense of futility.
This is the injustice of men and its resultant
pain. For a part of the wretchedness of the
human ant is that he is filled with ambition
and cross-purposes, and the clash of wills
brings injustice and suffering. Again Hamlet's
thinking is brought into sharp relief against
the easy-going optimism of the court. Polonius
gives his son a long speech of advice com-
posed of the wisdom of the world, showing
him how to advance himself and take care of
his own interests. It closes with that Stoic
idealism,

> This above all; to thine own self be true
> And it must follow, as the night the day
> Thou canst not then be false to any man.[45]

This concept that all men have a definite
place in the fixed pattern of the universe, and
that, if each is only true to the responsibilities
entrusted to him (his own interests, Polonius
would say), he will then never encroach upon

the interests of his neighbor, was a beautiful
part of the Stoic philosophy. It was based upon
the idea that the world was a perfect unit under
the guidance of divine providence. Seneca had
written,

> All this world, in which all divine and
> humane things are inclosed, is but one: we
> are the members and parcells of this great
> bodie. Nature hath created us akin, in form-
> ing us of the same Elements, and in the
> same enclosure. Shee hath planted mutuall
> loue in our hearts, and made vs sociable.
> She it is that hath composed iustice and
> equitie. . . . Let vs haue this Verse in our
> own mouthes:
>
> > I am a Man, and thinke this true to bee,
> > That nothing humane is estrang'd
> > from mee, . . .
>
> Human society resembleth a vault of stone,
> which would fall except the stones resisted
> one another; so that by this meanes it is
> sustained.[46]

It was beautiful idealism, but the theory of
the "arch of stones" supporting each other,
the perfect harmony of things, rang ironically
against the hard facts of life. Even as Polonius
spoke the Ghost was walking. There was the
revelation of a tragic clash of interests even
between brothers, in which injustice should
be so inextricably involved that, in order to
fulfill the demands of justice, the innocent must

suffer with the guilty and Hamlet fall through his uncle's guilt.

The aspects of injustice are myriad, ranging from trivial matters to the most profound. While this is only a minor problem in the play, Hamlet is yet keenly aware of the injustice of the world in its different forms. Against the envy of others no human goodness is proof. "If thou dost marry," he tells Ophelia, "I'll give thee this plague for thy dowry: be thou as chaste as ice, as pure as snow, thou shalt not escape calumny."[47] In the corrupted currents of this world merit goes unrewarded, while wealth and absurd pomp are licked and flattered, and young waterflies like Osric fill the courts of kings. But Hamlet with his inhuman cynicism sees through the sham of wealth and social prominence.

"He hath much land and fertile," he says of Osric; "Let a beast be lord of beasts, and his crib shall stand at the king's mess. 'Tis a chough; but, as I say, spacious in the possession of dirt."[48] So any fool raised to office, Hamlet observes, is immediately worshipped.

> It is not very strange; for mine uncle is king of Denmark, and those that would make mows at him while my father liv'd, give twenty, forty, fifty, an hundred ducats apiece for his picture in little. 'S blood, there is something in this more than natural, if philosophy could find it out.[49]

Montaigne, with whose work Shakespeare

may well have been acquainted, did attempt to explain the philosophy of it:

> I was now upon this point, that we need but looke upon a man advanced to dignity; had we but three daies before knowne him to bee of little or no worth at all; an image of greatnesse, and an Idea of sufficiency, doth insensibly glide and creep into our opinions; and we persuade ourselves, that increasing in state, and credit, and followers, hee is also increased in merit. We judge of him not according to his worth; but after the maner of casting-counters, according to the prerogative of his ranke. But let fortune turne her wheels, let him again decline and come down amongst the vulgar multitude; every one with admiration enquireth of the cause, and how he was raised so high. Good Lord is that he? will some say.[50]

While Montaigne attempts an explanation, Hamlet only broods with a sense of personal bitterness upon the fickleness of men. But painful as this misprizing of human worth and folly may be, it is perhaps trivial in comparison with other aspects of injustice, which make life intolerable and, except for the fear of the darkness after death, would drive men to self-destruction:

> For who would bear the whips and scorns of time,
> The oppressor's wrong, the proud man's contumely,

The pangs of dispriz'd love, the law's delay,
The insolence of office, and the spurns
That patient merit of the unworthy takes
When he himself might his quietus make
With a bare bodkin?[51]

In these lines the whole inhumanity of man
to man is summarized with the intense bitterness of one who has himself suffered.

But in addition to the injustice of men there
is still a deeper injustice, for man is also called
upon to suffer from the forces of the universe.
Not all the "whips and scorns of time" are
caused by his fellow sufferers, for the keenest
pain comes often from causes outside humanity itself. Sometimes those causes lie in birth,
sometimes in fortune, neither of which men
can control, and yet they mar and blight the
entire life.

So, oft it chances in particular men,
That for some vicious mole of nature in them,
As in their birth—wherein they are not guilty
Since nature cannot choose his origin—
By the o'ergrowth of some complexion,
Oft breaking down the pales and forts of reason
Or by some habit that too much o'erleavens
The form of plausive manners, that these men,
Carrying, I say, the stamp of one defect,
Being nature's livery, or fortune's star—
Their virtues else—be they as pure as grace,
As infinite as man may undergo—
Shall in the general censure take corruption
From that particular fault.[52]

These instances are, to be sure, a combination of both human and universal injustice, for it is the inhumanity of men that allows one defect to color or blot out all other virtues. But the fact that men are born with such defects, sometimes merely touching their outward appearance or manners, but sometimes affecting even sanity itself and breaking down the forts of reason, belongs to the injustice of the universe. For why should men suffer from their birth "wherein they are not guilty"?

These natural defects had been even more painfully described by Innocent III.

> For some come into this world so deformed and monstrous, that they seeme rather to be abominations than men: for whom peradventure it had bin better prouyded, if they had neuer come in sight, bicause they are set forth to be beholden as monsters. For manye of them are borne dismembered, and corrupt in their senses, to the heauiness and sorrow of their frendes, to the ignominie of their parents, and to the rebuke of their kinsfolk.[53]

Hamlet attempts no explanation; he is only pointing out the irony and injustice of things.

But along with the afflictions of birth are the circumstances into which men are forced, circumstances which are neither a part of their own making nor intended by others to involve them, but are merely a part of the complex movement and cross-purposes of life. It is the source of nearly all Hamlet's suffering. From dreams of idealistic philosophy he had been rudely awakened to find himself involved in a responsibility from which his nature recoiled with a cry of bitter pain.

> The time is out of joint: O cursed spite,
> That ever I was born to set it right![54]

This righting of a great wrong was not his own seeking, yet it must absorb the whole attention of his mind, erasing from it "all trivial fond records," all "forms and pressures" past. The commandment of the Ghost was like the voice of doom, changing the course and tenor of his life. He was helpless before its compelling force, for

> heaven hath pleas'd it so.
> To punish me with this and this with me,
> That I must be their scourge and minister.[55]

Food For Worms

With his awakened consciousness of the bitter injustice of things Hamlet's mind broods henceforth on the futility of human effort in conflict with the power of circumstance and fate. Even the supreme values of life are subject to the chance of fortune and of time.

As Mr. Robertson[56] has already pointed out there is a close similarity in Hamlet's thought and that of Montaigne on the helplessness of men against fortune and destiny. Montaigne says:

My consultation doth somewhat roughly hew the matter, and by its first shew, lightly consider the same: the maine and chiefe point of the work I am wont to resign to heaven . . . Good and bad fortune, are in my conceit two sovereigne powers. 'Tis folly to think that humane wisdome may act the full part of fortune. And vaine is his enterprise, that presummeth to embrace both causes and consequences, and lead the progress of his fact by the hand.[57]

Similarly Montaigne shows that fortune often improves our plans, and quotes Meander's statement that "Fortune has more judgment than we." Whether Shakespeare was here influenced by Montaigne as Mr. Robertson believes, or whether he is drawing from other sources, is not pertinent to this discussion. The idea is basically the old Stoic belief in the inevitability of fate, colored with a faint tinge of Christian providence. Against the decrees of destiny of what avail is human will? Hamlet finally surrenders even his better judgment to the direction of fate:

. . . we defy augury. There's a special providence in the fall of a sparrow. If it be now, 'tis not to come; if it be not to come, it will be now; if it be not now, yet it will come; the readiness is all.[58]

Fatalism is often the refuge of the weakened will, the faith of helplessness. Out of a will that desires but is powerless to act, bound by nothing but the mere negation of action, grows a conviction of the futility of effort and the tendency to leave the course of things to destiny.

But the philosophy of futility reacts in turn upon the will and further paralyzes its power of motion. Human effort seems useless and vain, and even the values for which men strive fade into distance and twilight. Hamlet experienced with pain this changing sense of values. Conscious of the reality of evil, and the impotence and frustration of desire, he became more and more convinced, not only of the futility of effort, but of the worthlessness of possible achievement. Greatness was only food for oblivion, and for even the great man's memory to outlive his life half a year he must needs build churches. The note of bitterness against religious enthusiasm is a part of the changed point of view. Human values have been largely swallowed up in the stark negation of evil. There is nothing in life worth living for, nothing worth achieving.

This is the essence of pessimism, and on its darkened horizon the avenging of his father becomes hazy and far away. Intellectually he still clings to its importance, but emotionally he would relegate it to the limbo of forgotten things, among the futilities of life. A gulf has opened between his intellect and will, or rather, between the old Hamlet and the new, the same gulf that separates him from Laertes and the court. To Laertes the value of vengeance was supreme.

To hell, allegiance! vows to the blackest devil!
Conscience and grace, to the profoundest pit!
I dare damnation. To this point I stand,
That both the worlds I give to negligence,
Let come what comes; only I'll be revenged
Most thoroughly for my father.[59]

This is a part of the "uses of the world," but
Laertes does not look beneath the surface of
things nor question customs and conventions;
he is perhaps emotionally incapable of pessimism, and for that reason retains his sense
of values and his power to act. Hamlet, however, has searched the heart of life and found
it vanity. He is forced to spur his dull revenge,
to convince himself anew of its importance. The
player actor has more tears for Hecuba than
he for his murdered father; he has indeed
grown "muddy-mettl'd." To build again a faith
in human values, he recalls the arguments of
his old philosophy, which he never wholly
abandons, but from which his mind has become estranged. If man's chief good is but to
sleep and feed, he is a beast, no more; but surely
with his "godlike reason" and "large discourse," he is called to nobler achievement. He
sees the imminent death of twenty thousand
men over a cause not worth a straw, yet for a
fantasy and trick of fame they go to their graves
like beds. It is the way of the world, the "im-
posthume of much wealth and peace," but in
the estimation of men the honor at stake has
value outweighing life itself. Against this
trifle his own cause seems great. For his honor

is involved, not over a paltry piece of land,
but in an act of justice demanded by both God
and his own conscience. For a moment he has
caught again the view of the world and time.
But only for a moment. At his next appearance
he is looking from the darkness of eternity,
and beside the grave all human values vanish
into nothing.

Fundamental in Hamlet's thinking, and
throughout the play, is the obsession with
Death. The story opens with the walking of the
ghost and closes with a funeral. Its pages are
painted with images of death, with murders and
yawning churchyards and graves filled with
skulls. Death follows us from scene to scene
and beats persistently upon our minds. It is the
mortality of things that Hamlet broods upon,
the decay of love, the corruption of death, and
the oblivion of the grave. He is like the voice
of death pronouncing judgment upon life; for
he looks beyond the vaunting greatness of the
present and weighs time in the balance of
eternity.

Again with consummate art Shakespeare
throws Hamlet into bold relief against the background of life around him. To the court, ab-
sorbed in its daily affairs, death was a matter
of little concern, a necessity of nature which
no man could shun and, therefore, not to be
long lamented. They held the soothing philosophy of Euphues:

Is it strange to see yt cutte off, which by
nature is made to be cut? or melten, which

is fit to be melted? or that burnt which is
apt to be burnt, or man to passe that is borne
to perish?[60]

This is the popular consolation drawn from
Plutarch, derived from the harsher Stoics,
softened and sentimentalized. Since fate is
inevitable, says Plutarch,

> Therefore it becomes men well educated
> to consider that those who have paid their
> debt to mortality have only gone before us
> a little time; that the longest life is but
> as a point in respect of eternity; and that
> many who have indulged their sorrow to
> excess have themselves followed in a
> small while those that they have lamented,
> having reaped no profit out of their com-
> plaints, but macerated themselves with
> voluntary afflictions.[61]

This is the philosophy of practical wisdom
and sound good health that refuses to be
bothered about the inevitable, and centers its
interest not on death but on life.

Hamlet, on the contrary, is obsessed with the
vivid reality of death, and tortured with exquisite pain at the thought of its power over
life. He is the antithesis of the Stoic. No nar-
cotic philosophy numbs the sensitivity of his
soul to the horror of this common end of man,
but he examines it with microscopic minute-
ness, analyzes and dissects and tries to read
its inmost secrets. His mother urges him to
give over his sorrow.

Do not forever with thy vailed lids
Seek for thy noble father in the dust,
Thou know'st 'tis common; all that lives must
 die,
Passing through nature to eternity.[62]

Hamlet replies, "Ay, Madam, it is common." But the contrast in point of view is painfully illuminating. To one the commonness of death dulls it with familiarity; to the other its commonness is the source of deepest pathos. To one who feels the tragedy of death it is no consolation to remember, as the King suggests, that it

 is as common
As any the most vulgar thing to sense,[63]

or that the common theme of nature is death of fathers; it only increases the universal horror and multiplies the pain of the particular by the infinity of the whole.

The universality of death is combined in Hamlet's thinking with its essential earthiness and its degradation of human greatness and pride. Death is the great leveler before whom beggars and kings are weighed in equal balance, by whom the high and the low are brought to a common end—to dust. When Hamlet kills Polonius, he drags "the guts" into the neighboring room, and explains to the courtiers that he has "compounded it with dust, whereto 'tis kin." Man at best is only "food for worms."

Your worm is your only emperor for diet;

we fat all creatures else to fat us, and we
fat ourselves for maggots. Your fat king
and your lean beggar is but variable service, two dishes, but to one table: that's the
end.
    King. Alas, alas!
    Hamlet. A man may fish with the worm
that hath eat of a king, and eat of the fish
that hath fed of that worm.
    King. What dost thou mean by this?
    Hamlet. Nothing but to show you how a
king may go a progress through the guts
of a beggar.[64]

The idea of man as food for worms, as coming
from the dust and going back to dust, is universal, to be sure. It is found abundantly in the
Hebrew scriptures, in some of the prayers and
songs of the church, and in popular proverbs. It
is found most vividly expressed in Augustine
and Innocent III. Augustine cries,

> What am I that speaketh wt thee: woe is me Lord:
> O Lorde spare me. I am but a rotten carcasse,
> Wormes meate, a stinkyng coffin, & foode for
> fire.[65]

Innocent III, as we have already seen, would
make both life and death so loathsome that the
soul would hate the world and long to escape
to heaven. He dwells upon the foulness of the
body and the gruesomeness of decay.

> But when man shall dye, his inheritance
> shall bee with brute beastes and serpents,

for all men shall sleepe in the dust, and the wormes shall eat their flesh. . . . O what a lothsome parentage is that, where rotten-nesse is the father? and what an vncleane stocke is that, which is vnited with worms? For man is conceiued in corruption, and in the burning heate of foul luste, vpon whose dead carkasse the wormes doe wait as mourners. In his life time he bringeth forth troublesome and tedious vermyne, & after death his flesh engendreth wormes; whilest hee liueth, his body yeldeth noysome and odious things: and when hee dyeth hee be-cometh a lumpe of foule and vncleane corruption. During this lyfe his only care is to nourish and maintaine one, but when he is dead, he shall feede & sustayne a number of wormes.[67]

The thinking of Hamlet is not so different from this gloomy preaching of the church, but there is a difference in emphasis, and as we shall see later, perhaps in implication. To Hamlet this return to the dust was not just a matter of course, to be accepted intellectually and ignored emotionally. It was an intense and painfully vivid reality, the one stupendous certainty, throwing its shadows backward over the whole course of life and swallowing its hopes and achievements in the darkness of oblivion. The grave-digger sings as he throws up the skulls from the earth. His rude song is filled with the tragedy of life, but it penetrates no deeper than his throat, and he drinks and laughs and jests with no thought of the skulls or his trade. "Has this fellow no feeling of his business, that he sings at grave-making?" asks Hamlet. Through Hamlet's daintier sense it is as if we see death for the first time in its stark reality, stripped of sentimental romance and sham glory, and the consolations of religion and philosophy. And through the ugliness of death we see the vanity and hollowness of life.

In the grave there is no distinction between the good and the bad. The skull buried in sacred ground is thrown out with no more circumspection than if it were "Cain's jaw-bone, that did the first murder." The politician whose shrewdness would circumvent God, and the courtier who could out-flatter lords, come to the same end, "chapless, and knock'd about the mazzard with the sexton's spade." "Here's revolution," exclaims Hamlet, "if we had the trick to see 't. Did these bones cost no more the breeding, but to play at loggats with 'em? mine ache to think on 't." No skill and tricks of the law, no deeds and conveyances of wealth can prevent the common end. As Hamlet holds up a skull he says,

> This fellow might be in 's time a great buyer of land, with his statutes, his recognizances, his fines, his double vouchers, his recoveries. Is this the fine of his fines, and the recovery of his recoveries, to have his fine pate full of fine dirt? Will his vouchers vouch him no more of his pur-

chases, and double ones too, than the length and breadth of a pair of indentures? The very conveyances of his lands will hardly lie in this box, and must the inheritor himself have no more, ha?[67]

Beauty and wit and power are equally helpless and frail before the corruption of death. Poor Yorick's infinite jests are still, and the flashes of merriment that were wont to set the table on a roar have frozen into the sickening grin of a skull, quite chop-fallen. The dust of the noble Alexander is worth no more than to plug beer barrels, and

> Imperial Caesar, dead and turn'd to clay,
> Might stop a hole to keep the wind away.[68]

This is the end, the goal of human power and glory, of wealth, learning, and wit. The soul of Hamlet sickens at the thought. "Now, get you to my lady's chamber, and tell her, let her paint an inch thick, to this favour she must come: make her laugh at that."[69]

With the vision of Death Hamlet sees the futility of life. Men rot in the earth in eight or nine years if they are not already rotten before burial, and even a man's life is no more than to say "one". Face to face with the degradation and the long oblivion of the grave, of what value is any human effort? All hopes of glory and power and achievement are swallowed up in the eternal silence of the tomb. Life itself is vain, and death the eternal fact.

The Rest Is Silence

The philosophy of futility is a philosophy of
pessimism. It is present in Job and Ecclesias-
tes, but the former closes with the spirit of
reverent submission and the latter in the spirit
of fideism, leaving a gulf between the doubt
and the single affirmation of faith at the end.
It is present in Innocent III and other religious
writers, and notably in the Dance of Death
tradition, but with a similar difference. These
can point out the futility of human effort and
the gruesomeness of death, because they possess a faith that lifts them above the tragedy
of the grave. They are separate and apart from
the despised flesh, and can glory from a distance over its suffering and degradation. But
it is an open question as to how far-reaching
Hamlet's pessimism may be. Is Shakespeare
presenting merely the conventional religious
idea, or must we understand a pessimism
reaching even beyond the grave? The religious
writer is careful to leave no doubt, but in *Hamlet* the question is more difficult.

The evidence may be briefly summarized.
The ghost returns from the realm of the dead;
and Hamlet speaks of his own "immortal"
soul, uses the conventional ideas of purgatory and heaven, and in his soliloquy, as he
sees the king at prayer, shows a belief in hell.
All this is in harmony with a normal faith.
On the other hand, this same soliloquy contains a strange inconsistency. Despite his
father's statement of his doom, Hamlet says,

> And how his audit stands who knows save
>   heaven?
> But in our circumstances and course of
>   thought,
> 'T is heavy with him.[70]

The ghost's statement is as completely ignored
as if it had never been made, and Hamlet is
merely using the popular surmise. A similar
"inconsistency" has been pointed out, in his
third soliloquy. With the ghost's appearance
still in his mind, he refers to the grave as

> The undiscover'd country from whose bourn
> No traveller returns. . . .[71]

Yet his father's ghost had returned and Hamlet had heard his voice. These inconsistencies,
about which so much has been made, are capable of explanation, to be sure. But on the other
hand, is it not possible that Shakespeare himself completely ignores the ghost as a living
reality, using it merely as a necessary tool
for the dramatic unfolding of the plot? In this
sense it would be dramatically real to Hamlet,
but at the same time would not be allowed to
interfere with the empirical reality of his
thought. And this need not be strange, for the
ghost belonged to a realm outside the use of
sense, and in contrast with the solid and tangi-
ble things of earth it is even unreal to Hamlet.
While he says after its appearance,

> There are more things in heaven and earth,
>   Horatio,
> Than are dreamt of in our philosophy,[72]

yet his own thinking is utterly uninfluenced by it. He is as empirical and free from supernatural domination as if no ghost had ever walked. He trusts his own experiment, the play "to catch the conscience of the king." He depends upon his own observations and those of Horatio's eyes, and the interpretation of his reason, above the revelation from another world. While he dramatically accepts the Ghost, he rationally ignores it.

Just how much faith would be involved in references to hell and purgatory, and how much convention, would also be a question. But on the whole Hamlet's thinking on death is singularly hopeless. The third soliloquy is distinctly pagan in tone. He questions death and its possible sleep as if no Christian resurrection and hell had ever been preached. There is a Stoic consideration of suicide as an escape from the troubles of life, combined with the natural fear of dreams after death, but there is no more certainty of an existence beyond, than any pagan might have felt. Even the Stoic contemplating death had to outface these natural fears. Lucretius says it is the fear of death inspired by poets' tales that make men endure the miseries of life:

> But if it once appear
> That after death there's neither Hope nor Fear,
> Then men might freely triumph, then disdain
> The Poets tales, and scorn their fancied pain:
> But now we must submit, since pains we fear
> Eternal after death, we know not where.[73]

Hence a major purpose in Epicureanism was to banish these fears and set men free by teaching the eternal sleep of death,

> For as we neither knew, nor felt those harms,
> When dreadful *Carthage* frighted *Rome* with
>   arms,
> So after Death, when we shall be no more
> What tho the Seas forsake their usual Shore,
> And rise to Heaven? what the Stars drop from
>   thence?
> Yet how can this disturb our perisht Sense?[74]

Philip de Mornay, in his *Six Excellent Treatises of Life and Death*, makes Socrates comfort Axiochus with the same philosophy in reference to the body. There will be no feeling after death for

> . . . your body shall bee dissolued as it was before your conception. And, as you felt no kind of euill, in that time, when *Draco* and *Calisthenes* gouerued the Commonwealth (for, then you were not existent, to feele either good or euill) so after death your body shall be sensible of nothing, it being then free from the touch of any discommodities.[75]

But De Mornay is careful to explain that, though the body perish, the soul is immortal and lives on. In Hamlet's soliloquy, however, there is none of the Christian certainty of life after death; there is only the longing for eternal sleep balked by the fear of a further existence. In other words, Hamlet has neither the comfort of Epicurean atheism nor the certainty and consolation of Christian faith, but only a tormenting doubt that palsies resolution.

In the grave scene, however, the doubt has changed to something deeper, for the insistence on death as the end of all is lightened by no gleam of immortality. The lines,

> Absent thee from felicity awhile,
> And in this harsh world draw thy breath in
>   pain
> To tell my story,[76]

coming after this scene, and from the philosopher of Death, may suggest only the felicity of eternal sleep.

But especially significant is Shakespeare's change in Hamlet's last words. In the First Quarto the dying Hamlet prays, "Heaven receive my soul." It was a conventional ending, fitting a man of faith and hopeful of the life beyond. It had the spirit of Ophelia's prayer, "God ha' mercy on his soul! And on all Christian souls, I pray God." But after the hopeless scenes by the grave and Hamlet's brooding over the oblivion of death, how profoundly suggestive is the substitution for this prayer with these strange, startling words—"the rest is silence!" In a single phrase, like an epitaph above his tomb, they crystalize his whole philosophy of Death, and suggest that profound negation at which his thought has finally arrived. After the struggle and pain of life, after its futile noise, "the rest is silence!"

But we must not make the mistake of confounding Hamlet's philosophy of pessimism and futility with Shakespeare's own thought. Our study has intentionally concentrated on Hamlet's broodings over the problem of evil and the form the world takes in the mirror of his mind. But in the play as a whole the intense pessimism is relieved by the doubts of optimism, and the gloom of Hamlet by the background of the court. Alongside the Prince is the Stoic confidence of Horatio. If "something is rotten in the state of Denmark," Horatio believes "Heaven will direct it," and to Hamlet's brooding over Alexander's dust, Horatio replies, "'T were to consider too curiously, to consider so."

Even Hamlet's own mind is not always consistent. Along with his sense of futility and the oblivion of the grave, there is a clear recognition of the Almighty who sets his canon against self-slaughter, and of a divinity that shapes our ends. He is divided between faith and negation, and much of his bitter cynicism and pain is the result of this self-estrangement. In the struggle against black negation, toward which the brooding on evil tends, he even questions his own senses, doubts his own doubts. For a time at least he accepts the doctrine of the skeptic that the criterion of good and evil is only in the mind, that "there is nothing either good or bad, but thinking makes it so."[77] As a pure skeptic he might escape the problem of evil entirely by doubting its existence. If there is no external fact of evil, but all is merely the reflex of our own thinking, then we can attain a peace of mind by doubting the evidence of the senses. This problem of the relativity of evil, however, belongs to the next chapter of this study. It is sufficient here to point out that Hamlet finds no relief through doubt. If "thinking" makes it bad, Hamlet nevertheless thinks, and to him it is bad; if he accepts the skeptic dictum theoretically, he cannot deny the evidence of his mind. Thus even the relief of skepticism fails him.

So through a drama of powerful human emotions reacting to a fundamental and universal moral problem, Shakespeare has concentrated our attention on this solitary, black-robed figure—the personification of all the troubled, suffering souls of every age—as he struggles to understand the meaning of "this harsh world" in which he draws his breath in pain. Job, facing the same problem of suffering and loss, had, through the revelation of divine majesty, been so overwhelmed with the insignificance of human knowledge that he was conscience-stricken at questioning the ways of God toward man, and his faith rose to a sublime and transcendent loyalty. But Hamlet finds no certainty. For him every ambition has been thwarted. Love has turned to lust, and friendship to treachery and hate. Despite his father's adjuration that he taint not his mind, in the tragic struggle his soul has become hardened and bitter, and his despair has grown deeper, till, standing by the grave, he feels life to be futility and death a hopeless silence. But the gloom toward which his mind has traveled is lightened by moments of calm, even Stoic, faith, and the ultimate conclusion is not utter despair, but rather passionate, penetrating doubt that nullifies the values and meaning of life.

But What of Shakespeare?

Is *Hamlet* with its profound thought and emotional intensity only an artistic presentation of a disillusioned soul as it awakens to the harsh reality of the world, or may it reflect something of the mood and feeling of its author? Why Shakespeare turned from delightful comedies and patriotic histories to tragedies and bitter comedies for the next eight years, has aroused much speculation.

No personal tragedy is known which could have brought this startling change. On the contrary he seems to reflect the changing mood of the times. Roughly the literature of England before 1600 was exuberant, optimistic, idealistic, joyous. The discovery and exploration of the New World, the close of the Civil Wars and establishment of a strong government, the succession of a young queen whom all admired, the defeat of the Spanish Armada, and perhaps above all the New Learning with its

emphasis on human perfection excited the
imagination and created visions of boundless
power and achievement. The outpouring of
morality plays, songs, sonnets, comedies, romances, and histories reflected the joyous
mood of the country.

After 1600, however, tragedies, critical literature, and satires that incited censorship by the
state reflected a spirit of disillusionment and
frustration. Contributing to this change of
mood were a growing disaffection with the
aging queen who refused to name a successor,
the tragic death of Essex, whom Shakespeare
admired, the imprisonment of Shakespeare's
patron Southampton and investigation of
Shakespeare's fellow players, the injustices
of the Star Chamber, the heavy taxes, the increasing poverty, the growing political and
religious unrest which would finally result
in another civil war, the increasing arrogance
of the court, and perhaps above all a change
from the optimistic philosophy of human
goodness and possible perfection to an increasing emphasis on the hopeless depravity
of humanity without special arbitrary grace.

It is inconceivable that a man who shows
such depth of emotion in his work should not
be grieved by the tragedy of those critical
times. The doubts of Hamlet may reflect
Shakespeare's own anxiety to find some rational answer to the problems of human suffering, injustice, and wrong—themes that dominate all the plays after 1600. If so, in the clash

of two world-views, the rising darkness was for years to eclipse the light for Shakespeare almost as completely as it did for Hamlet himself, while he continued his probing into the certainty or illusion of moral standards, the question of human and universal justice, and the ultimate meaning and destiny of evil.

FOOTNOTES AND REFERENCES

1. W. M. Hatch, *The Moral Philosophy of Aristotle*, consisting of the *Nichomachean Ethics* and of the Paraphrase attributed to Andronicus of Rhodes. (London: John Murray, 1879), pp. 82ff.

2. *Richard III*, II, i, 82.

3. *King John*, IV, iii, 140f.

4. *Ibid.*, III, iv, 107-111.

5. *Richard II*, V, v, 31-41.

6. *Troilus and Cressida*, III, ii, 82-90.

7. St. Augustine, *Certaine Select Prayers gathered out of St. Augustines Meditations*, 3rd ed. (London: John Daye, 1577) Sig. C., fol. 7.

8. Peter de La Primaudaye, *The French Academe*, trans. T. Bowes, (London: Edmund Bollifant, 1586), pp. 10f.

9. *Ibid.*, pp. 43, 14-17.

10. Giovanni Battista Gelli, *Circe*, trans. Thomas Brown (London: 1702), p. 289. An earlier English translation of this popular work appeared in 1557, with a second edition in 1558-9.

11. *Ibid.*, p. 294.

12. T. Bastard, "De Microsmo," in *Select Poetry, chiefly devotional of the Reign of Queen Elizabeth,*

ed. by Edward Farr for the Parker Society (Cambridge, England: University Press, 1845), II, 306.

13. Christopher Marlowe, *Doctor Faustus* (Cambridge, England: University Press, 1972) II, ii, 5-8.

14. Christopher Marlowe, *Tamburlaine,* I, (Cambridge, England: University Press, 1972) ii, 199f.

15. *Hamlet,* II, ii, 315-320.

16. *Ibid.,* III, i, 161f.

17. Andrew Cecil Bradley, *Shakespearean Tragedy, Lectures on Hamlet, Othello, King Lear, Macbeth,* 2nd ed. (New York: MacMillan Co., 1914).

18. Lily B. Campbell, *Shakespeare's Tragic Heroes—Slaves of Passion,* (Cambridge, England: University Press, 1930).

19. *Hamlet,* III, iv, 202-210.

20. *Ibid.,* V, ii, 58-62.

21. *Ibid.,* III, iv, 173-175.

22. *Ibid.,* V, ii, 67-70.

23. *Ibid.,* III, iv, 212, and IV, ii, 20f.

24. *Ibid.,* III, i, 79-88.

25. *Ibid.,* IV, iv, 64f.

26. *Ibid.,* IV, iv, 40-46.

27. *Troilus and Cressida,* II, ii, 47-50.

28. Thomas Beard, *The Theatre of Gods iudgments* (London: Adam Islip, 1631), pp. 1f. The first edition of this remarkable book appeared in 1597.

29. Edmund Spenser, J. C. Smith, ed., *The Faerie Queene* (New York: Oxford University Press, 1909), Prologue to Bk. V, See also Bk. IV, canto xviii, st. 32.

30. *Ibid.,* st. 1.

31. Edmund Spenser, *The Shepherdes Calender* (New York: B. Franklin, 1890), Feb. 11-13.

32. *Hamlet,* I, ii, 133-137.

33. *Ibid.,* I, ii, 11.

34. *Ibid.,* III, i, 46ff.

35. *Ibid.,* I, ii, 143-145.

36. *Ibid.,* III, iv, 71-81.

37. *Ibid.,* III, ii, 122-131.

38. St. Augustine, *Op. cit.,* Sig. A, III to Sig. B, I.

39. Edward Farr, *Op. cit.,* II, 344.

40. H. Kerton, trans., *The Mirror of Mans Lyfe* (London: Henry Bynneman, 1576), Bk. I, ch. 1.

41. *Ibid.*

42. *Ibid.,* Bk. I, ch. iii.

43. Michel de Montaigne, *Essayes,* trans. John Florio, 1603 (London: J. M. Dent, 1898), Bk. II, ch. xii.

44. *Ibid.*

45. *Hamlet,* I, iii, 78-80.

46. Lucius Annaevs Seneca, *The Works of Lucius Annaevs Seneca,* trans. Thomas Lodge (London: William Stansby, 1620), Wp st. XCV.

47. *Hamlet,* III, i, 149-141.

48. *Ibid.,* V, ii, 67-90.

49. *Ibid.,* II, ii, 380ff.

50. Montaigne, *op. cit.,* Bk. III, ch. viii.

51. *Hamlet,* III, i, 70-76.

52. *Ibid.,* I, iv, 23-36.

53. Kerton, *op. cit.,* Bk. I, ch. iv.

54. *Hamlet,* I, v. 189f.

55. *Ibid.,* III, iv, 173.

56. John M. Robertson, *Montaigne and Shakespeare and Other Essays on Cognate Questions* (London: Adam and Charles Black, 1909).

57. Montaigne, *op. cit.,* Bk. III, ch. viii. Similar ideas occur in Bk. II, ch. xii; Bk. I, chs. x, xi, xii, xvii.

58. *Hamlet,* V, ii, 230-234.

59. *Ibid.,* IV, v, 113-118.

60. John Lyly, *Complete Works,* 3v., ed. Bond, (Oxford, England: Oxford University Press, 1902), I, 310.

61. Plutarch, *Morals*. Trans. by several hands, with introduction by Ralph Waldo Emerson (Boston: Little Brown, 1870) I, 331.

62. *Hamlet,* I, ii, 70-73.

63. *Ibid.,* I, ii, 98f.

64. *Ibid.,* IV, i, 22f.

65. St. Augustine, *op. cit.,* Sig. A., fol. iii.

66. Kerton, *op. cit.,* Bk. III, ch. i.

67. *Hamlet,* V, i, 111-121.

68. *Ibid.,* V, i, 215f.

69. *Ibid.,* V, i, 212f.

70. *Ibid.,* III, iv, 82-84.

71. *Ibid.,* III, i, 79f.

72. *Ibid.,* I, v, 106f.

73. Lucretius (Titus Lucretius Carus), *Lucretius, His Six Books of Epicurean Philosophy,* trans. Thomas Creech, 3rd ed. (London: E. Blount, 1683), p. 5.

74. *Ibid.,* P. 92f.

75. Philip de Mornay, *Six Excellent Treatises of Life and Death* (London: William Stansby, 1607, Sig. A., fol. 5.

76. *Hamlet,* V, ii, 358ff.

77. *Ibid.,* II, ii, 256f. See also Hardin Craig, "Hamlet's Book," Huntington Library Bulletin, No. 6 (Nov. 1934), pp. 17-34 for a discussion of background material on this skeptic and Stoic doctrine.

Chapter 2

TROILUS AND CRESSIDA,
THE SEARCH FOR STANDARDS
IN A WORLD OF RELATIVITY

SINCE, in our twentieth century, moral standards have become widely questioned, and the concepts of "situation ethics" and the relativity of moral values have received increasing support, it is interesting to learn that Shakespeare long ago was also deeply concerned about these same problems. Hamlet's doubts demanded some kind of answer. Is it true that "There is nothing either good or bad but thinking makes it so," that there is no standard of right and wrong except what each decides in his own mind, or is there a definite standard outside ourselves, whether we recognize it or not? And why do we violate even the standards we ourselves accept? Those acquainted with present trends should be interested in Shakespeare's understanding of the earlier philosophies of relativity and his search in *Troilus and Cressida* for an answer to these questions.

Hamlet's statement that the "good or bad" is only in the mind was a natural impulse to avoid the depths of pessimism and despair. For skepticism, if once attained, heals that utter sickness of the mind which turns the whole world black. The early skeptics held that peace of soul, or imperturbability, can be attained only through the suspension of judgment about things. The method of the Pyrrhonists was to oppose contradictory ideas and concepts to each other and by considering the dogmatics of others to arrive at a state of mind that neither affirmed nor denied.

The principle, crystallized in the famous tropes of Aenesidemus and Sextus Empiricus, that all knowledge is uncertain, is applied in the Tenth Trope to the problems of good and evil. The customs, laws and beliefs of races and nations are brought into opposition. In one country, adultery is approved, in others condemned; in one, marriage of brother and sister is permitted, in others forbidden. Killing is permitted in the arena but condemned outside. By thus pointing out the wide and dogmatic differences in customs, religions, and morals of various peoples, the skeptic arrived at the conclusion that there is nothing in the nature of things themselves to make them good or bad, but that evil had relation only to the mind itself and is a matter of personal opinion.

The idea of relativity had already been somewhat similarly advanced by Epicurus, who held that injustice itself is no evil, for what is unjust in one country is just in another, and that the only evil is the fear of punishment inspired by conscience. Even before this Protagoras had held that man is the measure of all things, or "that things are to you such as they appear to you, and to me such as they appear to me. . . ."[2] The relativism of Protagoras was only slightly different from that of the skeptics; he affirmed positively the truth of the sense impressions, while the skeptics doubted their accuracy. They were alike, however, in holding that all values are matters of opinion, existing in the mind, but not necessarily in external fact.

Skepticism, after the attacks of Carneades, exercised a strong influence upon the later Stoics, who utilized the principle of the uncertainty of knowledge to free themselves from the troublesome problem of suffering and injustice. If all the suffering and injustice that happens to man is directed by a Divine Providence, and yet God cannot be the author of evil in any sense, then these things that happen to us are not really evil but only seem so. The opinions of men are based upon appearances, and the vital problem is to interpret the appearances correctly,[3] because it is the wrong interpretations that fill the mind with a sense of evil. There is no evil in external things themselves but only in our opinions, or "preconceptions," about them, and since we have the power to change these opinions or to suspend judgments of them, we can in this way abolish the idea of evil entirely.[4]

Though the Stoics used the logic of the skeptics in denying evil in external things, they held firmly to the positive reality of good and evil within the will. The universe, they held, is governed by a positive and unbending law implanted in the very nature of things. This universal law is the criterion of all good; the good or evil, therefore, for men is determined by whether or not the intention or actual choice of one's will is in harmony with this law. External things, whatever might happen to us, are neither good not evil, but only seem so through false appearances.

Skepticism, however, doubted all criteria for the judging of good and evil, and even undermined the Stoic concept of a natural moral law. To the skeptic there was nothing positive even about moral evil, but all was a matter of opinion. The difference between skepticism and positivism is basic in the judging of all human values. Positivism sees actual value within the object, action, idea, or principle itself; skepticism doubts all external values and places the worth of things in the opinion of the appraiser alone, not in things themselves.

The moral positivism of Aquinas, which included the Stoic idea of natural law, was undermined, as we have already seen,[5] by the voluntarism of Duns Scotus, which in turn threw open the doors to skepticism. For, if there exists no positive moral law implanted in the nature of things, and as a result our whole moral concept must be derived from the arbitrary and changing will of God, as Scotus held, then moral values have no permanent fixedness within themselves. With such a view Christian philosophy was blindly approaching the brink of skepticism, and only one more step was needed to plunge it into the abyss— doubt of the divine will, or of our understanding of the divine will. If things which appear evil to us were good in another age and under other circumstances, and cannot be said to be evil now except as God arbitrarily pronounces them so, we are forced to mistrust the evidence of our senses which proclaim them evil. The danger of such mistrust is its contagion; it is likely to question even the divine will, and finally arrive at the conclusion of pure skepticism, that there is no positive criterion for judging moral phenomena, that there is nothing either good or bad except as the mind itself believes it so, and we cannot even trust our senses or our minds. This would make the whole problem of evil a relative one, or rather would reduce it to a mere mental mirage.

Many of the Renaissance thinkers were strongly influenced by the skepticism of the Stoics regarding evil in external things. La Primaudaye, for instance, says our perturbations are "but opinions drawne from our will, through a judgment corrupted with the affections of the flesh," and we may rid ourselves of these opinions by "persuading ourselves that whatsoever we imagine to be good or euill in the world . . . is neither good nor euill, and so consequently, that it ought not in any sort to breed passions within us."[6]

Other Renaissance writers, however, in their

reaction against the positivism of the Scholastics were swept into all degrees of Skepticism, often apparently unaware of the depths beneath them. Cornelius Agrippa with his mixture of superstitious credulity and outright skepticism is an interesting example of the new uncharted movement. Moral philosophy, he says, consists rather in variety of use, custom, and observation of life than in rules, and is changeable according to the times, places, and opinions of men:

> ". . . for many things wax out of use through process of time, and consent of the people. Hence it comes to pass, that that was then a Vice, which is now accounted a Virtue; and that which is here a Virtue, in another place is counted a Vice; what one man thinks is honest, another man thinks dishonest; what some hold to be just, others condemn as unjust. . . ."[7]

This is the essence of skepticism, undermining, if carried far enough, the concept of a natural moral order, and making morality rest upon the changing opinions of men and the flux of time and circumstance. But Agrippa cannot follow the full length of his argument, for he denounces strongly the teaching of Teodorus, who held,

> That wise men would not stick to give their minds to Thieving, Adultery, or Sacriledge, when they found a reasonable opportunity: for there is not any one of these

that is evil by nature; and therefore if the
vulgar opinion generally conceiv'd concerning these things were set aside, there
is no reason but a philosopher might pub-
lickly go to a whore without a reproof.[8]

Nothing could be more wicked, says Agrippa,
than such opinions.

Giordano Bruno, in spite of his Platonism,
was also affected by skeptical thought and its
insistence upon the relativity of values. He
rejects the biblical story of the flood, the recent
creation of man, and the derivation of races,
and in ridiculing the simple faith of men he has
Momus propose to send Orion among men and
make them believe black is white, and

that human understanding, when it thinks
it sees best, is mere blindness, and that
what appears to Reason good, excellent,
and choice is base, wicked and extremely
evil; that Nature is a whorish baggage,
that Natural Law is knavery, that Nature
and the Divinity cannot concur to the same
end; that the justice of the one is not subordinate to the justice of the other, but are
things as contrary as light is to darkness.[9]

Bruno is attacking that type of faith made
prominent by William Ockham, and the revived Augustinism under the Calvinists, which
threw reason and the law of nature aside and
put its trust entirely in their particular interpretation of the Scriptures, even taking a satisfaction in opposing the Bible to nature and

reason as a means of exalting its authority
and rightness. John Bradford gives excellent
expression to this pious surrender to what he
understands as the will of God, when he says:

> There is neither virtue nor vice to be con-
> sidered according to the will and wisdom
> of man; but according to the will of God.
> Whatsoever is conformable thereto, the
> same is virtue, and the action that spring-
> eth thereof is laudable and good, howso-
> ever it appear otherwise to the eyes and
> reason of man; as was the lifting up Abra-
> ham's hands to have slain his son. What-
> soever is not conformable to the will of
> God, that same is vice, and the action
> springing thereof is to be disallowed and
> taken for evil; and that so much the more
> and greater evil, by how much it is not
> consonant and agreeing to God's will, al-
> though it seem far otherwise to man's wis-
> dom.[10]

Against this kind of faith Bruno champions
the validity of reason and natural law. Reason
itself, however, convinced Bruno that we do
not always allow our moral practice to be
governed by moral law, but constantly vary it
with times and circumstances. Like Plato he
did not think the current sex arrangements
perfect, for Jove might one day restore that
natural law by which every man is allowed to
have as many wives as he can maintain and
impregnate. In the practice of the world he

says, "We call those virtues which by a certain
trick and custom are so called and believed,
though their effects and fruits are condemned
by all sense and natural season; such as open
knavery and folly, the malignity of usurping laws and of possessors of *meum* and
tuum. . . ."[11]

Bruno's relativism did not reach the skeptical extreme of doubting the reality of good and
evil or that a criterion exists by which they
may be determined. But this criterion itself is
flexible and varies with times and circumstances. He is a pragmatist in morals, be-
lieving that the test of moral values is how
they work. Of chastity, which was always so
highly commended, he says,

> Of herself she is neither virtue nor vice,
> nor contains any goodness, dignity, or
> merit . . . when she yields to any urgent
> reason, she is called continence, and has
> the being of virtue, as partaking of such a
> fortitude and contempt of pleasure, which
> is not vain and useless, but improves hum-
> an society and the honest satisfaction of
> others.[12]

Bruno is here using the term "chastity" in
the sense of abstension from *all* sexual acts,
not in the modern sense of abstension from
unlawful acts. Loyalty and proper marital re-
lationships would be governed by his term,
"continence." Granting this distinction, Bruno
is defining the criterion of good and evil as,

under varying circumstances, the usefulness of things to human society.

It was thought by Benno Tschischwitz[13] that Shakespeare became acquainted with Bruno's comedy *El Candelajo*, which was written in London, and that his influence is observable in Hamlet's statement of the relativity of evil. It is not the purpose of this study to attempt to fix exact sources for Shakespeare's thought, but only to analyze it in the light of his intellectual background. By the time *Hamlet* was written the idea of relativity had become widespread, and he might have had access to it through many sources. Neither is it necessary that he should have received it through Montaigne, who, however, reproduces more nearly than Bruno the spirit and method of the older skeptics. Running throughout his "Apology of Raymond Sebond" is the Pyrrhonic thesis that there is no certain knowledge to be derived through reason or the senses. While he must grant that the senses are the beginning and the end of all our knowledge, they are nevertheless so imperfect and so easily deceived by false appearances that we may be said to have opinions rather than truth. Hence it comes that what one man considers good another pronounces evil; in some countries marriage between parents and children is permitted, children and the aged are put to death, parents are eaten by the children as an act of pious respect, robbing and stealing are encouraged, and "there is

nothing so extreme and horrible, but is found
to be received and allowed by the custome of
some nation. It is credible that there be natural
lawes; as may be seene in other creatures, but
in us they are lost. . . ."[14]

This skepticism about natural moral law together with the uncertainty of reason and the
senses, Montaigne believes, leaves the problem of moral values largely a matter of mere
changing opinion, influenced by environment.
For he says,

> . . . if nature inclose within the limits of
> her ordinary progress . . . the beliefes, the
> judgments, and the opinions of men; if
> they have their revolutions, their seasons,
> their birth, and their death, even as Cab-
> iches; if heaven doth move, agitate and
> rowle them at his pleasure, what powerful
> and permanent authority doe we ascribe
> unto them? . . . In such manner that as
> fruits and beasts doe spring up diverse and
> different; so men are borne, either more or
> lesse warlike, martial, just, temperate and
> docile; here inclined to superstition, there
> addicted to mis-believing, here given to
> liberty, there to servitude . . . grosse wit-
> ted or ingenious; either obedient or rebel-
> lious; good or bad, according as the in-
> clination of the place beareth, where they
> are seated; and being removed from one
> soil to another (as plants are) they take a
> new complexion.[15]

What abiding faith can we place in our beliefs and opinions, Montaigne would ask, when they as well as we ourselves are molded from the climate and soil in which we are born and, when, like cabbages or beasts, we are formed by natural environment to be warlike or docile, honest or thieving, chaste or licentious, good or bad? There can be no universal natural law to determine the good or evil, for men would then by nature all desire the good. The judgment of things then must be relative to the country, climate, and individual differences of men. Such, Montaigne concludes, is the relativity of moral evil. There is neither good nor evil in external things, but only in our judgment of them, which we can change at will.

> Therefore let us take no more excuses from external qualities of things . . . Our good and our evil hath no dependency but from ourselves.[16]

English thought was slower than the French or Italian to reflect the relativism of the new skeptical currents. Lyly plays with the idea and Spenser and others held to the relativity of good and evil in respect to physical things. But the most penetrating and skeptical statement is that of Chapman's Byron:

> There is no truth of any good
> To be discern'd on earth . . . all things here
> Have all their price set down, from men's
>   conceits,

Which make all terms and actions good or bad,
And are but pliant and well-color'd threads
Put into feigned images of truth:
To which to yield and kneel as true pure kings,
That pull'd us down with clear truth of their
    Gospel,
Were superstition to be hiss'd to hell.[17]

Byron analyzes from the skeptical point of view the whole problem of values. Externally the basic materials are furnished us for judgment; but these are then formed and interpenetrated by the mind, and given their price of truth, of good or evil. But it is we who set their price and not themselves. For nothing is either good or evil in itself. But when we name it so, and then fall down in worship of our mere opinion, we are guilty of a "superstition to be hiss'd to hell." This extreme of skepticism denies any certainty of values, either in external things or in the mind itself.

Opposing the evaluation of things in the mind alone, Erasmus had earlier satirized the platonic idealists in his famous *Ship of Fools*. He classifies those who use this policy with no regard for reality, as the happiest set of fools, for such fools are at no cost for happiness:

Whereas many things even of inconsiderable value would cost a great deal of pains and perhaps pelf to procure, opinion spares such charges, and yet gives us them in as ample a manner by conceit, as if we possessed them in reality. Thus he who feeds on such a stinking dish of fish, as another must hold his nose at a yard's distance from, yet if he feed heartily, and relish them palatably, they are to him as good as if they were freshly caught. . . .If a woman be never so ugly and nauseous, yet if her husband can but think her handsome, it is all one to him as if she really were so. . . . What difference is there between them that in the darkest dungeon can with a platonic brain survey the whole world in idea, and him that stands in the open air, and takes a less deluding prospect of the universe? If the beggar in Lucian, that dreamt he was a prince, had never waked, his imaginary kingdom had been as great as a real one. Between him therefore that truly is happy, and him that thinks himself so, there is no perceivable distinction; or if any, the fool has the better of it: first, because his happiness costs him less, standing him only in the price of a single thought; and then secondly, because he has more fellow-companions and partakers of his good fortune.[18]

This delightful satire against fools who allow their imagination to determine the worth of things points up the difficulty of the whole problem of values, one of the most difficult in philosophy. It is the age-old conflict between idealism and empiricism. The fool, or idealist, derives his values from within and has many companions in his foolishness, notably the Platonists, and, in the problem of evil, the Stoics. The empiricist derives his values from without, from external fact alone.

Shakespeare's Search for a Standard of Values

Byron's extreme skepticism denied any standard of values, either in external things or within the mind. What criterion, then, can be trusted in determining values and setting standards? How can we determine what is good and what is bad? The question demanded an answer, and after the searching doubts of *Hamlet*, Shakespeare turns to a penetrating study of this problem in *Troilus and Cressida*.

Shakespeare, to be sure, always recognized the importance of the mind in determining values. Iago, the champion of intellect and will over external circumstances, condenses the philosophy of wealth into a single epigrammatic statement:

> Poor and content is rich, and rich enough,
> But riches fineless is poor as winter
> To him that ever fears he shall be poor.[19]

Here he is speaking of material wealth. Of reputation, another but more abstract form of wealth, Iago says, "You have lost no reputation at all unless you repute yourself such a loser."[20]

This is a commonplace idea, to be sure: that, as far as each individual is concerned, no evil exists for him except what he himself knows or thinks. The concept of evil is only in the mind, and even if an idea or an act is perfectly good but one thinks it evil, to him it is evil.

This is the starting point for the Stoic consolation regarding external ills. The next step is to control the thought itself, and by reinterpreting doubtfully what appears to be evil, change it to a good. Thus John of Gaunt would have his son consider his banishment not a banishment but an escape from pestilence to a fresher climate, or a journey to purchase honor in foreign lands.[21]

Such Stoic consolations are found everywhere. They would close the mind to external fact and derive the truth from within. But Shakespeare ridicules such futile devices, for Bolingbroke exclaims:

> O, who can hold a fire in his hand
> By thinking on the frosty Caucasus?
> Or cloy the hungry edge of appetite
> By bare imagination of a feast?
> Or wallow naked in December snow
> By thinking of fantastic summer's heat?
> Oh no! The apprehension of the good
> Gives but the greater feeling to the worse.[22]

Such denial of plain fact, says Leontes, can be true only for those who are not themselves suffering:

> For there was never yet philosopher
> That could endure the toothache patiently,
> However they have writ the style of gods,
> And made a push at chance and sufferance.[23]

Though Shakespeare is an inveterate idealist, he has too profound a sense of reality to deny external fact. He would agree with Iago as well as with Bolingbroke and Leontes. His most pertinent discussion of values, however, is in *Troilus and Cressida*. In the council of war to decide the policy of Troy, Hector contends that Helen should be returned to the Greeks because she is not worth the cost of holding. But Troilus replies, "What is ought, but as 'tis valued?" Hector answers:

> But value dwells not in particular will;
> It holds his estimate and dignity
> As well wherein 'tis precious of itself
> As in the prizer; 'Tis mad idolotry
> To make the service greater than the god;
> And the will dotes that is inclinable
> To what infectuously itself affects,
> Without some image of the affected merit.[24]

Hector's common sense is similar to Byron's attack upon the superstition of worshipping our own opinions, but it differs from Byron in granting a value within the thing appraised. Hector would agree with Erasmus in counting as fools those who place all values within the mind. Yet this is exactly what Troilus does. He is an idealist of the Platonic type, and he replies that Helen is a pearl,

> Whose price hath launched above a thousand
>   ships,
> And turn'd crown'd kings to merchants.[25]

She is a "theme of honor and renown," and Troilus would not ask if she is worth it. If the price is set upon her by the kings of earth and underwritten by the blood of armies, what more is needed? It is the price that makes the value of the thing. But Hector takes the middle ground between outright empiricism and the idealism of Troilus. Real evaluation dwells as much within the thing itself as in the judgment of the prizer; there must be a basis in external fact for the concept in the mind.

This is the modified Aristotelianism of the later Scholastics, which held that all knowledge, or concept of values, is derived from external things through the senses. As Montaigne put it, "Senses are the beginning and the end of human knowledge."[26] Even Gelli, who is dominantly Neo-platonic, acknowledges that the beginning of knowledge comes from the senses, "for we can understand nothing, the first Idea of which we did not receive from the sensitive knowledge."[27] The external object must be mirrored by the senses as an "image" upon the mind, for without the "image of the affected merit" one would have no right basis on which to know it or to determine its value.

The principle is closely related to Ulysses' doctrine of "reflection." It is impossible for a man rightly to know his own worth merely from the estimation of his own mind, for he may underrate or overrate his value. No man can therefore boast of his merit until he sees his virtues reflected in the lives of others, and

he has an "image" outside himself on which
he can base a judgment of his virtues:

> Nor doth he of himself know them for aught
> Till he behold them formed in the applause
> Where they're extended, who, like an arch,
>   reverberate
> The voice again, or like a gate of steel
> Fronting the sun, receives and renders back
> His figure and his heat.[28]

It is the same principle stated by Brutus when
he says, "The eye sees not itself but by reflection, by some other things," and Cassius replies:

> And, since you know you cannot see yourself
> So well as by reflection, I, your glass,
> Will modestly discover to yourself,
> That of yourself which you yet know not of.[29]

Such knowledge, to be sure, requires a double process: first, the image of one's face, or
worth, in the mirror, that is, the applause or
condemnation of others; and second, the reflection of that image turned back again upon the
owner's mind. One instantly recognizes the
constant chance of error in such evaluation. If
one cannot know his own worth, neither can
he trust the estimation of others, the mirror
of whose minds may be warped.

In judging external objects, however, Aquinas believed the image registered upon the
mind of the beholder is identical with the object, while Ockham and later Scholastics af-

firmed only a resemblance, yet so close as to make knowledge authentic. But it is here that skepticism enters. For the mirrored image may be inaccurately reflected. The senses themselves are untrustworthy, as nearly all schools of philosophy admitted.

Shakespeare himself refers to the tricks the senses play upon the understanding, when "the error of our eye directs our mind."[30] Since also the mind itself is the mirror upon which the image rests, if this mirror is warped or untrue, the image will be distorted. But because no man can know that the mirror of his mind is accurate, each, in the last analysis, has to trust his best judgment, and his evaluations must always be relative.

This is the basis of skepticism, but skepticism may be of various degrees. In Shakespeare it never reaches the extreme of Pyrrhonism, which doubted all external values. On the contrary, if Hector and Ulysses express his views, then he has no doubt of the external reality and of its potential worth. In fact, this would be the fixed foundation of all evaluation, without which opinion would but "dote." But the mind of the "prizer" fuses with the external and judges its potential worth for him. It requires the "fusion" to make a real evaluation, and this is always relative to the accuracy of the senses, to the nature of one's own mind, and even to the circumstances or situation, for Portia says:

The crow does sing as sweetly as the lark,
When neither is attended; and I think
The nightingale, if she should sing by day,
When every goose is cackling, would be
    thought
No better a musician than the wren.
How many things by season season'd are
To their right praise and true perfection.[31]

Shakespeare's philosophy of values apparently recognizes a broad relativity of judgment. The actual "good or bad" for each one is in the mind and nowhere else, and as a man thinks, so is it for him. But this does not exclude the fact that outside of him is the external reality with which his judgment should correspond or be in error.

The Search for Moral Law

Relativity in the skeptical philosophies was chiefly directed at undermining faith in any moral law outside one's own mind. If no such law exists, and each may do whatever his mind desires, there is no problem of good and evil. Even the word "tragedy" would have no meaning, for comedy and tragedy would be the same.

Because of the difficulties involved in *Troilus and Cressida*, which made even Coleridge hesitate to express an opinion, one approaches it with a feeling of uncertainty. In general, however, the central theme of the play is the question of order and law. Nowhere else does Shakespeare express so definitely his faith in a universal moral law based on cosmic order, and nowhere else does he show so clearly how out of "square" the world is with this concept.

Much has been said of the difference between the Greek and Trojan heroes in the play; the Greeks, dominated by the cold, calculating intellectualism of Ulysses, and the Trojans, by the warm, passionate emotionalism of Troilus. The two groups are faced with two different problems, the Greeks with anarchy and the Trojans with a vital moral decision involving the principle of justice; yet beneath both problems lies the fundamental one of order and law. It could hardly have been accidental that Shakespeare presents so pointedly the difference between the two groups in reference to this basic problem of moral philosophy.

The Greek council, discussing their failure to take Troy, is regaled by Agamemnon with the conventional philosophy of human frustration. No decision on earth, he says, ever achieves its fullest hope; checks and disasters occur in even the greatest actions; no purpose was ever recorded in the past that "trial did not draw bias and thwart" away from its hoped-for end. But all these are trials sent by Jove to test the constancy of men and separate the hero from the coward, as the thresher winnows the chaff from the grain. Nestor, supposedly wise from age, is unable to add to this philosophy, and merely repeats it with varied illustrations; for, difficulties are like the tempest that destroys the bauble boats but lets go by the strong-ribbed bark.

With this elaborate preparation Ulysses begins his explanation, taking immediate issue with the conventional view and attributing the blame for their failure not to the gods but to themselves, for they had failed to conform to the order of the universe and had not obeyed the law of "degree," or rightful place, between the governor and the governed. With proper respect for order, the general should be like the hive to which all foragers repair, but when his authority is ignored, the order of the universe is broken and all things fall to chaos. This is true, he says, in the physical world:

> Degree being vizarded,
> The unworthiest shows as fairly in the mask.
> The heavens themselves, the planets, and this
>   centre
> Observe degree, priority, and place,
> Insisture, course, proportion, season, form,
> Office and custom, in all line of order;
> And therefore is the glorious planet Sol
> In noble eminence enthroned and spher'd
> Amidst the other; whose medicinable eye
> Corrects the ill aspects of planets evil,
> And posts like the commandment of a king,
> Sans check to good and bad. But when the
>   planets
> In evil mixture to disorder wander,
> What plagues and what portents
>   ....
> Divert and crack, rend and deracinate
> The unity and married calm of states
> Quite from their fixture.

Not only in the physical world, but also in the social and moral realm a violation of natural, universal order would bring disaster. Without universal order there would be no force to keep things in their rightful place, but each thing would meet "in mere oppugnancy."

> The bounded waters
> Should lift their waters higher than the shores
> And make a sop of all this solid globe,
> Strength should be lord of imbecility,
> And the rude son should strike his father dead.
> Force should be right; or rather, right and
>   wrong,
> Between whose endless jar justice resides,
> Should lose their names, and so should justice
>   too.
> Then everything includes itself in power,
> Power into will, will into appetite;
> And appetite, an universal wolf,
> So doubly seconded with will and power
> Must make perforce an universal prey,
> And last eat up himself.[32]

From the elaborate manner in which Ulysses' speech is introduced, from its heightened emotion, unusual with the speaker, and from the conviction which it carries in the council, one cannot escape the feeling that here Shakespeare is expressing his fundamental faith in an ordered world, in an order which makes inevitable a moral law.

For in Shakespeare's concept the two ideas are inseparable. The idea of the universe as an orderly arrangement of forms, each differing from the other in degree and ranging from the most insignificant detail up through the order of the planets to the highest—this concept of the universe was made prominent in Plotinus, was more elaborately developed by the Pseudo-Dionysius, was accepted by St. Thomas as the basis of his cosmology, and had become the usual view in the Renaissance.

Combined, however, with an ordered cosmos is the conviction of a moral law based upon and growing out of the cosmic order. This concept, as we have seen, was first made prominent by the Stoics in their struggle against Epicurean relativity. It was the conviction that there was something deeper than changing opinion to direct human conduct—a law fixed in the divine order of things and therefore inevitable. This concept of a universal moral law was also incorporated by St. Thomas in his philosophy, but with the additional Christian concept that it was only a phase of the Eternal Law of God. In the speech of Ulysses, however, we have only the Stoic concept.

The profound penetration of Ulysses reaches the depth of the problem of evil, for with no universal order there could be no problem. But if a universal order does exist, then each thing has its natural limits, its rights and prerogatives, which must not be molested by things around it. It is degree or place that marks the bounds of these natural rights, and between the endless jar of their opposing interests Justice sits as umpire, distributing to each person or thing the prerogatives which it by nature may claim, and defending it against encroaching wrong. "Right and wrong" are terms to distinguish that which each thing or person in this natural order should possess or against which it should be protected, and they take their meaning solely from the concept of order in the world. Were this concept of order blotted out and the bounds of things obliterated, there would be no moral law, no distinction between right and wrong, no meaning to the word "justice." Each thing with sufficient force would override all others; its power combined with its will, and its will driven by appetite or greed, would make an universal prey. The world would ultimately perish in chaos and anarchy —"eat up itself." For if no order is intended in the world, brute force without intellect would destroy even that which produced it—"beat its father down"—and would be as right as mercy; neither could be counted right or wrong, because these distinctions depend upon a faith in cosmic order.

Shakespeare's thought goes to the root of things. It clashes irrevocably with the Epicurean concept that the world is the result of chance and that moral law is wholly relative, growing out of the changing desires and fancies of men. It takes issue equally with the extreme skeptics' denial of any more fixed basis than the opinions and customs of nations. Both these schools of thought, by doubt or denial of planned order, escaped the problem of evil except as a mere relative notion in the minds of men. Shakespeare, on the other hand, with his deep conviction of order and natural law, is left with a full consciousness of the problem, and the realization that it has grown out of this very order.

The analysis of Ulysses is strikingly intellectual, and in his subsequent discussion he is scornful of the ignorant, such as the dull, brainless Ajax and the broad Achilles, who value brute force more than brains, and cherish the battering ram that beats down the walls more than the hands that made it or the intelligence that directs its work. This intellectual presentation is in the spirit of Greek philosophy, and from its point of view the failures and evils of men have close connection with their blockish ignorance.

Human Reaction to Moral Law

In the Trojan council we have a different atmosphere. The question facing the council is a moral issue, the discussion moves on an emotional and idealistic plane, and the decision reached is the result of emotion rather than reason. Shall Helen be returned and the war stopped? Hector says yes, for she is not worth the cost of keeping. Out of the decimated hosts of Greece and Troy each life lost is worth as much as hers, and what reason would deny the yielding of her up to stop the excessive cost? Troilus ignores the claim of reason, and comes directly to the question of values. Things are worth the value we place upon them; it is not from themselves but from us they take their price.

Yet it is not Helen's worth alone which is at issue, but the honor of the king, and who can weigh honor in common ounces, whose infinite worth cannot be buckled in

> With spans and inches so dimutive
> As fears and reasons.[34]

It was the voice of all the council, Troilus argues, that Paris should do some vengeance on the Greeks, and all approved his bringing Helen home. That was a reasoned decision, like the choosing of a wife, which is the act of will and judgment guided by the eyes and ears. After the choice is made, one cannot honorably turn back the goods, no more than silks upon the merchant when we have soiled them. To surrender Helen now would be an act of cowardice and disgrace.

Troilus' argument points up the complexity of human motives in which the "good" is often confused with the "bad," or rather two "goods" often conflict with each other. Here the value of honor and "saving of face," both good to those concerned, clashes with the demands of justice and moral law. In such conflicts is emotion or reason to prevail?

To Cassandra's prophecy of Troy's destruction and to Hector's appeal for reason and the "fear of bad success in a bad cause," Troilus replies:

We may not think the justness of each act
Such and no other than event doth form it.[35]

This is in harmony with his sense of sub-
jective values, for Troilus is an idealist, not a
pragmatist. Even on moral issues the extreme pragmatist, like Machiavelli, would decide his course of action by its probable success or failure, not by its justice or right. But
to Troilus success or failure mean nothing if
the act is right. We would have to agree with
him about that. Cassandra's brain-sick rap-
tures, he says,

Cannot distaste the goodness of a quarrel
Which hath our several honors all engaged
To make it gracious.[36]

Troilus does not reexamine the justness, or
the honorableness, of the council's decision
ten years before to steal the wife of a Grecian
king. Right or wrong, the action once taken
cannot be changed without loss of honor, and
honor outweighs right.

Paris adds his puny plea that it would be
treason to the "ransak'd queen,"

Disgrace to your great worths and shame to me
Now to deliver her possession up
On terms of base compulsion.[37]

But Hector sweeps aside the plea of honor
and disgrace as superficial glossing, and
brings the argument down to moral law:

The reasons you allege do more conduce

> To the hot passion of distemper'd blood
> Than to make up a free determination
> 'Twixt right and wrong, for pleasure and
>   revenge
> Have ears more deaf than adders to the voice
> Of any true decision. Nature craves
> All dues be render'd to their owners; now,
> What nearer debt in all humanity
> Than wife is to the husband? If this law
> Of nature be corrupted through affection,
> And that great minds, of partial indulgence
> To their benumb'd wills, resist the same,
> There is a law in each well-order'd nation
> To curb those raging appetites that are
> Most disobedient and refractory.
> If Helen then be wife to Sparta's king,
> As it is known she is, these moral laws
> Of nature and of nations speak loud
> To have her back return'd. Thus to persist
> In doing wrong extenuates not wrong,
> But makes it much more heavy. Hector's
>   opinion
> Is this in way of truth; yet ne'ertheless,
> My spritely brethren, I propend to you
> In resolution to keep Helen still,
> For 'tis a cause that hath no mean dependence
> Upon our joint and several dignities.[38]

This is a surprisingly inconsistent and yet a common decision. Hector voices with as complete conviction as Ulysses the moral law of nature and of nations, and he recognizes that under that law justice demands the return of

Helen to her husband, but after having made that "free determination 'twixt right and wrong" he turns deliberately away from it to uphold an empty "honor" which he knows is wrong.

The decision brings us face to face with the gravest problem of the play—the inconsistency of human conduct in relation to moral law. As the discussion indicates, the problem is inextricably connected with that of values, for it is what we value that decides our actions. In no other play except *Hamlet* is there such a penetrating analysis of the worth of things. Hamlet weighed life and found it vanity, but Hamlet had become a pessimist. Here, however, in the two great councils Shakespeare gives us an elaborate introduction to the fixed foundation of all moral values, the concept of order and natural law. Upon this platform of moral law he presents the huge drama of life in an action sung by poets from Homer down, famed through the ages for its glory and dignity, a war so important that gods fought alongside men on the battlefield. The result is as inconsistent as life itself.

Shakespeare shows that few in either host are concerned with order and moral law. Reason and natural justice, which should control the actions of men, are swept aside by ignorance and passion. The blockish Ajax is swollen with vanity, the butcher Achilles is swayed by pride and envy, and both are a prey to ignorance. Thersites, whose biting cynicism must be taken with a grain of salt but who yet carries conviction, comments that the fountain of Achilles' mind is not clear enough to water an ass, and that he himself had rather be a tick in a sheep than such a valiant ignorance. "If Troy be not taken till these two undermine it, the walls will stand till they fall of themselves," for they have such "little, little, less than little wit" that they cannot "in circumvention deliver a fly from a spider, without drawing their massy irons and cutting the web."[39]

Through their disregard of reason and natural law the whole Grecian camp is threatened with anarchy. The brute force of Ajax and Achilles cannot be controlled even by intelligence. To move them Ulysses must disregard reason and stoop to policy and tricks, which raises the distasteful problem of chicanery in government—the demagogy of the shrewd politician to influence the ignorant. His trick, however, as Thersytes points out, is only a makeshift, and in the end is "prov'd not worth a blackberry," for the cur Ajax becomes prouder than the cur Achilles; "whereupon the Grecians again proclaim barbarism, and policy grows into an ill opinion."[40] Such is the chaos wrought by ignorance and passion.

Even with the concept of a fixed moral law, there is always the problem of a relative interpretation of it in particular cases. The Trojan War grew out of a violation of the moral law, but immediately became involved with the ideals of honor and glory. In the play it is given the most penetrating criticism. Stripped of its glamor and viewed empirically for the thing it is, the motive of the war is not worth its cost. When Paris asks Diomedes who merits Helen most, Diomedes replies bitterly that there is no difference in the merits of the contenders:

> He merits well to have her, that doth seek her,
> Not making any scruple of her soilure,
> With such a hell of pain and world of charge;
> And you as well to keep her, that defend her,
> Not palating the taste of her dishonor
> With such a costly loss of wealth and friends.
> He, like a puling cuckold, would drink up
> The lees and dregs of a flat tam'd piece,
> You, like a lecher, out of whorish loins
> Are pleased to breed out your inheritors.
> Both merits pois'd, each weighs no less nor
>   more.[41]

Not only is the strife not warranted by the merits of the contenders, but she for whom they contend is not worth the cost:

> For every drop in her bawdy veins
> A Grecian's life hath sunk; for every scruple
> Of her contaminated carrion weight,
> A Trojan hath been slain. Since she could
>   speak,
> She hath not given so many good words breath
> As for her Greeks and Trojans suff'red death.[42]

The champion of empirical truth, however,

is the fool Thersites. For him no glory can hide the naked reality of things; his caustic cynicism burns its way to the center. He reduces everything to its basic elements, but in the reduction destroys its beauty and value. To him the war is patchery, juggling, and knavery. "All the argument is a cuckold and a whore; a good quarrel to draw emulous factions and bleed to death upon."[43] Those who would "war for a placket" deserve nothing but the bone-ache. He strips each hero of his glamor. Old Nestor is a mouse-eaten dry cheese; the shrewd Ulysses, a dog-fox; Agamemnon has less brains than ear-wax; Menelaus, the cuckold, is transformed into both bull and ass. "To be a dog, a mule, a cat, a fitchew, a toad, a lizard, an owl, a puttock, or a herring without a roe, I would not care; but to be Menelaus! I would conspire against destiny."[44] Diomedes is a knave who promises like Brabbler the hound, "but when he performs, astronimers foretell it. It is prodigious, there will be some change."[45] Patroclus is Achilles' male whore and a lecher.

To Thersites the whole war is nothing more. "Lechery, lechery; still wars and lechery; nothing else holds fashion. A burning devil take them!"[46] He sees no higher values in the duel of Troilus and Diomedes than the fight of two wenching rogues for the possession of a whore; and he shouts encouragement to Menelaus and Paris, "Now, bull! now, dog!" The whole group are fools, and he himself a fool and a rascal, "a scurvy, railing knave; a very filthy rogue." "I am a bastard begot, bastard instructed, bastard in mind, a bastard in valour, in everything illegitimate."[47] It is not surprising that from the warped, degenerate mirror of his mind the whole world should be reflected worthless—filthy, vile, corrupt. Yet who can say that he is entirely wrong about the Trojan War and its famous heroes? He is like a dog snarling at every rogue's heels, but a dog you would not want to kick, or question too closely, for his cynicism bites too deep.

Between Thersites, who sees no value in anything, not even in himself, and Troilus there is a universe of difference. Troilus is the idealist, and the idealism of his mind throws a halo around everything, attributes values beyond intrinsic worth. What should men need with reasons, he asks?

> Nay, if we talk of reason,
> Let's shut our gates and sleep. Manhood and honour
> Should have hare hearts, would they but fat their thoughts
> With this cramm'd reason. Reason and respect
> Makes livers pale and lustihood deject.[48]

He sees his course, his right and wrong, instantly, intuitively, and he is impatient of argument, which dulls the edge of action. If Helen alone were the issue of the fight, he "would not wish a drop of Trojan blood spent more in her defence," but she has become a symbol of an inner value, a "theme of honour and renown." Her price, though in herself not worth a straw, is rated with the honor of a king, and who can weigh the worth of honor and set a price upon the infinite. Troilus has instinctively, even unknowingly, substituted his inner values—glory and honor—for the external thing—a stained, disloyal wife. The fight has shifted from a cause he could not defend to one of infinite price, and because his values have no dependence on external things he can pursue them with a singleness of mind regardless of whether the result is success or failure.

In the same manner he also idealizes love. To Paris love may be only "hot thoughts" and "hot deeds," and to Thersites "lechery," but to Troilus it is infinite service, loyalty, and truth. The tragedy of love for him is "that the will is infinite, and the execution confin'd, that the desire is boundless and the act a slave to limit,"[49] that it is too often "food for fortune's tooth." His inner evaluation reaches beyond loss and change. He sees Cressida deliver to Diomedes the gift he had given her, and hears her lamely excuse the frailty of her sex:

> The error of our eye directs our mind,
> What error leads must err; O, then conclude
> Minds sway'd by eyes are full of turpitude.[50]

Thersites, who sees the thing for what it is, undeluded by any ideal sense, gives the logical interpretation:

A proof of strength she could not publish more,
Unless she say, my mind is now turn'd whore.[51]

But Troilus will not believe the testimony
of his eyes and ears. To record their truth
would be a lie, since yet there is a credence in
his heart, a hope so strong

That does divert the attest of eyes and ears,
As if those organs had deceptive functions.[52]

To account them true would not only deny his
faith in Cressida, but would shatter his ideal
of love and all his sense of values. Rather think
the girl he sees and hears speak is not she.
Thersites exclaims, "Will he swagger himself
out on's own eyes?" To preserve his inner
values, that is exactly what Troilus must do.
The girl he sees giving herself to Diomedes is
not his Cressida, but Diomedes'.

If beauty have a soul, this is not she.
If souls guide vows, if vows are sanctimony,
If sanctimony be the gods' delight,
If there be rule in unity itself,
This is not she.[53]

His whole world of values is at stake: faith
in beauty, truth, sanctity, God, even in unity
itself. When a similar shock comes to Hamlet,
who has like Troilus idealized love and the
wonder and beauty of the world, it leaves him
in pessimism and despair, sick of life and longing for death because he cannot close his eyes
to the unexpected evil and corruption. In con-

trast, Troilus is not a thinker. In the struggle
of his soul against his senses, reason is helpless, taking either side with a kind of bifold
authority. A thing inseparable has suddenly
divided "wider than the sky and earth," and
yet this spacious opening is too narrow to ad-
mit the point of a broken spider's web. Contrary to reason Cressida's action is a division
in absolute unity—an impossible concept, yet
necessary to the mind of Troilus, who, to retain his faith against the evidence of eyes and
ears, must, unlike Hamlet, close his mind
against reality: "This is, and is not, Cressida."

Shakespeare has given us in *Troilus and
Cressida* a picture of the world in which there
is not only a cosmic order, but an order in
human affairs, implanted, as the Stoics would
say, in the very nature of men and recognized
by nations—an order which carries a conviction of right and wrong, and a justice which
guards the bounds of each and decrees appropriate punishment for their violation. Though
the moral law is fixed and immutable, the
interpretation of it by human minds may vary
as widely as the cynicism of Thersites and the
idealism of Troilus—all the space between
earth and heaven. But differences in interpretation in no way abrogate the moral law.

To Thersites with his warped mind the world
is corrupt, and he feels no shame in baring its
corruption and his own. Troilus, on the contrary, suffers, but closes his eyes to reality.
In the strength of his ideals he can live above

and apart from the world, superior to loss and change.

Between these two extremes Hector recognizes the Trojans' breach of moral law and suggests the decision which justice demands; then, like millions of others, deliberately takes the face-saving course to preserve their "several dignities." And Hector suffers the penalty of violating the law he recognizes.

Finally, Ulysses, who is of course not under the pressures of Hector, guiding himself calmly by reason in harmony with the cosmic law, directs the course of the war to a successful close for the Greeks. Recognizing the demands of law, he tries in vain to move others to the same conviction. When he fails through reason and moral law to move Ajax and Achilles to fight, he stoops to trickery and plays on their selfishness and conceit. He is personally less admirable than Troilus, who, though blinded by his ideals to the demands of law, would hardly have knowingly used false motives to induce men to right action. But Ulysses, guided by reason, and with his ability to see both right and wrong, seems more eminently fitted for the "tough world" which Shakespeare pictures, with its confusion of ideals and realities, and its tragic mixture of good and evil.

FOOTNOTES AND REFERENCES

1. Epicurus, *Morals*, trans. John Digby (London: Sam Briscol, 1712), Mx. xxiii.

2. Benjamin Jowett, trans. *The Dialogues of Plato* (New York: Macmillan Co., 1892), IV, 205. For Plato's brilliant reply see IV, 217.

3. George Long, trans. *The Discourses of Epictetus* (London: George Bell, 1906), pp. 12, 84.

4. George Long, trans., *Thoughts of the Emperor Marcus Aurelius Antoninus* (London: George Bell, 1901), p. 129.

5. *Supra*, p. 21f.

6. La Primaudaye, *op. cit.*, p. 35f.

7. Heinrich Cornelius Agrippa von Nettesheim, *The Vanity of Arts and Sciences* (London: R. M. for R. B., 1684), ch. LIV.

8. *Ibid.*

9. William Boulting, *Giordano Bruno, His Life, Thought, and Martyrdom* (London: Kegan Paul, Trench, Trubner & Co., 1914), p. 160.

10. John Bradford, *Writings, containing Sermons, Meditations*, etc. Ed. for the Parker Society (Cambridge, England: University Press, 1853), p. 310.

11. Boulting, *op. cit.*, p. 153f. See also Bruno's *Spaccio*, Dial 1.

12. Boulting, *op. cit.*, p. 153.

13. Benno Tschischwitz, *Shakespeare's Hamlet vorzugsweise nach historischen Gerichspuncten erlautert* (Halle, E. Germany: 1868).

14. Montaigne, *op. cit.*, Bk. II, ch. xii.

15. *Ibid.*

16. *Ibid.*, Bk. I, ch. i.

17. George Chapman, *The Conspiracy of Charles, Duke of Byron* (Urbana: U. of Illinois Press, 1970) III, i, 42-62.

18. Desiderius Erasmus, *In Praise of Folly* (London: Everyman edition), p. 171f.

19. *Othello*, II, iii, 256f.

20. *Ibid.*, III, iii, 339-343.

21. *Richard II*, I, iii, 270f.

22. *Ibid.*, I, iii, 284-299.

23. *Much Ado About Nothing*, V, i, 35-38.

24. *Troilus and Cressida*, II, ii, 53-59.

25. *Ibid.*, II, ii, 82f.

26. Montaigne, *op. cit.*, Bk. II, ch. xii throughout; Bk. III, chs. xi, xii.

27. Gelli, *op. cit.*, p. 262.

28. *Troilus and Cressida*, III, iii, 95-123.

29. *Julius Caesar*, I, ii, 52f, 67-70.

30. *Troilus and Cressida*, V, ii, 110. See also *Venus and Adonis*, II, 1064ff; *Lucrece*, 368ff; *Cymbeline*, IV, ii; *A Midsummer Night's Dream*, V, i, 2-22.

31. *Merchant of Venice*, V, i, 102f. See also Sonnet CII.

32. *Troilus and Cressida*, I, iii, 63-126.

33. For its possible Platonic origin and its Renaissance currency see James Holly Hanford, "A Platonic Passage in Shakespeare," *Studies in Philology*, XIII (1916), pp. 100-109. Thomas Elyot in *The Governour*, II, 209, and 211f, has a similar discussion of degree and chaos. See also Lyly, *op. cit.*, I, 273f, and Justus Lipsius, *Sixe Books of politickes or civil doctrine* (New York: De Capo, Reprint, 1594) p. 109. For the anarchy of uncontrolled license see *II Henry IV*, IV, v, 131ff.

34. *Troilus and Cressida*, II, ii, 31f.

35. *Ibid.*, II, ii, 119f.

36. *Ibid.*, II, ii, 132-135.

37. *Ibid.*, II, ii, 151-153.

38. *Ibid.*, II, ii, 168-193.

39. *Ibid.*, II, iii, 171.

40. *Ibid.*, V, iv, 12ff.

41. *Ibid.*, IV, i, 55-65.

42. *Ibid.*, IV, i, 69-74.
43. *Ibid.*, II, iii, 78-80.
44. *Ibid.*, V, i, 67-70.
45. *Ibid.*, V, i, 98-100.
46. *Ibid.*, V, ii, 195-197.
47. *Ibid.*, V, vii, 18f.
48. *Ibid.*, II, ii, 64-50.
49. *Ibid.*, III, ii, 88-90.
50. *Ibid.*, V, ii, 110-112.
51. *Ibid.*, V, ii, 113f.
52. *Ibid.*, V, ii, 122f.
53. *Ibid.*, V, ii, 138-142.

Chapter 3

MEASURE FOR MEASURE AND
TIMON OF ATHENS
The Via Media

EVEN WITH a fixed and universal moral law, which Shakespeare affirms in *Troilus and Cressida*, the differences between the minds and the experiences of men can lead to radical variations in their understanding and application of it. What standard, then, if any, can guide men in choosing the right course of action in a given situation? In *Measure for Measure* and *Timon of Athens* this seems to be the central theme.

Aristotle had long ago attempted to define the right course between good and evil as the way of moderation, the *via media*. In the *Nichomachean Ethics* he says:

> We can only indicate the more general features of good and evil. . . . There is, then, this most characteristic impression which right causes; that it is a "fitness" of things, an exact adjustment between means and ends, a moderation, in absence of all extravagance whether of excess or defect. It is analogous to what health is in the body—freedom alike from superfluity or from want.[1]

Whatever act, then, possesses this perfect fitness and moderation is good, and whatever digresses from this medium, either to excess or to defect, is evil.

The single act, however, is of much less importance, Aristotle asserts, than the general attitude or habit of conduct to which the principle applies. Those habits which establish a state of mind characterized by fitness and moderation, a conformity to a reasonable standard, are called virtues, and those that are characterized by irregularity and lack of measure are vices.

Virtue is, therefore, a formal state of mind united with the assent of the will and based upon an ideal of what is best in actual life— an ideal set by Right Reason, according as the moral sense of the good man would determine its application. This ideal or standard of right is "a mean state" between two vices, one in the direction of excess, the other in the direction of defect: it is a mean state also from the fact that vices fall short or else go beyond what is fitting both in feeling and conduct, whereas virtue has an instinct to find out and the resolution to prefer "the mean," the true fitness of things.[2]

With this definition of Virtue, or the good, as the mean between two vices, Aristotle proceeds to illustrate and define different virtues. *Courage* is the mean between the two vices of

cowardice and *recklessness*, *liberality* the
mean between *prodigality* and *stinginess*,
temperance the mean between *sensuality* and
the *insensate*, *magnificence* the mean between
ostentation and *meanness*, *high-mindedness*
the mean between *vainglory* and *littleness* of
soul.

The *via media*, says Aristotle, is not easy to
attain, because it is relative. It is not a mathe-
matical point equally distant from the two extremes, because it must vary with different
persons, purposes, points of view and circumstances.[3] What would be the perfect mean of
liberality for one person or for one purpose
would be too much or too little for another.
Right Reason is the only guide to the attainment of the perfect standard, and because this
standard is unique and at the same time variable it is much easier to miss than to attain it.
Aristotle accepts the dictum of the Pythago-
reans that wrong is infinite, while right belongs
to law; it is easier to shoot at random into infinite space than to hit a narrow mark.[4] But
since one extreme is usually worse than the
other, one should at least withdraw himself
from the worse extreme, and, if he cannot hit
the perfect mark of life, at least avoid the worst
evils.[5]

This doctrine of "the mean" was gradually
connected with the Stoic's idea of the law of
nature, which was conceived as determining the
proper mean through the use of Right Reason.[6]
The rigidity of the Aristotelian definitions also

gradually gave way, and the "golden mean"
became confused with temperance, or rather
temperance was exalted as the dominant virtue
embracing all the others and with the help of
reason keeping them all within measure and
bounds.[7]

Furthermore all the passions of the mind
were subject to its control. As La Primaudaye
expresses it:

> Temperance (saith Plato) is a mutual con-
> sent of the soule . . . causing all disor-
> dered and vnbridled desires to take reason
> for a rule and direction . . . This vertue
> then of temperance is stedfast and moder-
> ate rule of reason ouer concupiscence,
> and ouer other vehement motions of the
> mind.[8]

Thus temperance and reason came to be inseparably connected as the basis of all virtue.
Lipsius says:

> As for virtue she ever marches in the mid-
> dle path, and is cautiously heedful lest
> there should be anything of Excess or De-
> fect in any of her actions. For still she
> directs herself by the Ballance of Right
> Reason, and hath that alone for her test.
> Now this Right Reason is nothing else but
> a TRUE APPRECIATION AND JUDGE-
> MENT OF HUMANE AND DIVINE MAT-
> TERS, AS FARR AS THEY APPERTAIN
> TO US: Contrary hereunto is Opinion

which is a FUTILE AND FALLACIOUS
JUDGEMENT CONCERNING THE SAME
THINGS.[9]

Lipsius combines the Aristotelian "mean"
with the Stoic concept of reason and opinion,
and the Christian idea of "humane and divine
matters" as the basis of this judgment.

It would be useless, however, to multiply examples of this idea in Renaissance times. It
appears everywhere and is applied to all
phases of life. Pico della Mirandula decided
upon this basis that the simple life was the life
of virtue, and giving up his wealth and social
position, he retired from the affairs of the
world.[10] The principle is prominent in Spenser,[11] and indeed is a fundamental ideal in all
the moral philosophy, applicable alike to the
trivial matters of dress[12] and to the most
powerful passions of anger, grief, or joy. That
man is of highest wisdom, writes Bruno, who
says, "I was never less gay than now, or never
less sad."

Because both the contraries in excess—
that is, in as far as they exceed—are vices,
because they pass the line; and the same,
in so far as they diminish, come to be virtues, because they continue within limits . . . the vice is there where the opposite
is; the opposite is chiefly there where the
extreme is; the greatest opposite is the
nearest to the extreme; the least or nothing
is in the middle, where the opposites meet,

and are one and identical; as between the coldest and hottest and the colder and hotter, in the middle point is that which you may call hot and cold, or neither hot nor cold, without contradiction. In this way whoso is least content and least joyful is in the degree of indifference, and finds himself in the habitation of temperance, where the virtue and condition of a strong soul exist, which bends not to the south wind nor to the North.[13]

The soul which is continually swayed between the extremes of passion, as Hamlet was, is both dead and living, and suffers from distractions within itself. As Bruno expresses it,

Devoid of hope, I reach the gates of hell,
And laden with desire arrive at heaven:
Thus am I subject to eternal opposites,
And, banished both from heaven and from hell,
No pause nor rest my torments know,
Because between two running wheels I go,
Of which one here, the other there compels.[14]

The only way of escape, says Bruno, is through temperance, which keeps to the middle ground. But when passion leads to either extreme it becomes a double vice, which consists in this, that the thing recedes from its nature, the perfection of which consists in unity, and there where the opposites meet its composition and virtue exists.[15]

This suggests the further concept of the self-

destructiveness of extremes. For any good
departs from its true nature and becomes an
evil when carried to excess. Lipsius says even
of religion itself that "we ought still to vse a
mean, *least the people fall to superstition*,
which is an utter enemie to religion."[16]

The self-destruction of extremes is emphasized by Shakespeare, when the King, perhaps from his own sensual experience, says
to Laertes:

> There lives within the very flame of love
> A kind of wick or snuff that will abate it,
> And nothing is at a like goodness still;
> For goodness, growing to a plurisy,
> Dies in his own too much.[17]

Friar Laurence moralizes upon the mingled
structure of life and the world with its mixture
of potential good and evil, each depending on
its reasonable use:

> For nought so vile that on the earth doth live
> But to the earth some special good doth give,
> Nor ought so good, but, strained from that fair
>   use,
> Revolts from true birth, stumbling on abuse,
> Virtue itself turns vice, being misapplied.[18]

So Claudio, imprisoned, recognizes that
even liberty itself may turn to bonds unless
restrained. His imprisonment, he says, comes

> From too much liberty, my Lucio, liberty.
> As surfeit is the father of much fast,

So every scope by the immoderate use
Turns to restraint. Our natures do pursue,
Like rats that ravin down their proper bane,
A thirsty evil; and when we drink we die.[19]

The ideal, of course, was that temperance
should not merely govern the isolated act,
but should become the character of the man.
It was considered a quality of mind, related to
reason, which should determine the action
and course of life. The man who lacks the
temperate soul becomes a menace to his fellows and an evil in society. It is from the point
of view of moderation that the Humanists condemned Hedonism. Pleasure in itself was not
taboo. Sir Thomas More represents the Utopians as advocating pleasure, safeguarded by
reason, as the end of life:

For joyful life, that is to say a pleasant life
is either evil: and if it be so, then thou
shouldst not onlye helpe no man thereto,
but rather, so much as in you lieth, with-
drawe men from it, as noysome and
hurtful, or els if thou not only mayste, but
also of dowty art bound to procure it to
others, why not chiefly to the self? To
whome thou art bound to show as much
favoure and gentlenesse as to other. For
when nature biddeth the to be good and
gentle to other she commandeth the not to
be cruell and ungentle to the selfe. Therefore even very nature (say they) prescrib-
eth to us a joyful life, that is to say, pleasure

as the end of all our operations, And they define vertue to be life ordered according to the prescripte of nature.[20]

Though many in England, and particularly the growing number of Puritans would not have agreed with More's Utopians, Shakespeare apparently would have no quarrel with them. He has the puritanical Malvolio, who would forbid all cakes and ale, appropriately exposed and condemned.[21] But he also strongly disapproves carrying pleasure to the extreme of libertinism and vice. It is significant of Shakespeare's philosophy of moderation that in *Julius Caesar*, Antony, in spite of the element of treachery in his character, is presented in heroic proportions; but after he has allowed his pleasures to run riot in Alexandria, he is pictured as the shattered remnant of his former self, a libertine in his dotage.

The ideal of moderation is a fundamental principle in Shakespeare's moral philosophy. It underlies the characterization of Prince Hal, Hotspur, and Falstaff in their attitudes toward honor. It underlies the tragedy of Coriolanus, for his acknowledged courage is carried to the extreme of recklessness, and his magnanimity, which makes him refuse the spoils of war, is lost in the extreme of haughtiness. He cannot "temperately transport his honors." But the principle is nowhere so elaborately developed as in *Measure for Measure* and *Timon of Athens*.

Justice and Law in Measure for Measure

The moral problem presented in *Measure for Measure* is a complex one. It involves the principle of moderation, or temperance, as it applies not only to sensual conduct, but also to the more fundamental problems of justice and law. Temperance and justice were intimately associated in Renaissance thinking, because both seemed to govern the *via media* so perfectly. Many regarded temperance as the supreme virtue which embraced all others and determined the mean for them. Others, however, associated justice with it as a necessary and equal virtue, or even gave it the supreme place. Lyly apparently gave them equality:

> Honestie my olde Graundfather called that,
> when menne lyued by law, not lyst; obseruing
> in all thinges the means which we name ver-
> tue; and vertue they account nothing else
> but to deale iustly and temperately.[22]

Though La Primaudaye says temperance is the "foundation of all the virtues," he gives justice an equal place as "mistress" and "ground-work" of them all.[23] Agrippa says that the virtues are in some respects antagonistic to one another, as mercy opposes justice and magnanimity opposes humility, and unless they are reconciled in a harmony they become vices:

> Now that wherein they ought all to concur,
> is Justice, according to the Opinion of

Ambrose and *Lactantius*, who together with *Macrobius*, have followed the Opinion of Plato in his Commonwealth. Others take it to be Temperance, that imposeth a mean in all things.[24]

Gelli agrees in making justice the "Assembly of all virtues,"[25] and Hurault concurs in placing justice or "righteousness" as "the chiefe of the virtues which containeth all vertues," and regulates the course of moderation. Even liberality cannot be exercized without justice, for liberality must reward men according to their worth and the giver's ability. But temperance is inseparably connected with justice, for it is justice, or righteousness, which gives temperance its perfect moderation:

If we intend to speak of Temperance, we shall find that it is vnited vnto righeousness, and that the Intemperate person which is subject to his passions, cannot doe anything aright, so long as he is intangled in that vice . . . Insomuch that no man can be called a temperate or staied person, vnless he be righteous.[26]

In *Measure for Measure*, therefore, it is not surprising to find the two ideas of justice and temperance inseparably connected. Shakespeare's basic purpose in the play is apparently to define ideal justice, but since the abuse of justice comes from related extremes, he bases his plot upon a problem of morals and law in which the principles of intemperance and injustice can be most clearly and strongly presented.

The organization of his characters is almost a schematic dramatization of Aristotle's statement that

⌈ The man who pursues the excesses of what is pleasant, or pursues even necessary pleasures to an extravagant point and pursues them from a definite conviction (i.e. for gratification), such an one is a dissolute man: his will being abandoned to pleasure he is necessarily past repentance and so incurable, since without repentance there can be no moral cure.

On the other hand, the man who is defective in his desire for pleasure, is the exact opposite of the dissolute man, and is an ascetic: while, again, the man who steers
⌊ a mid course is the temperate man.[27]

Again Aristotle adds a fourth classification:

Intermediate between dissoluteness and temperance is the mixture of good and evil called weakness. That is to say, there is a character which, through the ascendency of passion, is easily led astray contrary to Right Reason . . . a character which, though it be so overmastered by the feeling of the moment, is yet not so utterly overborne by evil as to alter its nature and form a conviction that it ought without stint or curb to pursue bodily pleasures as a duty. [28]

In *Measure for Measure* all four of these
classes are represented. At one extreme are the
dissolute frequenters of the brothels, Mrs.
Overdone who runs one, Pompey her pander,
and the libertine Lucio; at the other extreme is
Angelo, who has crucified all natural impulses, which he considers evil; in the middle is
the temperate Duke, who is the ideal of moderation; and between the Duke and Lucio are the
"weak" lovers, who have not allowed reason to
govern.

Angelo is not to be considered a villain in the
sense that he is essentially evil. He is possessed of most excellent qualities—purity, sin-
cerity, love of justice and law and a zeal to uphold it; but his evil arises from carrying his
ideal of purity and justice beyond the limits of
reason, and stifling all natural impulses as
vices. The Duke describes him as "A man of
stricture and firm abstinence," and adds further:

> Lord Angelo is precise
> Stands at a guard with envy, scarce confesses
> That his blood flows, or that his appetite
> Is more to bread than stone.[29]

It is evident that Shakespeare wants us to
understand the extreme nature of the man, for
he repeats the characterization continually.
Lucio says in the same scene.

> Lord, Angelo, a man whose blood
> Is very snow-broth, one who never feels
> The wanton stings and motions of the sense,

But doth rebate and blunt his natural edge
With profits of the mind, study, and fast.[30]

To the libertine Lucio such extreme abstinence is utterly contrary to nature, and sets
Angelo apart as not entirely human.

They say this Angelo was not made by man
and woman after this down-right way of
creation. Some report a mermaid spawn'd
him; some, that he was begot between two
stockfishes. But it is certain that when he
makes water his urine is congeal'd ice; that
I know to be true; and he is a motion gener-
ative; that's infallible.[31]

With this elaborate insistence upon Angelo's
impassiveness, his rigid control of all emotions and sensitive impulses, his extreme
"rightness," Shakespeare has prepared what
many might regard as an ideal justicer, one
who could not be bribed or moved from justice
by human weakness. Even his name suggests
the righteousness of the angels.

The motives of the Duke in withdrawing and
turning the government over to Angelo have
often been severely condemned. He mentions
two reasons for doing so. First, he is plainly
dissatisfied with his own government and with
its apparent failure in law enforcement. Those
strict statutes and "biting laws," which are
"the needful bite and curbs to headstrong
steeds," he has let slip, till like a whip that is
never used, they are more mocked than feared:

> So our decrees,
> Dead to infliction, to themselves are dead,
> And liberty plucks justice by the nose,
> The baby beats the nurse, and quite athwart
> Goes all decorum.[32]

The Duke is perhaps exaggerating the condition of affairs because of criticism he has heard, but the chief point is his own dissatisfaction. In failing to execute the laws as rigidly as they should have been executed, he has even encouraged crime:

> For we bid this be done,
> When evil deeds have their permissive pass
> And not the punishment.[33]

His discouragement indicates that he has thought deeply about the problem of justice and law. With a conviction of his own failure he might tighten the reins of government himself, but there were two reasons to discourage such a course. The people had regarded him as lenient, and if he suddenly announced a stringent enforcement of the laws, many would hardly believe it and would continue to presume upon his leniency. There would be more infractions of the law and more penalties than if another took charge. It would be better, therefore, to adopt the plan used by all rulers, and recommended by Justus Lipsius and by Machiavelli, of letting a new man carry out the change. People would more readily believe a new official, especially if he had a reputation for strictness. There would be less tendency to challenge the change.

The Duke's second reason for turning the government over to Angelo rather than enforcing the law more rigidly himself, is apparently a desire to try Angelo's theory of government. The Duke knows his leniency has been criticized, quite possibly by Angelo himself. One of the most difficult problems of government is how severe the penalties should be for violations. If law interferes too intimately in the lives of people, it breeds resentment and rebellion; if penalties are too severe, courts do not enforce them and crime increases despite the penalties. No law can be enforced effectively which the people do not support. Honestly dissatisfied with his own attempts, yet distrustful of Angelo's rigidity, the Duke decides to give his subordinate full power to rule as his own judgment directs while he can quietly watch in disguise the progress of events. It is to be noticed that the Duke does not place upon Angelo any obligation to increase the stringency of the laws. His sole commission is to give Angelo absolute freedom to enforce the law as he himself sees fit:

> Your scope is as mine own,
> So to enforce or qualify the laws
> As to your soul seems good.[34]

In his tongue would be both life and death.

One is justified in assuming, therefore, that the Duke expects a more rigid enforcement of laws merely because of Angelo's nature. He is in fact conducting an experiment in government and in human nature; and he adds,

> Hence shall we see,
> If power change purpose, what our seemers be.[35]

There can be little doubt that Shakespeare's purpose in such an elaborate experiment was to expose to his beloved England the dangers in the growing extremes of puritanism. It is true that Shakespeare is too magnanimous or too tolerant to wage the bitter war against the puritans that Jonson did. He is almost strangely silent about this most disturbing of contemporary movements. The two pointed references to puritans are both humorous. The gull Aguecheek would beat Malvolio if he thought him a puritan, but Maria assures him: "The devil a puritan that he is, or anything constantly, but a time pleaser . . ."[36] Yet one cannot ignore the puritan element in Malvolio's character, especially in his austere and "virtuous" condemnation of hilarity and cakes and ale. And according to some of their critics even the "time serving" might not be amiss in satirizing the puritans.

The second reference to puritans is the clown's good-natured raillery at the common marital fate of all men, even the most religious and the most widely antagonistic—all cuckolds with horns:

> If men would be contented to be what they
> are [cuckolds], there were no fear in mar-
> riage; for young Charbon the puritan and
> old Poysam the papist, howsome'er their
> hearts are severed in religion, their heads
> are one; they may joul horns together,
> like any deer in the herd.[37]

But if Shakespeare was too tolerant to be
excited over the puritans as a religious group,
he might still be concerned over the more
vital question of the extreme spirit of puritanism. It would be in harmony with his
breadth of mind and his penetrating understanding to go at once to the heart of the puritan danger—the extreme rigidity with which
they would legislate and control the lives of
men. It would also be in harmony with his
broad tolerance and wisdom to avoid per-
sonalities and to deal with the basic problem
of intolerance.

Consequently the term puritan is never used
throughout the play. Angelo, to be sure, is
called "precise," a term widely applied to
puritans, and the whole description of his extreme asceticism and rigidity was considered
characteristic of the puritans. Yet Shakespeare
gives him the name Angelo, which would popularly associate him with the papists and would
not have been approved by many puritans.
With great tact Shakespeare seems to be suggesting that his play is not an attack on puritans as a group, but is an examination of a

philosophy of law and government and of moral extremes, characteristic not only of puritans but of many groups and individuals in every age. But the problems involved are particularly related to the spirit of intolerance which was then growing in England, and which was associated with puritanism.

Calvin had taught an asceticism different from the medieval Catholic ideal, but almost as extreme. Instead of a withdrawal from the world he advocated a life of great activity but with the severest self-discipline.[38] Perhaps no group of people have ever felt such responsibility for the lives of others. They had the zeal of reformers and the consciousness of being their brothers' keepers, and they were never content to legislate for themselves alone.

In London the war against the theaters, bear baitings, and amusements of every sort was continuous and severe. In Geneva, when Calvin gained almost complete control of the city, he at once set about toning up the morals of the people. Penalties, including imprisonment, were meted out for dancing, playing cards on Sunday, frequenting taverns, cursing, swearing, trying to commit suicide, for saying *requiescat in pace* over a husband's grave, for eating fish on Good Friday, for laughing during the sermon, for arranging a marriage between a woman of seventy and a man of twenty-five, or for saying the pope was a good man.[39]

Even the names of children were regulated

by law, and such good Catholic names as
Claude, Baptist, Evangelist, Sunday, Easter,
Pentecost, Sepulchre, and Angel were forbidden under penalty,[40] as "Angelo" would
have been. In 1546 the council ordered all
taverns closed because they were sinks of
iniquity, and substituted "abbayes" instead,
where people could buy food and drink at cost,
but where it had to be consumed in company
with the Bible, to the tune of religious con-
versation, and without the appetizing in-
decency and profanity of the taverns.[41] The
"abbayes" soon failed and went out of business.

The penalties against the more grievous sins
of adultery and fornication, strange to say,
were much lighter than one might expect or
than Calvin himself approved. If unmarried,
the culprits were imprisoned for six days on
bread and water and fined sixty sous. If married, the imprisonment was for nine days and
the fine according to the seriousness of the
offence. But Calvin apparently thought this
punishment entirely too light. Though he does
not say flatly that adultery should be punished
by death, he is fierce in denouncing the adul-
teress:

She injures her husband, exposes him to
shame, despoils also the name of her family, despoils her unborn children, despoils
those whom she has already borne in lawful wedlock. When a woman is thus in the

hands of the devil, what remedy is there except that all this be exterminated.[42]

He refers pointedly to the stoning of adulterers in Deuteronomy 22:21, as an example that those who have lived in such scandal should teach us by their deaths to keep chaste, and then adds, "Do you not see that it is an insufferable crime, and one which ought to be punished to the limits."

Though Calvin did not increase the severity of the laws against adultery, he did, as Harkness says, through the consistery and council, "cause many more offenders to be brought to justice . . . or at least to punishment; for he demanded the full and stringent execution of the laws." He felt keenly a responsibility for his neighbors' conduct. To permit sin in others was the same as to participate in it, and to allow brothels was the same as operating them.

If we suffer them and let them be nourished by our indifference, we shall be held before God as brothel-keepers and procurers.[43]

The puritan tendency to rigid asceticism, and to hew to the line and letter of the law, with severe penalties for violation, is antagonistic to the ideal of moderation. How it will work when put to the test of power and opportunity is apparently what Shakespeare wants to show. The result might easily have been foretold by any Aristotelian or Humanist.

Angelo's ideal of asceticism in the play

quickly fails because it would maintain an extreme beyond the bounds of nature. It tolerates no weakness, and, lacking the strength and resiliency of moderation, it is unprepared for temptation. Angelo is supremely self-assured. When, despite remonstrances, he condemns Claudio to death, he defends himself:

> 'Tis one thing to be tempted, Escalus,
> Another thing to fall. . . .
> When I that censure him, do so offend,
> Let mine own judgment pattern out my death,
> And nothing come in partial.[44]

This is the overconfidence of the extremist. In his feeling of security Angelo is safe until he meets a kindred soul whose saintly purity is the fulfillment of his own ideal. For Isabella herself has at first much of the coldness and severity of Angelo. She is a novice in one of the strictest orders of the church, excluded from all contact with men, yet she would wish more strict restraint upon herself and the votaries of St. Clare rather than relax a single rule. When she begins the petition for her brother's life, she pleads with half a heart and is at war within herself "twixt will and will not," because she has no sympathy with those who have so sinned. It is the libertine Lucio, who knows—and loves—the weakness of the flesh, that urges her forward. While to Lucio and his licentiousness, Isabella belongs to a world above all weakness of the flesh, "a thing enskied and sainted," to Angelo she is a kindred

spirit, clothed with the saintly purity to which
he aspires, and which in a measure he feels
that he possesses. To hear her spotless virtue
plead for one guilty of adultery and demand
that Angelo knock at his own heart and ask
"what it doth know, That's like my brother's
fault," stirs unexpected emotions against
which he has no defence. He might be proof
against all other lures.

> Never could the strumpet,
> With all her double vigor, art and nature,
> Once stir my temper.[45]

But the purity of Isabella, who would bribe him
only

> with true prayers
> That shall be up at Heaven and enter there
> Ere sunrise,[46]

arouses in him not only admiration for her
goodness, but stirs also a natural human emotion, which to his perverted ascetic ideal seems
wholly evil. In his thinking there has been no
distinction between illicit and legitimate love,
for love, as Pope Innocent pointed out, involves
the flesh and the flesh seemed evil. Repudiating his marriage vows to Mariana on the pre-
text of her lack of dowry may have increased
his revulsion to sex as a measure of self-
justification. As Isabella pleads, he is suddenly
bewildered by the clash of emotions—the base
mingling with the pure—and he feels himself
"that way going to temptation where prayers

cross." To his consternation he desires Isabella "foully" for the very qualities that make
her saintly, and he is faced with the moral
paradox that he is goaded into sin by loving
virtue. In anguish he exclaims,

> O cunning enemy, that, to catch a saint,
> With saints dost bait thy hook.[47]

His whole moral world has suddenly crashed,
evil has changed places with good, and the
state on which he had prided himself has
turned "sear'd and tedious." Emotions he had
long condemned were aroused in him by a
saint's petition. Blood was triumphant, and he
must "write good angel on the devil's horn"
for it was no longer the devil's crest.

The penalty of extreme asceticism is its
wrong sense of moral values in which the extremist loses his way and becomes uncertain
of his course. In the intensity of temptation
Angelo cries,

> Alack, when once our grace we have forgot,
> Nothing goes right; we would, and we would
>   not.[48]

It is a mistake to think of Angelo as a hypo-
crite. This was Ben Jonson's characterization
of the puritan. Shakespeare sees more deeply.
Angelo is perfectly sincere and honest, and
in his conflict of emotions he suffers intensely. He has merely carried his "goodness" to an
excess which throws his sense of values into
confusion when the temptation comes. For to

be "overgood," to think of one's self as above human weakness, Shakespeare would say, has as many dangers as to be bad, and Mariana expresses the doctrine of moderation when she pleads for Angelo's life:

> They say, best men are molded out of faults,
> And, for the most, become so much the better
> For being a little bad; so may my husband.[49]

And no one can doubt that the Angelo who has measured the depths of his own weakness and begs for sudden death to atone for his sin is a better and wiser man than the Angelo who boasted that he could not fall.

What of Justice and Law?

The problem of justice and law, which is even more fundamental in the play than the moral extremes, is also connected with the ideal of moderation. Aristotle had said that justice, assuming the equality of persons, attempts to measure the difference between "right" and "wrong" and bring them to an equal balance.

> The "equal," therefore, is a mean point between "too much" and "too little," and "gain" is too much and "loss" too little in inverse ratio to one another—too much of good and too little of evil, or too little of good and too much of evil; the mean point between the two being, as we have shown, the "equal" which we assert to be "the just." Corrective Justice will, consequent-

ly, be a mean between "loss" and "gain."
Hence when men are at issue between one
another, they betake themselves to the
judge, since to have recourse to justice, the
very purpose and *raison d'etre* of a Judge
being, as it were, to act as a living embodiment of Justice.[50]

The judge, who represents justice, is often
called a "mediator," says Aristotle, because
men find in him an ideal "mean" or standard
of reference, where justice resides. Hurault,[51]
Gelli,[52] and others describe justice in much the
same manner. William Baldwin in his *Treatise
of Moral Philosophe* (published some time
before 1564) defines it as a "measure, which
God hath ordained vpon the earth, to definde
the feble from the mightye, and the true from
the vntrue: and to roote out the wicked, from
amonge the good."[53] It is justice also that
makes the laws, he declares, and not the laws
justice, for he who knows justice can discern
what is right or what is wrong, what is equal or
vnequal, "which, expressed in writing, may be
called a law."[54] La Primaudaye says justice
is the mean between injustice and severity;
and it is as much a vice to refrain from punishing those who deserve it as to punish too
severely, for justice distributes to every man
what he ought to have.[55]

Shakespeare's treatment of justice in *Measure for Measure* has been strongly condemned
by some and questioned by others; however,

correctly understood, it is surprisingly modern and certainly centuries beyond the popular concept of his time. In *Troilus and Cressida* Ulysses speaks of

> right and wrong
> Between whose endless jar justice resides.[56]

This picture of its office as "mediator" between struggling inequities, is again humorously expressed in regard to the justice of the braggart Armado,

> Whom right and wrong
> Have chose as umpire of their mutiny.[57]

Both statements emphasize the medial position occupied by justice. In *Measure for Measure* also the Duke emphasizes the exactness with which the inequalities are to be measured and balanced. Each wrong or loss must be compensated for by an equivalent right or gain. Angelo commits the same sin for which he condemns Claudio; consequently, justice demands

> An Angelo for Claudio, death for death!
> Haste still pays haste, and leisure answers
>   leisure;
> Like doth quit like, and *Measure* still *for
>   Measure*.[58]

Such may be absolute justice. But the practical difficulty always lies, not in determining the amount of the injury or loss, but in the voluntariness of the act. An injustice may be done involuntarily, or with varying degrees of the will involved. Plato in *The Laws* en-countered this difficulty, and finally decided that in civil government the punishment must be determined not by the voluntariness or involuntariness, but by the distinction between injustice and hurt. When there is hurt, it must be made good by law.[59] This solution of the difficulty, though it may be as near justice as human society can ever come, is nevertheless capable of great injustice because it takes no account of the complex world of motives, human passions, weaknesses, and ignorance.

Shakespeare is keenly aware of its limita-tions. "Measure for Measure" justice, to be sure, was far superior to the practice of the Elizabethan age, when petty thieves, or even innocent debtors, could be long imprisoned, and sometimes die forgotten in dismal dun-geons. Rightly understood, however, the law of "an eye for an eye, tooth for tooth, and life for life" required that the punishment be exactly commensurate with the injury, never more severe. But, as Plato recognized, this often overlooked the human factors. Hence Shake-speare supplements "Measure for Measure" justice with the ideal of the Sermon on the Mount:

Judge not, that ye be not judged. For with what judgment ye judge, ye shall be judged; and with what measure ye mete, it shall be measured unto you. And why beholdest thou the mote that is in thy brother's eye, but considerest not the beam that is in thine own eye.[60]

From this point of view, though justice must make equalities of right and wrong, and for every loss mete out a gain to match, it is at the same time tempered by a knowledge of one's own infirmities and may not go beyond the bounds of human weakness.

The failure of Angelo is that he has disregarded the "temperate" element in justice, as well as in his private life. He has never recognized that he might have a beam in his own eye, and he exacts more than justice should demand in the light of human strength and weakness. The result is not justice but the gravest injustice, which is all the worse because it is considered just. Claudio is condemned to death for a fault, which was "almost no fault" in Elizabethan eyes, for in Elizabethan England a betrothal was considered as binding as marriage, and under the circumstances surrounding Claudio and Juliet, actual marital relations, though clearly not approved by the Duke in the play, would not have been severely condemned. In fact, because Angelo had been betrothed to Mariana earlier and had no just reason for repudiating the contract, the Duke arranged for Mariana to supply Isabella's place in the assignation. Such an arrangement would have been considered a "common law" marriage.

But the inequity of Angelo's punishment

of Claudio is immediately apparent. He condemns Claudio to death, though Juliet is
equally guilty. Habitual frequenters of the
brothels are merely imprisoned; Mrs. Overdone, the keeper of a brothel, is untouched,
and Pompey, who has been her pander for
years, is helped to the honorable position of
assistant hangman. While all the brothels in
the suburbs of Vienna are pulled down, those
in the City are left standing for seed, because
some good burgher "put in for them." This
suggests one of the most difficult problems
in the enforcement of law. For where laws
and penalties are too extreme for public
approval, they can not be enforced, and injustice and corruption result even in the law-
enforcement officials.

Claudio's bitterness against such partiality
reaches even beyond the human problem and
indicts the justice of heaven:

> Thus can the demigod authority
> Make us pay down for our offence by weight
> The words of heaven: on whom it will, it will;
> On whom it will not, so; yet still 'tis just.[61]

The Calvinist doctrine of arbitrary justice
could not more concisely have been condemned. Such justice, no matter how the Calvinist might defend it theologically, in human
affairs stirs inevitable bitterness. Angelo
makes its best defence when he contends that,
in spite of its partiality, it is still just to the
man condemned:

> I not deny
> The jury, passing on the prisoner's life,
> May in the sworn twelve have a thief or two
> Guiltier than him they try. What's open made
>   to justice,
> That justice siezes. What knows the laws
> That thieves do pass on thieves? 'Tis very
>   pregnant,
> The jewel that we find, we stoop and take 't
> Because we see it; but what we do not see
> We tread upon, and never think of it.
> You may not so extenuate his offence
> For I have had such faults.[62]

But it is the tragedy rather than the glory of human justice that Angelo is right. The law would never be enforced if it must wait till every juror is without offence and every crime is known. Yet the fact that we cannot be impartial does not relieve the pitiful spectacle of human error, whose blundering results are so clearly expressed by the temperate Escalus: for where earthly justice reigns, too often

> Some rise by sin, and some by virtue fall,
> Some run from brakes of vice, and answer
>   none:
> And some condemned for a fault alone.[63]

The extreme with which Angelo would execute justice also defeats its very purpose. All the old penalties that had hung on the wall like rusty mail while nineteen zodiacs went round he immediately revived and put to execution.

When Justus Lipsius pleaded for the Prince to check the dissoluteness of the people in Europe and bring about a new and healthier manner of living, he granted it would be difficult, but it could be done if the Prince himself would conform to the same restraints which he imposed upon the people, and if he would try not to reform all at once, "but by little and little, reduce them to the ancient order. For there is none amongst us all that can be so soone reformed, nor change so suddenly his disposition or alter his course."[64] The advice of Lipsius would check the extreme and keep justice within human limits. But Angelo's policy is to execute all laws immediately with the utmost rigor.

It is to be noted, however, that in *Measure for Measure* the equitable enforcement of the law is not condemned; rather it is approved and encouraged. The condemnation placed throughout is upon the extreme nature of the penalties, which violates the very principle of justice. In Lucio's opinion there is no equality between the death penalty of Claudio and his error; he is condemned merely for "untrussing"; "why, what a ruthless thing it is in him [Angelo], for the rebellion of a codpiece to take away the life of a man!"[65] And the gentle Provost says,

> He hath but as offended in a dream
> All sects, all ages smack of this vice; and he
> To die for it![66]

The essence of injustice is to make the penalty greater than the offence; and, when justice is carried beyond the extreme of human nature, it is destroyed in its own extremity and changes to injustice. Pompey's comment when he is told of the penalty for bawdry is unfortunately pregnant with truth:

> If you head and hang all that offend that way but for ten year together, you'll be glad to give out a commission for more heads. If this law hold in Vienna ten year, I'll rent the fairest house in it after three-pence a day.[67]

Of a piece with this is Lucio's comment to the Duke, ". . . the vice is of a great kindred, it is well allied; but it is impossible to extirp it quite, friar, till eating and drinking be put down."[68]

With public feeling like this laws cannot be executed nor penalties imposed, for law enforcement requires the approval and cooperation of the majority of the people. Without this there may be a law for every trifle, but all will be evaded, and hypocrisy and corruption will take the place of honest justice. Watching the violent reforms of Angelo, the Duke says,

> . . . There is so great a fever on goodness, that the dissolution of it must cure it. Novelty is only in request; and it is as dangerous to be aged in any kind of course as it is virtuous to be constant in any undertaking. There is scarce truth enough alive

to make societies secure; but security enough to make fellowships accursed.[69]

This is a condemnation of that zeal for reform that outruns all reason, discards safe, established forms for novelties, and ignores the basic truths that make society secure. Yet while there is no security for society, there is enough security or power in factional fellowships to make them a curse.

The Duke had been dissatisfied with his own attempts at justice but the failure of Angelo's extreme ideal, with its severity against some, its laxity with others, and its hypocrisy even in the seat of highest judgment, makes his own fault small. Here in Vienna, he says,

> I have seen corruption boil and bubble
> Till it o'errun the stew; laws for all faults,
> But faults so countenanc'd, that the strong
>   statutes
> Stand like the forfeits in a barber shop,
> As much in mock as mark.[70]

With the failure of Angelo we come to the ideal of the Duke, and apparently of Shakespeare, which is moderation. The Duke himself is described as "a gentleman of all temperance," and "one that, above all other strifes, contends especially to know himself."[71] These two statements suggest the basis for Shakespeare's definition of justice. It must contain within it the element of moderation and must be measured by self-knowledge. It must see the

beam within one's own eye. Escalus is surprised at Angelo's "lack of temper'd judgment," and he pleads with him to weigh his
own weakness and to balance the condemnation with the offence:

> Let but your honor know,
> Whom I believe to be most strait in virtue,
> That, in the working of your own affections,
> Had time coher'd with place or place with
>   wishing,
> Or that the resolute acting of your blood
> Could have attained the effect of your own
>   purpose,
> Whether you had not sometime in your life
> Err'd in this point which now you censure him,
> And pull'd the law upon you.[72]

A knowledge of human infirmity is a standard to help measure the greatness of a wrong
and to gauge the severity of the penalty. Were
there no frailty in men, the severest penalties
might be just. "We are all frail," says Angelo,
and Isabella replies, "Else let my brother die."
A man's self-knowledge is, therefore, one
measure of his justice. So long as his judgments do not condemn himself he is not tyran-
nous; but when his penalties for others are so
severe they pass upon himself, he becomes unjust. The Duke defends Angelo on that ground:

> His life is parallel'd
> Even with the stroke and line of his great
>   justice.

> He doth with holy abstinence subdue
> That in himself which he spurs on his power
> To qualify in others. Were he meal'd with that
> Which he corrects, then were he tyrannous.[73]

But, finally, ideal justice is self-condemning. Out of one's self-knowledge comes, not only a measure of others' guilt, but, when brought face to face with one's own act, the measure of one's own. The King in *Hamlet* describes the perfectness of heavenly justice as self-condemning, for "there is no shuffling," but at the bar of heaven each action lies

> In his true nature, and we ourselves compell'd
> Even to the teeth and forehead of our faults,
> To give in evidence.[74]

This is the ideal apparently which guides the Duke in his distribution of justice at the close. Some have been surprised at his treatment of Barnardine, a convicted murderer who should have been hanged without mercy under English law. It is understandable that Shakespeare would not want to mar a comedy, if *Measure for Measure* can be so called, by carrying out a death sentence. But he could easily have avoided this by never introducing Barnardine on the stage, and by merely mentioning his death, as he does that of Ragozene, the pirate. Evidently the prominence he gives Barnadine is Shakespeare's effort to define more clearly his concept of justice. He is concerned about the beastliness of the fellow:

A man that apprehends death no more
dreadfully but as a drunken sleep; careless, reckless, and fearless of what's past,
present, or to come; insensible of mortality, and desperately mortal.[75]

To put him to death in such a state, the Duke
says, would be damnable. The fellow is too
densely ignorant to apprehend the meaning of
life and death, and cannot therefore be judged
by laws he does not understand. The Duke explains the difficulty:

Sirrah, thou art said to have a stubborn soul,
That apprehends no further than this world,
And squar'st thy life according.[76]

To destroy his soul when he knows nothing
of the soul nor of its laws would not be justice,
but unintelligible injustice. The Duke, therefore, pardons his "earthly" faults and places
him on a form of "probation" to be instructed
by the friar for "better times to come."

Though many in our twentieth century would
still not approve such leniency, for "rehabili-
tation" of criminals is yet in its infancy, no
other judgment would have been in harmony
with the concept of justice as self-condemning, as equated with the criminal's intelligence
and understanding of his act. In this concept
Shakespeare was centuries ahead of his time.

With Angelo the judgment is the same, for
out of his own mouth comes his condemnation.

With fine irony the Duke prepares him for it.
It would be beyond all reason, he says,

> That with such vehemency, he should pursue
> Faults proper to himself. If he had so offended,
> He would have weigh'd thy brother by himself,
> And not have cut him off.[77]

In condemning Claudio for a sin he too commits Angelo pronounces judgment on himself,
and, when faced with his own guilt, he begs
immediate sentence and instant death. Lucio
too stands self-condemned and would slip
away from a sentence that "may prove worse
than hanging."

Thus Shakespeare's justice seems measured
exactly by the offense and yet so adjusted to
human frailties and the voluntariness of the
crime that each offender stands self-condemned.

But we have not understood *Measure for
Measure* unless we recognize within it the
impossibility of such justice in our present
world. This constitutes part of the bitterness
of the play. In *Hamlet* the King recognizes that

> In the corrupted currents of this world
> Offence's gilded hand may shove by justice;
> And oft 'tis seen the wicked prize itself
> Buys out the law.[78]

In *Measure for Measure* we have this truth
almost tragically presented, and in the fine
closing scene the author with matchless subtle-
ty contrasts the farce of human justice with the

ideal. Here is all the "shuffling" and subter-
fuge, false testimony, and the arrogance of
authority, hurried and prejudiced judgments,
hearts crying in vain for justice being tried by
the criminal himself, as a lamb might ask
justice of the wolf. In comparison with the
impossible ideal, it is Shakespeare's picture
of the world as it is, where crime allied with
power may shove by justice, and where frail
men, whose fragile essence is as glass, assume
a severity beyond the mercy of the gods. The
whole pitiful spectacle is well summarized in
Isabella's tragic lines:

> . . . but man, proud man,
> Dress'd in a little brief authority,
> Most ignorant of what he's most assurred,
> His glassy substance, like an angry ape,
> Plays such fantastic tricks before high heaven
> As makes the angels weep.[79]

TIMON OF ATHENA and
"The Middle of Humanity"

Among the dramas of pessimism *Timon of
Athens* stands like an unfinished ruin almost
too vast and rugged in its conception for
symmetrical completion. As a philosophical
indictment of the world it held possibilities
greater than those of *Hamlet*, because the
theme has a broader perspective and greater
variety in points of view, but perhaps partly on
this very account it lacks the emotional intensity of Hamlet, and thus, fails to carry the

same conviction. Nowhere in Shakespeare is the attack on human society filled with such bitter, intense hatred, but the effect is lost through the weakness of Timon, and the ultimate pessimism breaks down into a pathetic apology for our common human frailties.

Briefly, the play is a study in misanthropy in which the world is viewed through the eyes of an extreme idealist, a cynic, and a practical man of action. In its hate theme it is akin to *Hamlet* and *Lear*; in its three points of view—the ideal, the practical, and the cynical—and in its love theme, it is akin to *Troilus and Cressida*; and in its treatment of the central character, as well as the whole problem of world depravity, it follows the philosophy of the *via media*.

The play opens with all interest centered on Timon. Even before he appears we learn of his extreme liberality, which has made him the most popular man in Athens, and we have a warning also of the change of fortune which often follows such hero-worship.

When Timon appears we see his liberality exemplified. He redeems Ventidius from prison at a cost of five talents[80] and, in the spirit of Seneca's *Of Benefits*, refuses to be repaid;[81] for he is not of that feather to shake a friend off when he is in need, and if one receives again, he cannot be truly said to give. He even wants Ventidius brought to him when he is free, for

> 'Tis not enough to help the feeble up,
> But to support them after.[82]

He settles a fortune on his servant that he may marry an heiress, because "'tis a bond in men." He rewards the painter and the poet for their "counterfeits" and "feignings," and entertains his friends with lavish feasts. He is clearly violating the Elizabethan, and the Aristotelian, ideal of moderation. Hurault says:

> The dutie of liberalitie consisteth in distributing a mans good measurably, to such as haue need; if he go beyond that, it is vice, whether it be in the ouermuch or in the ouer little. For in the one consisteth prodigalitie, and in the other nigership, which is an incurable disease. . . .[83]

Sir Thomas Elyot, in the discussion of liberality, magnificence, and beneficience repeats that liberality is a mean and may be turned into a vice if it "lacks the bridle of reason":

> Semblably liberalitie (as Aristotle saith) is a measure, as well in gyuing as in taking of money and goodes. And he is only liberall, which distributeth accordinge to his substance, and where it is expedient. Therefore he ought to consider to whom he shulde gyue, howe moche, and whan.[84]

He adds also:

> Tulli calleth them prodigall, that in inordinate feasts and bankettes, vayne playes,

and huntinges, do spende al their substance, and in those thinges wherof they
shall leaue but a shorte or no remem-
braunce.[85]

Timon was guilty, from this point of view,
of the excess of prodigality, which Aristotle
had regarded not as a depraved or wicked disposition, but a foolish one.[86] If one wants gold,
said a senator, let him but steal a beggar's dog
and give it Timon, and the dog coins gold immediately.

> If I would sell my horse and buy twenty more
> Better than he, why give my horse to Timon,
> Ask nothing, give it him, it foals me straight
> And able horses. . . .
>   It cannot hold; no reason
> Can found his state in safety.[87]

Timon's steward grieves because he will not
cease his flow of riot. He tells him the world
to him is but a word:

> Were it all yours to give it in a breath,
> How quickly were it gone.[88]

Yet Timon, strange to say, is no mere spend-
thrift. His liberality proceeds from a far nobler
quality—an excess of love. He is the Prince of
lovers. His heart is great enough to include
the world, and his trust in the goodness of men
is infinite. It is true, he tells the painter, that
"since dishonor traffics with man's nature, He
is but outside," but this truth for him is merely
unfelt theory. He has never known a friend un-

true. For him love is an ideal that levels all barriers between "mine" and "thine." What else is friendship for if not to share wealth: "we were born to do benefits; and what better or properer can we call our own than the riches of our friends?"[89] In this perfect union of hearts Timon "could deal kingdoms" to his friends and "ne'er be weary."[90] His love possesses that ideal perfection that makes his friend as dear to him as himself. It is the Platonic idealization which permeated so much early Renaissance thought and which Shakespeare had made prominent in the Sonnets, where he offers to give his mistress to his friend, and which triumphed over selfishness in *The Two Gentlemen of Verona.*

Timon is a Platonic idealist not only in his attitude toward love, but, like Troilus, in his sense of values. These come from within; and in his inner soul he idealizes love and measures the truth of all his friends by his own heart:

> I weigh my friend's affections with my own.
> I'll tell you true.[91]

The tragedy of Timon, then, is not due primarily to excess of giving, but to excess of love and trust in men. Even Lucullus grants that Timon's only fault is "honesty." Out of this strange fact arises Shakespeare's indictment of the world, as well as his condemnation of Timon. That such infinite love and trust should turn to tragedy, and good result in harm, is a part of the strange limitations of humanity from which only the gods are free. Flavious says:

> Poor honest lord, brought low by his own heart,
> Undone by goodness! Strange unusual blood,
> When man's worst sin is, he does too much
>   good!
> Who, then, dares to be half so kind again?
> For bounty, that makes gods, does still mar
>   men.[91]

Timon's tragedy, then, is that his goodness is too good for the world in which he lives. It is through the eyes of Apemantus in the first three acts that Shakespeare gives us a view of Timon's world. Of the same strain as Thersites, but of a more philosophical mind, he sees life with no idealistic coloring, and his acrid intellect penetrates the disguise of superficial manners and reveals the hidden baseness. To him all men are knaves or fools. Timon's friends are knaves merely because they are Athenians; to knock out the brains of one of them would be "doing nothing"; the painter himself is but "a filthy piece of work"; and in all of them

> The strain of man's bred out
> Into baboon and monkey.[93]

Apemantus, to be sure, is "opposite to humanity," but his judgment in too many instances is correct. He sees both Timon and his friends more truly than they see themselves:

Who lives that's not depraved or depraves?
Who dies, that bears not one spurn to their
    graves
Of their friends' gift?
I should fear those that dance before me now
Would one day stamp upon me. . . . .[94]

In Timon's friends he sees the dregs and flattery, and in Timon he sees a fool laying out wealth on curtsies. His friends are dipping their meat in his blood, and he only cheers them on.

But the ingratitude of Timon's friends is denounced with even greater intensity by his servants. Lacking the cynic's philosophy of human baseness, they are still appalled at the unspeakable depravity of men. The servant who flings back the money at Lucullus feels something of his master's passion that one who has fed at Timon's cost should so deny him. But even strangers, who have known him only by report, are shocked by the depth of the ingratitude.

Why, this is the world's soul; and just of the
    same piece
Is every flatterer's spirit. Who can call him
His friend that dips in the same dish? for, in
My knowing, Timon has been this lord's father,
And kept his credit with his purse,
Supported his estate; nay, Timon's money
Has paid his men their wages. He ne'er drinks,
But Timon's silver treads upon his lip;
And yet—O, see the monstrousness of man,
When he looks out in an ungrateful shape.[95]

The betrayal of Timon's friends is of a piece
with the treachery of Judas to the Christ, for
they had all dipped with him in the dish, had
carried his purse, and used his money as if it
were their own. The very servants who were
sent to collect from Timon the debts he owes
their masters revolt at their ingratitude. To
wear Timon's jewels, and then demand the
money which he owed to purchase them was
something worse than theft.

But the theme of ingratitude is broadened
further by the subplot. After all his service to
the state, Alcibiades is banished, not for a
crime but for pleading the cause of a friend.
He had kept back the Senate's foes while they
counted their money in safety and let out their
coin on interest, and he had received only in-
sults and banishment.

The multiplying of such instances suggests
a fundamental flaw in human nature. At the
ingratitude and treachery of Timon's friends
a servant exclaims that their villanies will
finally cheat the devil himself:

> The devil knew not what he did when he
> made man politic; he crossed himself by't;
> and I cannot think but, in the end, the
> villainies of man will set him clear.[96]

But to show their depravity still worse, they
are so devoid of every sense of shame that they
can come back for further gifts after they have
betrayed the giver; and to reach the lowest
depths of all, after Timon has driven them out,
they return to hunt through his house for the

jewels and other gifts he had given them.
Nothing could be added to blacken the picture
of human baseness. The repeated instances,
with their cumulative effect, one piled upon
another, and all leading to that climax of unbelievable depravity, become a universal indictment of the world; and the opening words
of the play take on a new and somber meaning:
"How goes the world." asks one; to which another answers, "It wears, sir, as it grows."

We are interested not alone in Shakespeare's
presentation of world depravity, but in the
philosophical reaction to it. Three different
reactions are distinguished and contrasted. To
the cynic it is the normal course of things and
merely food for hate; to the idealist it brings
a profound shock that wrecks, not the ideal,
but his relation to the external world; and to
the practical man it is a call for action.

Timon's immediate reaction is a change
from a love that knew no bounds to a hate that
is equally boundless. The unexpected baseness
of his friends is thrown into sharp contrast
with his ideal of love and his faith in human
goodness. His world within is suddenly out of
joint with the world outside, and being an
idealist he instinctively hates the outside
world to retain the truth which he values within. The more extreme these inner ideals are,
the more completely does he find himself at
odds with life; and the pain of the continual
clash between the world and his own mind
fills him with hate for all humanity.

So Timon becomes the supreme hater of the world because he had been the supreme lover. The world had been unworthy of his love and could not measure up to his ideals. The beauty of unselfishness within his own mind had been met with a greed so profound that it seemed to dominate the natures of men. Were the gods themselves, he says, to borrow of men, they would renounce the gods. Wealth so corrupts that no one can escape unless he despises his very nature with its weakness:

> Twinn'd brothers of one womb,
> Whose procreation, residence, and birth
> Scarce be divident, touch them with several
>   fortunes,
> The greater scorns the lesser; not nature,
> To whom all sores lay siege, can bear great
>   fortune
> But by contempt of nature.[97]

The attack upon the injustice and corruption of wealth which runs through so much of Shakespeare's social satire from *Richard II* and *King John* through *Hamlet* and *Lear* reaches its bitterest tone in Timon. Gelli had denounced the injustice of wealth in a way that might well have suggested the passages in *Hamlet*[98] and *Othello*.[99]

Alas! my dear friend, how many Sots and Blockheads are there in the world, who if they were poor, would be . . . insulted, lampoon'd and ridiculed for dull unthinking Fools; who because they have abundance of dirty Acres they can call their own, are deified in Epistles Dedicatory, are respected in all Companies, have the upper Seat given them at all publick Entertainments, are call'd your Excellence and your Honor, and have their Levies crowded every morning with store of humbel Servants, who applaud all their actions and admire every sottish saying that drops from them, tho' they are the arrantest coxcombs in Nature. 'Tis a plain case that you despise Virtue by the daily Proverbs you daily teach to children. Get money, my Son, honestly if thou canst, however get money. Virtue won't keep the wolf from the door, she's so sheepish-hearted.[100]

Falconbridge in *King John* had set forth the doctrine that it is wealth or "commodity" that throws the world out of balance and brings all its evils:

Commodity, the bias of the world;
The world, who of itself is poised well,
Made to run even upon even ground,
Till this advantage, this vile-drawing bias,
Makes it take head from all indifference,
From all direction, purpose, course, intent.[101]

But Falconbridge checks his railing against the rich because of its futility, and being a man of the world, he decides to seek "commodity" and fit himself for the world as he has found it.

In Timon we have the same denunciation,
but with the added intensity and bitterness of
personal hate. Wealth makes the distinction between the beggar and the lord and reduces all
men to flatterers and villains:

> The learned pate
> Ducks to the golden fool; all is oblique;
> There's nothing level in our cursed natures,
> But direct villany.[102]

Unlike Falconbridge Timon's hate is too deep
for compromise, and it drives him into solitude
away from the sight of men.

Yet Timon is still the antithesis of Apemantus. They agree only in a hatred of the world,
but their reasons are as separate as the poles.
Apemantus, like Thersites, has no ideals, sets
no value upon anything; his beggarly life has
made him what he is, a cynic who takes a poor
delight in castigating the pride of men. He
feeds upon misfortunes and loves his misery.
"Willing misery," he preaches to Timon,

> Outlives incertain pomp, is crown'd before;
> The one is filling still, never complete;
> The other at high wish.[103]

He dislikes the world because he is incapable
of loving anything. He stands even below the
flatterer in baseness because he lacks the element of good, the human aspiration, that makes
the other flatter. Timon says,

> If thou hadst not been born the worst of men,
> Thou hadst been a knave and flatterer.[104]

To Timon's pure idealism nothing could be more opposite than the cynic, and he expresses his natural repugnance when he says: "Were I like thee, I'd throw away myself."[105]

But Timon's hatred comes from the opposite pole—an idealism too lofty for the world. With his bare realism Apemantus thinks Timon's hate is nothing but

> A poor unmanly melancholy sprung
> From change of fortune,[106]

of no benefit to him or injury to his flatterers. Apemantus is right from the world's point of view, for why should Timon let his disappointment in his "friends" turn him against the whole world? If he is to live in the world, of what value is it to withdraw from the society of men? Will he receive better attendance from the trees and frozen brooks? His withdrawal indicates no change of heart; for, if he still had wealth, he would give it all to rascals. Apemantus is right again when he says: "The middle of humanity thou never knewest, but the extremity of both ends."[107] The way of moderation Timon has never known, but only a love too great for the world to merit and a hate much bitterer than the world deserved. Each extreme was madness, and made him unfit for living among men.

The tragedy of Timon is not the loss of paltry wealth, for when he discovers wealth again, he gives it recklessly to all who come. The tragedy is the discrepancy between the

world and his ideal. This was the cleavage that
left him hopelessly estranged from life, and for
which there could be no healing, for each new
contact only drove him farther from the world
and locked him more securely in himself. Alcibiades expresses a sincere love and sympathy, but is only repulsed. He is too much
like the world which Timon hates, and there is
no point of contact for their minds. Alcibiades'
march against Athens is induced by personal
selfishness, a desire for vengeance and power,
as much as by a sense of justice in punishing
the Senate for its wrongs, and when he has
conquered he will be satisfied. But to Timon
the evil of men is so great that only its complete eradication can cure the world.

Yet his hate is basically unselfish because it
would include all men in death, even himself.
He hates the world, not so much because it
has injured him, but because it is evil, and to
destroy the evil all must be destroyed. It is a
hatred growing out of love—love of goodness,
love for an ideal, even love for Athens. A
strange but logical contradiction and harmony
of extremes when love for his country makes
him hate his country, when the ideal is saved
only by destruction of the real, when he would
help with his gold to exterminate his countrymen, and yet curse the man who was born to
conquer his country.

> I am sick of this false world, and will love
> naught

But even the mere necessities upon 't.
Then, Timon, presently prepare thy grave;
Lie where the light foam of the sea may beat
Thy grave-stone daily; make thine epitaph
That death in me at others' lives may laugh.[108]

The bandits prove to him again that the whole
world is given to robbery, and that they are
only more honest than others in the open profession of their villainy. Even the physical
world examples men in stealing, for the moon
steals from the sun, the earth from all living
things, and the laws from all men. When ru-
mors circulate of his new-found wealth, the
poet and the painter come again with flattery
and show him that the depravity of the world
remains unchanged. In their terror from the
vengeance of Alcibiades, the Senators with
their penitent request also confirm his hate.
They hope that time and grief have changed
him, and if they offer again the fortunes of his
former days, he will return and protect them.
They speak of their penitence and love.

Together with a recompense more fruitful
Than their offence can weigh down by the dram;
Ay, even such heaps and sums of love and
     wealth
As shall to thee blot out what wrongs were
     theirs,
And write in thee the figures of their love,
Ever to read them thine.[109]

It seems a fair and moving invitation to re-

turn to Athens, as well as a confession of
wrong and a desire for atonement. But Timon
is suspicious and would lead them on:

You witch me in it,
Surprise me to the very verge of tears.
Lend me a fool's heart and a woman's eyes,
And I'll beweep these comforts, worthy senators.[110]

His trap succeeds. The Senators' next speech
reveals the ugly truth that all their sorrow and
love are not purely for their former wrongs nor
for Timon's sake, but for their own ends, to gain
his help against the threat of Alcibiades. It is
still the old world with its old selfishness and
depravity, and Timon's reply is filled with
withering hate and scorn.

It is in vain to plead with him for any earthly
ends; he is already writing his epitaph. The
world has been unworthy of his love and he
must therefore find his peace in death. Henceforth he sets his "everlasting mansion" upon
the "verge of the salt flood."

My long sickness
Of health and living now begins to mend,
And nothing bring me all things.[111]

Yet he loves his country, he declares, as he
loves himself, and does not rejoice in the common wreck, but would teach his countrymen
how to prevent the wrath of Alcibiades and ease
their griefs. There is a tree near his cave which
he had planned to cut. Let all the Athenians

come quickly, from the least to the greatest,
and hang themselves on his tree and they will
escape the vengeance of Alcibiades!

The fact that Shakespeare drew from Plutarch for this incident does not change its significance. It is the logical conclusion of extreme pessimism, like that of the ancient
Hegesias, who encouraged suicide as an escape
from the miseries of life and whose teaching
resulted in such a flood of deaths that it was
stopped by order of the king. Timon's optimism about the world had changed to a pessimism so deep that life was to be hated and
death to be desired. His hatred of men as they
are and his love for man the ideal could unite
in no better gift than death to all.

In this change from extreme optimism to
extreme pessimism, however, lies Shakespeare's condemnation of Timon. His vision
had been too lofty for the earth, his love and
his hatred both too great. He had never known
the middle way himself, nor did he see the
truth of Plato's statement "that few are the good
and few the evil and that the great majority are
in the interval between."[112] Men were not the
angels Timon had dreamed, nor were they all as
depraved as he came to think.

Timon's servants and the younger generation
of Athenians redeem mankind from the general
curse and bring a ray of brightness in the
gloom. Even Timon recognized, in spite of his
doubts, the honesty and love of his steward:

Forgive my general and exceptless rashness,
You perpetual-sober gods! I do proclaim
One honest man—mistake me not—but one;
No more, I pray, —and he's a steward.
And thou redeemst thyself.[113]

After Timon's curses that would exterminate
the race of men, the plea of younger Athens
to Alcibiades comes with singular pathos:

We were not all unkind, nor all deserve
The common stroke of war. . . .
    All have not offended;
For those that were, it is not square to take
On those that are, revenge; crimes, like lands,
Are not inherited.[114]

A new generation repudiates the injustices of
the old to both Timon and Alcibiades and pleads
for mercy. Shakespeare is saying that the
"tough world" which he has pictured in *Measure for Measure* and *Timon* is after all not
wholly black, but is a mixture of good and evil.
It contains the most shameless ingrates, even
worse than thieves; it is filled with injustice
even in high office, with greed and lust, and
with such hypocrisy that even the pagan
priest "who scolds against the quality of the
flesh" does not believe himself. But it contains also the simple honesty of Timon's servants, the moderation of the Duke, the friendship and mercy of Alcibiades, the penitential
tears of the younger Athens, and even the
glorious vision of a Timon.

For such a world Alcibiades, though far from admirable, is well suited, for he knows and has the faults of other men, and can meet toughness with equal toughness. Though he is banished with an injustice as great as Timon had suffered, he nevertheless finds no place for despair. In exile he takes his courtesans with him; he loves his friends and hates his enemies, and fights and forgives. He stands in the great "interval between" the very good and the very bad, and because he has no visions above the level of the world, he is fitted to administer its justice, to make "war breed peace," and "peace stint war." He is like Ulysses in keeping his eyes upon the earth and its practical affairs, and he loves the world because he belongs to it.

We have in *Timon* a medley of Renaissance ideas rather chaotically developed. There is the new emphasis upon the earth and its practical affairs; there is the skepticism and dissatisfaction with government and justice, and the abuse of wealth; there is the insistence upon moderation as the way suited to practical living; but there is also both blame and admiration for the restless souls, the souls too great for earth, whose longings Bruno expresses in his *Gli Eroici Fuori*.

Such a soul is Timon. He belongs to another world for his idealism is too high for this, and it makes his life a sickness to be cured only by the health of death. But his tragedy leaves its trail of glory. To his servants, and to many sympathetic readers, he is like a vision from above, or a religious ideal which binds them in a common brotherhood of sorrow, and will remain through the storms til death. Their hearts wear "Timon's livery" till the end:

> We are fellows still,
> Serving alike in sorrow. Leak'd is our bark,
> And we, poor mates, stand on the dying deck,
> Hearing the surges threat: we must all part
> Into this sea of air.[115]

FOOTNOTES AND REFERENCES

1. Hatch, *op. cit.*, p. 61.
2. *Ibid.*, p. 64.
3. *Ibid.*, p. 90.
4. *Ibid.*, p. 93.
5. *Ibid.*, p. 105f.
6. See Plutarch, *op. cit.*, III, 470.
7. See Pierre Charron, *Of Wisdome* (London: E. Blount, 1612), p. 676.
8. La Primaudaye, *op. cit.*, p. 181.
9. Justus Lisius, *A Discourse of Constancy*, in two books (London: E. Blount, 1670), p. 21f.
10. W. E. Campbell, ed. *The English Works of Sir Thomas More* (London: Eyre & Spottiswode, 1931), I, 370.
11. See *The Faerie Queene*, II, ii, but especially Bk. II throughout.
12. On dress, see Elyot, *op. cit.*, II, 20; Lyly, *op. cit.*, I, 189, 286; II, 83; *Hamlet*, I, iii, 80ff.
13. Giordano Bruno, *The Heroic Enthusiasts and Ethical Poems*, 2v. (London: George Redway, 1887), I, 88f.
14. *Ibid.*, I, 60f.

15. *Ibid.*, I, 6.

16. Lipsius, *Sixe Bookes of politickes and civil doctrine*, p. 5.

17. *Hamlet*, IV, vii, 133ff.

18. Romeo and Juliet, II, iii, 171ff.

19. *Measure for Measure*, I, ii, 129ff.

20. Sir Thomas More, *Utopia* (London: Everyman ed., 1910), p. 108.

21. *Twelfth Night*, II, iii, 108ff.

22. Lyly, *op. cit.*, II, 44.

23. La Primaudaye, *op. cit.*, p. 390.

24. Agrippa, *op. cit.*, p. 151.

25. Gelli, *op. cit.*, p. 231.

26. Jaques Hurault, *Politicke, Moral, and Martial Discourses*, trans. Arthur Golding (London: Adam Islip, 1895), p. 170f.

27. Hatch, *op. cit.*, p. 393f.

28. *Ibid.*, p. 397.

29. *Measure for Measure*, I, iii, 50ff.

30. *Ibid.*, I, iv, 57ff.

31. *Ibid.*, III, ii, 111ff.

32. *Ibid.*, I, iii, 27ff.

33. *Ibid.*, I, iii, 37ff.

34. *Ibid.*, I, i, 65ff.

35. *Ibid.*, I, iii, 53ff.

36. *Twelfth Night*, II, iii, 160.

37. *All's Well That Ends Well*, I, iii, 53ff.

38. Robert Nigel Hunt, *Calvin* (London: The Centenary Press, 1933), p. 13.

39. Georgia Elma Harkness, *John Calvin: the Man and His Ethics.* (New York: Henry Holt, 1931), p. 26f.

40. *Ibid.*, p. 29.

41. *Ibid.*, p. 28.

42. *Ibid.*, p. 130.

43. *Ibid.*, p. 131f.
44. *Measure for Measure*, II, i, 17f, 29f.
45. *Ibid.*, II, ii, 183ff.
46. *Ibid.*, II, ii, 151ff.
47. *Ibid.*, II, ii, 180f.
48. *Ibid.*, IV, iv, 36f.
49. *Ibid.*, V, i, 444f.
50. Hatch, *op. cit.*, p. 264.
51. Hurault, *op. cit.*, pp. 178ff, 186.
52. Gelli, *op. cit.*, p. 236ff.
53. William Baldwin, *The Treatise of Moral Philosophie, containyng the sayinges of the wyse, nevvly sette forthe and enlarged by Thomas Paulfreyman* (London: 1560), Sig. E, fol.
54. *Ibid.*
55. La Primaudaye, *op. cit.*, pp. 391, 502.
56. *Troilus and Cressida*, I, iii, 116ff.
57. *Love's Labour's Lost*, I, i, 169f.
58. *Measure for Measure*, V, i, 414ff.
59. Jowett, *op. cit.*, IX, 860-862.
60. Matthew 7:1-3.
61. *Measure for Measure*, I, ii, 124-127.
62. *Ibid.*, II, i, 18-28.
63. *Ibid.*, II, i, 38ff.
64. Lipsius, *Sixe bookes of politickes or civil doctrine*, p. 107.
65. *Measure for Measure*, III, ii, 121ff.
66. *Ibid.*, II, ii, 4ff.
67. *Ibid.*, II, i, 251ff.
68. *Ibid.*, III, ii, 108ff.
69. *Ibid.*, III, ii, 235ff.
70. *Ibid.*, V, i, 321ff.
71. *Ibid.*, III, ii, 246ff.
72. *Ibid.*, II, i, 8ff.
73. *Ibid.*, IV, ii, 82ff.

74. *Hamlet*, III, iii, 61ff.

75. *Measure for Measure*, IV, ii, 148ff.

76. *Ibid.*, V, i, 485ff.

77. *Ibid.*, V, i, 108ff.

78. *Hamlet*, III, iii, 57ff.

79. *Measure for Measure*, II, ii, 117ff.

80. Approximately $6,000. Timon's extremely prodigal and impractical nature is suggested by the immense sums represented in his gifts and by his request for a 1,000 talents from the Senate, approximately $1,200,000.

81. *Timon of Athens,* I, i, 95, 110; ii, 10f.

82. *Ibid.*, I, i, 107f.

83. Hurault, *op. cit.,* p. 230. See also Baldwin, *op. cit.,* Sig. H. fol. 1xiii.

84. Elyot, *op. cit.,* II, 112f.

85. *Ibid.*, II, 118.

86. Hatch, *op. cit.*, p. 196.

87. *Timon of Athens*, II, i, 7-13.

88. *Ibid.*, II, ii, 162f.

89. *Ibid.*, I, ii, 106f.

90. *Ibid.*, I, ii, 226f.

91. *Ibid.*, I, ii, 222f.

92. *Ibid.*, IV, iii, 37ff.

93. *Ibid.*, I, i, 239f.

94. *Ibid.*, I, ii, 145ff.

95. *Ibid.*, III, ii, 71ff.

96. *Ibid.*, III, iii, 28ff.

97. *Ibid.*, IV, iii, 3ff.

98. *Hamlet*, V, ii, 86ff.

99. *Othello*, I, iii, 336ff.

100. Gelli, *op. cit.*, p. 240f.

101. *King John*, II, ii, 574ff.

102. *Timon of Athens*, IV, iii, 17ff.

103. *Ibid.*, IV, iii, 242ff.

104. *Ibid.*, IV, iii, 275ff.
105. *Ibid.*, IV, iii, 219.
106. *Ibid.*, IB, iii, 213ff.
107. *Ibid.*, IB, iii, 300f.
108. *Ibid.*, IB, iii, 376ff.
109. *Ibid.*, V, i, 153ff.
110. *Ibid.*, V, i, 158ff.
111. *Ibid.*, V, i, 180ff.
112. Jowett, *op. cit.*, II, 234.
113. *Timon of Athens*, IV, iii, 502ff.
114. *Ibid.*, V, v, 21ff.
115. *Ibid.*, IV, ii, 18ff.

Chapter 4

THE PSYCHOLOGY OF EVIL
THE MORAL INSURRECTION

IN Shakespeare's attempts to grasp the problem of evil we have seen the doubts and pessimism of *Hamlet* grow hopelessly bitter in *Timon of Athens*. We have seen, in *Troilus and Cressida*, his belief in a universal moral law implanted in the natures of men, subject to different interpretations according to the variation in human experience and understanding. Finally Shakespeare has also shown in *Measure for Measure, Timon* and other plays how difficult it is for those who accept the moral law to attain the right standard of conduct, which requires a fine sense of temperance and justice and a moderation determined by Right Reason.

Now a new phase of the problem emerges. From Hector's inconsistency in *Troilus and Cressida* had come the question: Why do men act contrary to the standard of right which they themselves understand and accept? Are they puppets in the irresistible sway of traditions, customs, and social pressures; are they helpless victims of "original sin" or heredity, or are they actually free to choose the right? If this last is true, why do they choose the evil rather than the good when theoretically Reason declares the good more desireable than the evil?

A full discussion of freedom would involve us unnecessarily in all the ramifications of original sin, foreknowledge, predestination, grace, and election; Shakespeare's thought moves on a plane above such theological controversy.

In general, the denial of freedom of the will, going back to Augustine, held that since the fall of Adam, man's nature and will had become so vitiated by this original sin that he could not choose good but only evil, for out of "the corrupt nature of man proceedeth nothing but damnable."[1] For man to be able to choose the good his will and nature had to be regenerated by a free and arbitrary gift of grace from God, and there was nothing a man could do to merit or incline God toward conferring this grace on him. It was reserved for the few whom God arbitrarily elected.

The doctrine of grace and arbitrary election was also connected with predestination, which held that no act could take place, even the fall of Adam, without God's foreknowledge and predetermining or allowance of it. Many recognized the danger of these doctrines which logically made God responsible for the evil as well as the good in human conduct. For if he withholds men from sin by the gift of his grace, why did he not by the gift of his grace withhold Adam from the first sin with all its consequences? And why does he deny his grace to all except the few "elect"?

John Philpot speaks of those, who on the basis of this reasoning, excuse their wickedness, saying, "If I be elected of God to salvation, I shall be saved whatsoever I do."[2] If they were not of the "elect" they might as well do whatever they wished for they were damned anyway. Calvin was troubled by the same problem, but encouraged all to aspire to goodness though they were compassed about with most "miserable necessity."[3]

In opposing the Spiritual Libertines, however, Calvin was strangely inconsistent with his own teaching. The Libertines were a fairly numerous sect in France who believed in the predeterminism of the will no less rigidly than Calvin did, but they connected with this a pantheistic view of the world. Calvin at once saw that their doctrine made God the Author of evil as well as of good; that it actually blotted out the distinction between good and evil because "nothing can be blamed as bad, since everything is the work of God." To illustrate he says,

> Some one has committed adultery? One cannot chide him for it; for that would be to blaspheme God. A man covets his neighbor's wife. Let him enjoy her if he can; for he would only be doing the will of God, and even that would be a divine act.[4]

Calvin relates an incident that happened in

Geneva, when "that great hog Quintin," a leader of the Libertines, slew another man in the street, and one of the faithful coming up asked him why he had done it.

> Forthwith he [Quintin] replied in his Pickardy dialect, "Since you want to know, I did it."
>
> The other, much astonished, said to him, "How could you be such a villain?"
>
> To which he replied, "It isn't me; it's God."
>
> "What?" said the other, "are crimes to be imputed to God which he commands to be punished?"
>
> Then the rotten thing disgorged some more venom and said, "Yes, it's you; it's me; it's God. For what you or I do God does; and what God does, we do, since He is in us."[5]

The pantheism in the Libertine belief would naturally be an abomination to the Calvinists, but the Libertine doctrine that God determines the will of each man and leads him to choose and to act as he does, should have been thoroughly in harmony with Calvin's teaching.

While the number of the Libertines as a religious group was always small, their philosophical ideas, which excused men from responsibility for moral conduct, were rather widely received. They were in harmony with the tendency of the age toward naturalism, which counted those things right which are prompted by the impulses of nature. This combination of libertinism and naturalism is seen, as Busson points out, in Marguerite of Navarre's *Heptameron*, as well as in her private life. With her mystical religious spirit she combined a conscience none too delicate and a belief in nature as the divine will; hence she urges women to follow the instincts of their natures, and makes their refusal to do so a vice.[6]

The freedom of the Libertines seems also to have influenced the Family of Love groups in England, which Strype says, "began now mightily to take place with many in this kingdom."[7] Unlike the Libertines, they were champions of free will, but they also denied the possibility of sin among the "saved." There were evidently many fanatical off-shoots from this group. A Mrs. Dunbar originated a Family of Essentialists who also taught that there is no sin, but that God does everything that is done, of whatever nature it may be. A tailor by the name of Lockley used to say, "Sin? what sin, man? There is no man sinneth at all." He held many meetings through the country at considerable cost. A gentleman named Mackworth was also said to have had two wives, and defended his course as lawful, but upon being imprisoned he not surprisingly "became somewhat reformed touching that detestable opinion. . . ."[8]

Roger Hutchinson, in refuting the idea of fixed or fatalistic determinism, as well as the teaching of the Family of Love, describes their doctrine as approving any act:

> If we think all things to be governed by destiny, we must needs agree with the Libertines, which make no difference between light and darkness; but defend all things to be lawful and honest, calling notable vices vocations commanded of God: If they spy a thief, they blame him not, but exhort him to continue in his vocation; they bid the bawd, the strong whore, apply their vocations: for St. Paul saith, all things bee lawful unto him; if unto him, to us.[9]

Between the two extremes of the Calvinists and Libertines regarding freedom and responsibility, the Humanists, however, steered a middle course. Sir Thomas More, in his attack on Tyndale, argues that Luther and the reformers, in emphasizing too far the grace of God and denying the possibility of human choice, really make God responsible for all acts, evil as well as good.[10] Giordano Bruno[11] and Montaigne[12] also denounce the reformers for denying the efficacy of works and placing all their hope in mere faith. Even Roger Hutchinson, one of the more moderate reformers, places the responsibility for each man's salvation within himself: "God leaveth in our power to will and nil, to take or to forsake."[13]

The Humanists in general accepted freedom

of the will as a definite fact, and on it based
their faith in the perfectability of men. John
Picus della Mirandula speaks of the struggle
against the evils and temptations of the world
as a

> conflict in which no man may be over-
> come against his will, and in which we need
> none other strength to vanquish but that
> we list ourselves to vanquish.[14]

Even with such complete acceptance of freedom, however, the Humanists, conventionally
at least, recognized the necessity of divine
grace in overcoming evil and attaining perfection. To deny any such need would have been
atheism. Pomponazzi went further than most
in denouncing the idea of efficient grace, even
as it was mildly expressed by St. Thomas, and
proclaimed the idea more impious than Stoicism,[15] but Pomponazzi was one of the few.

Falstaff's "Vocation"

Shakespeare's general attitude toward the
questions of freedom, responsibility, and grace
is apparently in harmony with the more advanced thought among the Humanists. He
shows no influence of Calvinism unless it is
a reaction against it. Though he was aware of
the religious controversies raging over the
questions of freedom, election, and grace, his
own attitude seems to have been one of respect-
ful, good-humored irony. The licentious Lucio
and the two gentlemen in *Measure for Measure*

jest about grace and religious controversy. "Grace is grace, despite of all controversy," says Lucio, "as for example, thou thyself art a wicked villain, despite of all grace."[16] Theological controversy does not affect the quality of grace; neither does grace affect the villainy of the first gentleman. Lucio had no quarrel with grace, for if it fell where it would fall, why should he or the first gentleman worry?

There are many hints that Falstaff's libertinism is conceived in the light of this deterministic background and becomes an excuse for it. Though he has long forgotten what the inside of a church is like, it is evident from his numerous scriptural allusions that he has had a religious background. His reference to weavers and the singing of psalms, and to losing his voice by "halloing and singing of anthems," though hilariously untrue, indicates an acquaintance with the enthusiastic singing or "shoutings" of some religious groups. His repeated attacks of penitence, which leave as quickly as they appear, carry a suggestion of that "working of grace" which was so prominent an idea in Calvinistic redemption. Falstaff makes Hal his bad angel, able to corrupt a saint:

Thou hast done much harm upon me, Hal; God forgive thee for it! Before I knew thee, Hal, I knew nothing; and now am I, if a man should speak truly, little better than one of the wicked. I must give over this life, and I will give it over; by the Lord, an I do not, I am a villain; I'll be damn'd for never a King's son in Christendom.[17]

Before he knew Hal he was in a state of innocence and knew nothing, but now he is *little better than* one of the "wicked." He clearly means the "reprobate," or the "massa damnata," of Calvinist theology. It is equally clear that he does not consider himself one of the "wicked" but one of the "elect." In the next instant, therefore, he is ready to snatch a purse, and easily defends his thievery: "Why, Hal, 'tis my vocation, Hal; 'tis no sin for a man to labour in his vocation."[18]

Out of his long-forgotten, church-going past Falstaff apparently remembers the fulminations of some preacher like Roger Hutchinson against the Libertines for encouraging thieves and whores to follow their "vocations," for St. Paul had said "all things are lawful." As one of the elect, and unworried about damnation, Falstaff can humorously defend his "vocation" with the Libertine doctrine which was anathema to Calvin, but which was logically an outgrowth of the deteriministic philosophy.

Again, when caught in his lies, he defends himself glibly with theological terms:

Dost thou hear, Hal: thou know'st, in the state of innocency Adam fell; and what should poor Jack Falstaff do in the days of villainy? Thou see'st I have more flesh than another man; and therefore more frailty.[19]

Like Hal, however, Shakespeare does not excuse Falstaff's lying and thievery, for he later
consigns him to a punishment which has
aroused the ire of a number of his critics;
and in spite of Falstaff's implications that he
belongs to the elect, he places his final resting
place only "in Arthur's bosom,"[20] wherever
that may be!

'Tis in Ourselves

In harmony with the Humanists Shakespeare's references to grace in his early plays
shift after 1600 to a greater emphasis on the
will. In *Love's Labour's Lost* Biron says men
cannot overcome their natural affections except by "special grace."[21] In *Romeo and
Juliet* Friar Laurence moralizes on the "grace
and rude will" which struggle to dominate
each life.[22] Henry V asserts that his passions
are subject to his "grace."[23] But in *Julius
Caesar* Cassius says "the fault" that he and
Brutus are "underlings" is not "in their stars,
but in ourselves."[24] Edmund in *Lear* also
ridicules attributing our weakness to the stars
when we ourselves are responsible.[25]

Cassius and Edmund refer to the influence
of the stars, for these, like grace, exerted an
influence externally. Iago, however, pours
the most withering scorn on the idea of "virtue," the supernatural grace given to help control the passions. When the weak Roderigo
pleads that it is not in his "virtue" to amend
his passion for Desdemona, Iago says,

Virtue! a fig! 'tis in ourselves that we are
thus and thus. Our bodies are our gardens,
to the which our wills are gardeners; so
that if we will plant nettles, or sow lettuce,
set hyssop and weed up thyme, supply it
with one gender of herbs, or distract it with
many, either to have it sterile with idele-
ness, or manured with industry, why, the
power and corrigible authority of this lies
in our wills. If the balance of our lives had
not one scale of reason to poise another of
sensuality, the blood and baseness of our
natures would conduct us to most pre-
posterous conclusions: but we have reason
to cool our raging motions, our carnal
stings, our unbitted lusts, whereof I take
this that you call love to be but sect or
scion.[26]

Iago continually converts truth to bad ends
and gives to innocent things an emphasis that
makes them evil. So his turning the truth
about the supremacy of reason and the will into
a sneer at divine aid was a trick that neither
the Humanists nor Shakespeare would have
approved. The emphasis that both he and Edmund gives to the will in controlling one's
life is, of course, a fine dramatic touch which
deepens their own villainy and leaves them
without excuse.

Yet when we remember Hamlet's pessimism
about the power of virtue to "innoculate our
old stock;" and when, in harmony with humanistic thought, we see the increasing emphasis

on reason and the will, we may be justified in feeling that, whatever pessimism Shakespeare may have had about ultimate perfection, he has a growing tendency to place the hope and responsibility for it more and more in humanity itself.

The Genius and The Mortal Instruments

If the will and reason, however, are chiefly responsible for attaining human perfection, it remains to explain those antagonistic forces which, against the dictates of reason, move the soul to the choice of evil. The answer involves us in all the intricacies of Elizabethan psychology. Since Miss Anderson[27] and Miss Campbell[28] have already made such excellent analyses of the psychological theories of the period, we need consider only those aspects necessary to the present problem.

In Elizabethan psychology, with which Shakespeare seems thoroughly familiar, it was generally held that the soul came from God completely good, but in the womb it came under the curse of original sin. From this curse Calvin and many of the reformers held that it could be freed only by a supernatural infusion of divine grace, and this was granted only to the few "elect." The Humanists and others, however, seemed less concerned with original sin, which was supposedly removed by the baptism almost universally administered to infants, and were more concerned about the struggle of the soul to retain its pristine purity.

The soul, like a prince within his castle, was considered impregnable against all attacks from outside. Yet it was constantly under assault by an almost infinite variety of influences both physical and metaphysical, or supernatural. These included variations in the four humors which give the body its natural qualities, the influence of heredity, all the passions and desires of the flesh, even differences in climate, race, and nation, foods and drink, differences in age from youth to dotage, and even the planets, days of the week, and hours of the day. But against all such influences the soul was secure unless it voluntarily yielded to its own corruption.

Shakespeare uses many of these theories for dramatic effect, though there is a question as to how much credit he gave them for affecting the lives of his characters. He includes numerous references to the stars as yielding good or evil influences. Falstaff recommends a good store of good sack to give a man courage, and temperance. Iachimo excuses his treachery by the influence of the dull English climate on his quick Italian brain, and Othello's trust and jealousy are associated with his climate and race.

The influence of heredity, however, is the one most vital in the forming of character and personality. To Perdita and the sons of Cymbeline it gives royal graces even in a shepherd's hut or in the wilderness.

On the other hand, it was thought that evil

might be infused into the embryo of the child from a variety of sources. It could come from the condition of the parents at the time of coition. Hurault says the drunkard is "vnmete for generation because it is likely that his pro-creation shall be unequal, crooked and un-stable, as well in members as in manners."[29] It was a common belief also that illegitimate children inherited violent, wayward, or evil natures as a result of the irregularity and pas-sion of their conception. Henry VIII, if you can believe it, had parliament pass a law that any man who had unlawfully known his wife before marriage, and did not confess it, should be counted little better than a traitor if it should later be discovered. Strype explains that he was concerned for the welfare of the realm and knew that the sins of the parents descended to the children and through these to the govern-ment which they administer.[30]

Shakespeare seems to have followed this popular belief in characterizing his bastards, Thersites, Don John, and Edmund. Thersites is "ill-gotten," illegitimate in mind as well as body. Don John is described as a "bastard, whose spirits boil in frame of villainies," and who is "compos'd and framed of treachery."[31] The bastardy of Edmund is especially empha-sized; it rankles in his mind and fills him with jealousy of his brother and hatred for his father. Coupled with these hereditary in-fluences, however, is his father's preferential treatment of Edgar and his keeping Edmund

away from home to conceal his bastardy, conduct which alone would breed the boy's jealousy and hatred. Falconbridge in *King John* is
an exception, for his father's noble qualities
counterbalance the rude wildness derived from
his illegitimate birth.

The evil influences entering into conception,
which were sometimes of a nature to suggest
demoniacal tampering, might cause misshapen bodies as well as souls. A close relation
was felt between beauty of soul and perfection
of body, a Platonic influence especially strong
in the Renaissance and prominent in Shakespeare. It was thought the soul had power to
choose a body like itself, or to shape the body
to its own perfection.[32] All, of course, recognized exceptions to the rule, either through
chance, or through a stubbornness in the
bodily material which would not yield to the
efforts of the soul, or through the arbitrary
choice of God, displaying his power.[33]

Shakespeare recognizes this relation of soul
and body,[34] with similar exceptions,[35] and
uses it in characterizing Richard III, as well
as Thersites, Caliban, and others. Richard is
described as one whose villainy is inborn, with
body and soul framed alike for evil. He himself
blames his deformed body for his villainy. He
has been "cheated by dissembling nature" and
sent into the world before the time, deformed,
unfinished, "scarce half made up," a thing for
dogs to bark at as he passed. With such a body
he was unfit for the life of courtly grace and

was determined to become a villain. Queen
Margaret curses him:

> Thou elvish-mark'd abortive, rooting hog!
> Thou that was seal'd in thy nativity
> The slave of nature and the son of hell![36]

There is implication of even fiendish influence in his birth: "Sin, death and hell have
set their marks on him." He is a hell-hound
born with teeth already grown, whose poisonous bite would rankle to the death; a black in-
telligencer of hell; a cacodemon. His beastliness
and lack of human soul is continually suggested by epithets of savagery: "Poisonous
hunch-back'd toad," "bottl'd spider," "bloody
dog," and "wretched, bloody, and usurping
boar," that

> Swills your warm blood like wash, and makes
>   his trough
> In your embowll'd bosoms.[37]

Such blots of nature might run all the degrees from Caliban's complete earthiness or
Richard's misshapen fiendishness to Hamlet's
"single defect," which nevertheless degrades
infinite virtues to its own baseness. Between
these extremes lies Antony's inheritance, for
he has not

> Evils enough to darken all his goodness;
> His faults, in him, seem as the spots of heaven,
> More fiery by night's blackness; hereditary,
> Rather than purchased; what he cannot change,
> Than what he chooses.[38]

Though men are almost helpless in overcoming these inborn evils, they are not excused from responsibility. The Elizabethans
divided the soul into three levels: the lower
soul, or the mere life principle, shared alike
by plants and animals; the middle soul, or the
senses with their appetites and passions,
which were often at war with the reason; and
the higher, or immortal soul, which was the
reason, or intellect, and the will. Of this higher
soul Sir John Davies writes:

> In nature she hates *ill* in deede, or show
> And in the true, or false *good*, doth delight;
> If ill for *good* shee choose, hence it doth gro
> Because *ill* seeming *good*, shee takes it so.[39]

Just as the reason may be deceived by the
false reports of the senses in arriving at values,
so it may also be in determining good or evil.
The flesh with its senses is called a veil, a
"muddy vesture of decay" which shuts out the
music of the spheres,[40] a prison,[41] a tomb.[42]
Its senses, though naturally good, are deceived continually by appearances and do not
see the inner truth. When they do take issue
with the reason, the passions, which are also
good within themselves, may become so
aroused as to become "perturbations" or
"diseases," and in this extreme they help the
senses tyrannize over the reason. In the tyranny of passion it is impossible for the brain to
see aright,[43] and with the judgment thus
blinded there is no safeguard to the will, which

may consequently run to all excess. In this struggle the will, says Bruno,[44] is the captain and reason is its guide. It may conquer the passions by playing one against another. But if it loses, it becomes enslaved and degraded, and "altogether brutish."[45]

Charron distinguishes three degrees of corruption, or brutishness. The worst are those who have become "utterly abandoned" to evil, the "whole bent of their wills are fixed entirely in its Interests." They have a "Strong and Vigorous Mind" but so "corrupted throughout", that vice has "become a part of its Temper and Constitution." The least culpable are those who have only "intervals of Folly," when they are "surprised, and carried away forcibly, by a current too strong for them to stem." Between these two extremes are those, also of strong mind, who "have a right Notion of Vice," but "go to work in cold blood, and with great deliberation," and "drive a Bargain as it were." They know "the Heinousness of the Sin" they are tempted to commit, but put the "Profit it brings, into the contrary Scale; and thus they barter away their souls, and are content to be wicked at a certain Price."[46]

Shakespeare is intimately acquainted with the intensity of this moral struggle and the difficulty of the Will and Reason in overcoming the passions. Brutus says,

Since Cassius first did whet me against Caesar,
I have not slept.
Between the acting of a dreadful thing

And the first motion, all the interim is
Like a phantasm, or a hideous dream:
The Genius and the mortal instruments
Are then in council; and the state of a man
Like to a little kingdom, suffers then
The nature of an insurrection.[47]

Brutus is undergoing a nightmare of emotions. His Genius, or Immortal Soul, is in council with the Passions, which are called "mortal instruments" because they are connected with the flesh and perish with it. His Reason and Will, stirred by Cassius, by Caesar's imperial ambitions, and by the universal danger of giving any man too much power, have decreed the death of Caesar as the only way to save his country from tyranny. But his love for Caesar and gratitude for all the favors Caesar has shown him are in rebellion against the stern decree. In this case of insurrection the Soul is victorious over the senses, though we may feel that Reason was here blinded in its judgment.

In too many instances, however, the passions are victorious. Angelo is a perfect example of Charron's least culpable weakness, for he is normally upright, but is suddenly surprised and overcome by a passion too strong for him to resist.

Iago is a perfect example of those who are already so abandoned to evil that "the whole bent of their will is fixed entirely in its interest." As Charron says, he has a "strong and vigorous mind," understands how to manipu-

late people, and executes his plots with bril-
liance. He is pictured as an atheist and utterly
self-centered from the first. If he has ever had
a conscience it was dead long before the action
of the play begins; so he reflects no inner
struggle. On the contrary his reason and will
are in perfect harmony with the senses and
urge them on. He has no allegiance to anyone
but himself. He follows the Moor but to serve
himself, and he has only scorn for those who
feel an obligation to any other. Self-worship is
the basis of the evil in his nature. All is good
that profits him. That this may happen to be
evil to others makes it no less good to him. It
is inevitable that his egoism should sacrifice
all those around him and feel perfectly at ease
in so doing. He is denied the lieutenantship
when he felt his price deserved it; Othello
therefore must suffer for it. He is "belee'd and
calm'd" by Cassio, and Cassio must suffer for
it. Love of self is naturally accompanied by
suspicion and hate of those who thwart it. An
abnormal sex obsession turns his thought that
way for revenge, where with a single act of
double knavery he can displace Cassio and
avenge himself upon the Moor. He will abuse
Othello's ear that Cassio is too familiar with
his wife.

As with Launcelot Gobbo and Tarquin, the
subtle sophistry by which the reason justifies
its union with the baser passions also enters
here. Under its alchemy mere suspicions turn
to certainties:

> I hate the Moor;
> And it is thought abroad that 'twixt my sheets
> He has done my office: I know not if 't be true,
> But I, for mere suspicion in that kind,
> Will do as if for surety.[48]

The thought, harbored, becomes conviction
that gnaws his innards like a poison. From
Cassio's handsome person, "fram'd to make
women false," his mind jumps to the desired
conclusion that Cassio has already won Desdemona's affections:

> That Cassio loves her, I do well believe 't;
> That she loves him, 'tis apt, and of great
> credit.[49]

He is like one who tells a lie till he believes
his own falsehood. He even fears Cassio with
his "night-cap" too—an after-thought, no
doubt, but one sufficient to justify revenge. All
these are sophistries that win the reason to
complete cooperation with his hate. They multiply his motives; yet only one is needed—that
all these stand in the way of his self-interest.
In carrying out his revenge, Iago takes a
keen delight in the ingenuity with which he
masters every situation. Up all night in a
carousal that ruins Cassio, he exclaims,

> By the mass, 'tis morning.
> Pleasure and action make the hours seem
> short.[50]

He enjoys holding the perfect confidence of
those whom he is torturing. Cassio declares

he never knew "a Florentine more kind and honest," and Othello greets Iago's "love, not with vain thanks, but with acceptance bounteous."

His delight is further increased by the shrewdness with which he can confuse all moral values and to others make evil appear good. He calls his skill a

> Divinity of hell!
> When devils will the blackest sins put on,
> They do suggest at first with heavenly shows,
> As I do now. For whiles this honest fool
> Plies Desdemona to repair his fortunes,
> And she for him pleads strongly to the Moor,
> I'll pour this pestilence into his ear,
> That she repeals him for her body's lust.
> And by how much she strives to do him good,
> She shall undo her credit with the Moor.
> So will I turn her virtue into pitch,
> And out of her own goodness make the net
> That shall enmesh them all.[51]

Out of Iago's self-interest grows also the second aspect of his evil nature. He must not only destroy all obstacles to his will, but he is proud of the cunning with which he devises the kind of destruction that will bring him the keenest delight. Cassio must feel the disgrace of losing the lieutenantship through his own fault. He can blame no one but himself. He knows that Othello is so "enfetter'd" by his love for Desdemona

> That she may make, unmake, do what she list,

> Even as her appetite shall play the god
> With his weak function.[52]

Othello's torture then must be inflicted where he will suffer most. As Othello rushes raging from Desdemona's side, Iago gloats over the torture he is inflicting on him:

> Not poppy, nor mandragora,
> Nor all the drowsy syrups of the world,
> Shall ever medicine thee to that sweet sleep
> Which thou owedst yesterday.[53]

And as he sees Othello, overcome by passion, fall into a trance, he stands over him in both joy and contempt:

> Work on,
> My medicine, work! Thus credulous fools are
>   caught,
> And many worthy and chaste dames even thus,
> All guiltless, meet reproach.[54]

Iago's motives have often been discussed. To be sure, he coveted the lieutenantship and felt himself wronged in losing it. He has a contempt for Othello's race and his trusting nature and little, if any, belief in the chastity of women. But back of all is his colossal egoism, his sadistic enjoyment of torture, and his pride in the skill with which he can inflict it and yet retain the confidence of his victims.

In the same class with Iago, but with different personal qualities, are Aaron, Richard III, and Edmund, while Macbeth finally identifies himself with them through "long custom," as

Charron says. All have strong and vigorous minds, some even brilliant; their wills and reason have grown incorporate and of a piece with evil. There is no longer any struggle in the soul, because no part protests against the wrong. As Charron writes, even the distinctions between good and evil are "obliterated and worn away; and consequently the Will can be under no solicitude to restrain, or refuse."[55] Having set aside the laws and moral standards of God and men, their own wills become their only law. In thought they cut themselves loose from all social obligations and owe no duty but to themselves. Richard boasts of his self-interest, "Richard loves Richard; that is I am I,"[56] and his only heaven is to dream upon the crown.[57] Edmund too discards the gods and follows the wayward law of his own nature. "All with me's meet that I can fashion fit,"[58] express not only his philosophy but that of all the others.

Iago, Richard, Edmund, and Aaron all fall more or less within the class of Machiavellians as popularly understood. Machiavelli's philosophy is really state-centered. The object or end of all conduct is the good of the state, and actions are to be judged good or bad only "in so far as they promote or hinder its well being."[59] The virtue of an action has nothing to do with divine or natural law, but is determined by its usefulness in attaining the desired end. The end thus justifies the means. But this violates no moral law, for the end is the good of the state, and the state itself makes the moral law. When the good of the state demands it, lying, deceit, breaking of faith, cruelty, and slaughter are praiseworthy and good.[60]

It is aside from our study to trace the influence of Machiavelli on Elizabethan thought. The pertinent fact here is the shift in the central idea of the philosophy. In popular conception it changed from a state-centered to an ego-centric system. The Machiavellian considered himself the end of all action, and judged a thing good if it contributed to his own welfare. His own will was the moral law. Hence he scoffed at religion,[61] as Edmund and Iago do, and justified deceit, treachery, poisoning, and murder if they furthered his own ends. However, it was necessary to maintain with those who respected divine law, an outward show of compliance.

With men of this type, repentance, as Charron says, usually has no place. They have no sense of remorse, which comes from "acting against our better judgment," for these are acting in harmony with their own philosophy of right and wrong. Richard is troubled with conscience the night before his death, but only while his will and reason are relaxed in sleep. To him conscience is a "word that cowards use," devised to keep the strong in awe. Edmund too at the moment of death would do some good despite his own nature, for the cataclysm of suffering has finally awakened a spark of remorse. But those whose wills are more completely "incorporated" with evil may die impenitent like Iago, or like Aaron, cursing because they cannot do more villainy.

Between this group whose consciences no longer trouble them and those who may be only rarely surprised and overcome by a passion too strong to resist are those whose passions rebel constantly against the conscience, reason, and the will. Hamlet admires the "man who is not passion's slave," for he himself, Othello, Lear, and Timon are all too much enslaved by overmastering passions. Shakespeare pictures desire so strong as to become a madness, caring nothing for expense or havoc, and not to be satisfied except through action:

> The expense of spirit in a waste of shame
> Is lust in action; and till action, lust
> Is perjured, murderous, bloody, full of blame,
> Savage, extreme, rude, cruel, not to trust;
> Enjoy'd no sooner but despised straight;
> Past reason hunted, and no sooner had,
> Past reason hated, . . .
> All this the world well knows; yet none knows
>   well
> To shun the heaven that leads men to this
>   hell.[62]

The last two lines suggest the strangeness of the problem of moral evil, when even knowledge that the "heaven" of lust is in reality a "hell" is still no deterrent. Passion sweeps the

will on inspite of knowledge. As the clown expressed it when asked why he desired to marry: "I am driven on by the flesh; and he must
needs go that the devil drives."[63] Even knowledge that certain destruction awaits can make
no difference. Claudio says:

> Our natures do pursue,
> Like rats that ravin down their proper bane,
> A thirsty evil; and when we drink we die.[64]

When passion so blinds the judgment that it
is unable any longer to direct the will, and
reason is set aside, then the man is diseased
as with a fever and is past hope of cure. So
Shakespeare describes his passion for the
Dark Woman:

> My love is as a fever, longing still
> For that which longer nurseth the disease;
> Feeding on that which doth preserve the ill,
> The uncertain sickly appetite to please.
> My reason, the physician to my love,
> Angry that his prescriptions are not kept,
> Hath left me, and I desperate now approve
> Desire in death, which physic did expect.
> Past cure I am, now reason is past care,
> And frantic-mad with evermore unrest.[65]

In all moral evil there is this same rebellion
of the passions against reason and will, an
internal insurrection in which one part of the
soul becomes a traitor to the other. The young
Bertram had supposedly enticed a gentle-
woman of Florence to an assignation, and one

of the lords exclaims: "God delay our rebellion! As we are ourselves what things are we!"
Another replies:

Merely our own traitors. And as in the common course of all treasons, we still see
them reveal themselves, till they attain to
their abhorr'd ends, so he that in this action contrives against his own nobility, in
his proper stream o'erflows himself.[66]

The Heaven that Leads to Hell

In the struggle of the passions against reason and will Shakespeare laments the fact that
"none knows well to shun the heaven that leads
men to this hell." Even when men know "hell"
is the end, they still plunge on. Shakespeare
explains this strange contradiction of knowledge in two ways: first, by the intensity of the
passions, which become a sickness or fever
that infects the reason and enfeebles the will, as
we have seen in the sonnet above; and second,
by a blinding of the reason through a subtle
shift in the meaning of terms, until that which
is evil appears to be good. As Sir John Davies
said the soul "hates ill," and would never
choose it unless "ill seeming good, she takes it
so." Shakespeare humorously shows this not-
so-subtle shift in terms in the temptation of
Launcelot Gobbo to run away from his master
Shylock:

The fiend is at mine elbow and tempts me,
saying to me, Gobbo, Launcelot Gobbo,

good Launcelot," or "good Gobbo," or "good Launcelot Gobbo, use your legs, take the start, run away." My conscience says, "No, take heed, honest Launcelot, take heed, honest Gobbo," or, as aforesaid, "honest Launcelot Gobbo, do not run, scorn running with thy heels." Well, the most courageous fiend bids me pack. "Via!" says the fiend, "away!" says the fiend, "for the heavens, rouse up a brave mind," says the fiend, "and run." Well, my conscience, hanging about the neck of my heart, says very wisely to me, "My honest friend Launcelot, being an honest man's son"— or rather an honest woman's son, for indeed my father did something smack, something grow to, he had a kind of taste—well, my conscience says, "Launcelot, budge not," says my conscience. "Conscience," say I, "you counsel well." "Fiend," say I, "you counsel well," To be ruled by my conscience, I should stay with the Jew my master, who, God bless the mark, is a kind of devil; and to run away from the Jew, I should be ruled by the fiend, who, saving your reverence, is the Devil himself. Certainly the Jew is the very Devil incarnal, and, in my conscience, my conscience is but a kind of hard conscience to offer to counsel me to stay with the Jew. The fiend gives the more friendly counsel. I will run, fiend, my heels are at your command. I will run.[67]

So evenly balanced are the fiend tempter and the Devil Jew that it takes Launcelot some time to reach a decision. The fiend flatters with "*good* Launcelot," and conscience counters with "*honest* Gobbo." The *courageous* fiend urges a "*brave* mind," which is a challenge that would appeal to a man in a good cause, while conscience is beginning to feel like a burden around his neck. The appeal of conscience to remember his father has little effect when he thinks of how his father "smacked." As he balances the counsel of the two, he sees the fiend counseling him to run away from the Devil Jew and conscience telling him to stay with the Devil. So conscience now, instead of being a "good" conscience is a "hard" one, which is bad, and he is ready to follow the friendlier counsel, which seems good.

Perhaps no one has pictured more vividly the psychology of temptation than Shakespeare has done in *Lucrece* and *Macbeth*. In *Lucrece* no supernatural influence is present, but the first suggestion of evil comes by way of the senses. Tarquin is moved by the praise of Lucrece, and at first sight her beauty stirs the passions of desire and lust, but reason warns him against the dangers of attempting to seduce her. It tells him of the sorrows that may follow, of the shame of polluting so pure a shrine with his uncleanness, of the dishonor to his reputation as a soldier, to his ancestry, to this posterity, of the fleeting worthlessness of what he gains, as if he would sell eternity to get a toy; of the vileness of the deed, which would live forever in his face.

But ever balancing the voice of conscience is "hot-burning will."[68] Even as the conscience reaches the climax of its plea, a change begins and desire becomes supreme:

> Shameful it is; ay, if the fact be known;
> Hateful it is; there is no hate in loving;
> I'll beg her love; but she is not her own:
> The worst is but denial and reproving:
> My will is strong, past reason's weak
>   removing,
> Who fears a sentence or an old man's saw
> Shall by a painted cloth be kept in awe.[69]

At this climax of temptation we notice a confusion of good and evil. To oppose the shame is the hope of secrecy; hatefulness is removed by the sophistry that there is no hate in love. By substituting the term "love" for "lust" he now has a suit he can pursue with honor, one that even calls for resolution and courage. The sophistry of passion urges the "worser sense for vantage still," using right words with wrong meanings, until the "pure effects" are so destroyed "That what is vile shows like a virtuous deed."[70] This inversion of good and evil, the turning topsy-turvy of the moral world, is the final step in the struggle of the passions to overcome the reason.

Thus the word "love" transforms the deed to one of honor and virtue. "Beauty" is a plea before which orators are dumb, and when affection leads even cowards will fight. With such a leader and such motive, why should he wait on reason, which belongs to age? His will has now definitely mutinied against reason and joined forces with passion.

> Desire my pilot is, beauty my prize;
> Then who fears sinking where such treasure lies?[71]

From the moment of complete surrender every obstacle becomes an earnest of the hoped-for good. Warnings and discouragements are only tests of strength, for pain must pay "the income of each precious thing."[72] So complete has become the inversion of good and evil that base desire appears a blessing for which to pray:

> So from himself impiety hath wrought,
> That for his prey to pray he doth begin,
> As if the heavens should countenance his sin.[73]

This is a most significant phase of the struggle. Shakespeare, thinking of the moral awakening which follows an intense emotional experience, wrote:

> Love is too young to know what conscience is;
> Yet who knows not conscience is born of love?[74]

This moral awakening is so profound in the experience of evil that it may change one's whole relations to the gods, at least temporarily, and perhaps permanently. In the intensity of desire the object becomes the only good in the universe, and everything else a means to attain this end. Religion, prayer, and the gods are only servile instruments to aid one's purpose. But if one suddenly sees, as Tarquin does, that the "powers to whom he prays abhor this fact," these gods themselves are set aside and others created that will aid his desire. For in the crisis of temptation the will itself, "back'd with resolution," is the supreme and ultimate criterion of its good and evil, in comparison with which the opposing gods are to be ignored. One's own will becomes his god. When this conviction becomes a permanent philosophy, we have the motivation of the Elizabethan atheist or Machiavellian. In this way Edmund sets aside the gods and chooses Nature for his deity because Nature is always in harmony with his will.[75] Richard III and Iago have no gods but themselves and see no good but what their own wills choose. Tarquin chooses Love and Fortune for his guides, and hopes to patch up with absolution what sin the gods may see through the darkness;[76] Macbeth is ready to "jump the life to come." Such is the profound moral change when desire clashes with ideals; it leaves a

> wound that never healeth,
> The scar that will, despite of cure, remain.[77]

With complete triumph of desire and passion over reason and the will, the insurrection within the soul is still; all things work in harmony again and fear gives place to action. The eye can send its order to the heart, the heart give its hot charge to the swelling veins, and the hand, "smoking with pride," march on to do the bidding of the eye. One can then face danger without fear.[78] So after "long Custom" with evil, as Charron puts it, even the souls tormented between passion and conscience are at ease because the will has surrendered and conscience is dead.

Shakespeare, to be sure, recognizes that heredity, defects of birth, illegitimacy, racial prejudice, and social pressures of many kinds influence the lives of men. They may extenuate one's guilt, as Antony's heredity explains his faults, but they do not relieve one of responsibility; for men are free to choose the right and must suffer the penalty of choosing the wrong. No one has shown more poignantly than Shakespeare the profound changes that can come when the passions overwhelm the reason and will. Such tragedies bring a hardening within, an isolation of the soul from the beautiful and good, a repudiation of all restraint and the substitution of one's own mind and will for God and moral law, and ultimately, as with the Macbeths, the haunting torture of a guilty conscience before the final dissolution.

FOOTNOTES AND REFERENCES

1. John Calvin, *Institutes of the Christian Religion* (Cambridge: J. Clarke and Co., 1957), Bk. II, ch. iii. See also Henry Bullinger, *Fiftie Godlie and Learned Sermons*, ed. for the Parker Society (Cambridge, England: University Press, 1849), LLL, 102f; John Jewell, *Works*, ed. for The Parker Society (Cambridge, England: University Press, 1845-50), III, 168.

2. John Philpot, *Examinations and Writings*, ed. for The Parker Society (Cambridge, England: University Press, 1843). p. 233.

3. Calvin, *op. cit.*, Bk. II, ch. ii.

4. Harkness, *op. cit.*, p. 76.

5. *Ibid.*, p. 78.

6. Henri Busson, *Les Sources et le Development du Relationisme dans la Literature Francaise de la Renaissance,* Paris: 1922).

7. John Strype, *Annals of the Reformation and Establishment of Religion,* 4v. (London: Oxford University Press, 1824), II, ii, 282.

8. *Ibid.*, II, ii, 300f.

9. Roger Hutchinson, *The Works of Roger Hutchinson*, ed. for The Parker Society (Cambridge, England: University Press, 1942), p. 79.

10. Campbell, *op. cit.*, II, 206, 291, 299f.

11. Boulting, *op. cit.*, p. 157f.

12. Montaigne, *op. cit.*, Bk. III, ch. xii.

13. Hutchinson, *op. cit.*, pp. 59, 85.

14. Campbell, *op. cit.*, I, 364.

15. Busson, *op. cit.*, p. 41f.

16. *Measure for Measure*, I, ii, 24-27.

17. *I. Henry IV*, I, ii, 102-109.

18. I am aware that Falstaff's statement may be

interpreted as a sly dig at the "professional" thievery of soldiers, of whom Falstaff is a disreputable representative. But coming in such close connection with his "penitence" and "praying," being "saved by merit," and echoing Hutchinson's words so closely, it seems rather his humorous defense of being the leader of an organized band of highwaymen, the highest "professional" thieves of the time.

19. *I. Henry IV*, III, iii, 185-189.
20. *Henry V*, II, iii, 5.
21. *Love's Labour's Lost*, I, i, 150-153.
22. *Romeo and Juliet*, II, iii, 23-30.
23. *Henry V*, I, ii, 241-243.
24. *Julius Caesar*, I, ii, 139-141.
25. *King Lear*, I, ii, 128-145.
26. *Othello*, I, iii, 318-330.
27. Ruth L. Anderson, *Elizabethan Psychology, and Shakespeare's Plays*, University of Iowa *Humanistic Studies*, Vol. III, No. 4 (University of Iowa Press, 1927).
28. Lily B. Campbell, *op. cit.*
29. Hurault, *op. cit.*, p. 315. See also Plutarch, *Morals*, I, 3.
30. Strype, *op. cit.*, II, ii, 303.
31. *Much Ado About Nothing*, IV, i, 183f.
32. Edmund Spenser, *Complete Poetical Works* (Boston: Houghton Mifflin, 1908), p. 481.
33. *Ibid.*
34. *Pericles*, V, i, 121f; *Tempest*, I, ii, 457ff.
35. *Macbeth*, I, iv, 11f.
36. *Richard III*, I, iii, 228ff, 293; *II Henry VI*, V, i, 187f; *III Henry VI*, II, ii, 135ff, where he is described as a "foul undigested lump, crooked in manners and shape," and marked by the destinies to be avoided.

37. *Richard III*, V, ii, 8f.

38. *Antony and Cleopatra*, I, iv, 10ff.

39. Sir John Davies of Hereford, *Microcosmos, in Works in Verse and Prose*, ed. by Alexander Grosart (New York: AMS Press, Inc., 1878), p. 25.

40. *Merchant of Venice*, V, i, 60ff.

41. *King John*, III, iv, 19.

42. *Richard II*, I, iii, 196.

43. Davies of Hereford, *op. cit.*, p. 39.

44. Bruno, *op. cit.*, I, 43f.

45. La Primaudaye, *op. cit.*, p. 633.

46. Charron, *op. cit.*, Bk. II, p. 97f.

47. *Julius Caesar*, I, i, 61-69.

48. *Othello*, I, iii, 378-382.

49. *Ibid.*, II, i, 277-278.

50. *Ibid.*, II, iii, 384f.

51. *Ibid.*, II, iii, 331-343.

52. *Ibid.*, II, iii, 327-329.

53. *Ibid.*, III, iii, 330-332.

54. *Ibid.*, IV, i, 45-48.

55. Charron, *op. cit.*, p. 99f.

56. *Richard III*, V, iii, 183.

57. *III. Henry VI*, III, ii, 147f.

58. *King Lear*, I, ii, 200.

59. R. M. Carew, "The Ethics of Machiavelli," *Hibbert Journal*, XXVII (1926-29), 1-142.

60. Nicolo Machiavelli, *The Prince* (London: J. M. Dent, Everyman ed.), p. 122f.

61. Christopher Marlowe, *The Jew of Malta*, Prologue, 11, 14; *Massacre at Paris*, II, 65ff, in *Works and Life of Christopher Marlowe* (New York: Gordian Press, 1966).

62. Shakespeare, *Sonnet* 129.

63. *All's Well That Ends Well*, I, iii, 30ff.

64. *Measure for Measure*, I, ii, 132ff.

65. *Sonnet* 147.

66. *All's Well That Ends Well*, IV, iii, 23ff.

67. *Merchant of Venice*, II, ii, 2-32.

68. "Will" is more strictly confined to the higher part of the soul, and associated with the reason as the "intellectual appetite"; but when it is dominated by the baser passions it is used to refer to the "sensual appetite" out of which the passions grow. In this sense it is distinguished by Sir John Davies as "wilful-will."

69. *Lucrece*, 239ff.

70. *Ibid.*, 252.

71. *Ibid.*, 278f.

72. *Ibid.*, 330-336.

73. *Ibid.*, 341-343.

74. *Sonnet* 151.

75. *King Lear*, I, ii, 1.

76. *Lucrece*, 344-357.

77. *Ibid.*, 731f.

78. *Ibid.*, 491-504.

Chapter 5

SUFFERING AND UNIVERSAL JUSTICE IN *KING LEAR*

The Significance of Suffering

WE HAVE seen in *Troilus and Cressida* Shakespeare's belief in a cosmic order, including a universal moral law implanted in the natures of men and an innate sense of justice to guard the bounds of right from wrong. But in *Measure for Measure* he has shown the difficulty, or even the impossibility, of expecting absolute justice in human affairs.

If perfect justice, however, is impossible for humanity to administer, the next logical question seemed to be whether there is a justice in the universe itself, above the blindness and self-interest of men? This is the theme of *King Lear*. It resolves itself into two problems: the causes of suffering, and its relation, if any, to the heavens.

This brings us full circle again to all the doubts and questionings of Hamlet. For suffering in itself may have no meaning; its significance philosophically lies in its relation to a world order. If the universe is directed by a sympathetic intelligence, why should suffering be permitted?

That Shakespeare was early troubled by the question is indicated by the passage in *Lucrece:*

Why should the worm intrude the maiden bud?
Or hateful cuckoos hatch in sparrows' nests?
Or toads infect fair founts with venom mud?
Or tyrant folly lurk in gentle breast?
Or kings be breakers of their own behests?
   But no perfection is so absolute
   That some impurity doth not pollute.[1]

Metaphysically, as we have already seen in
the meditations of *Richard II*,[2] Shakespeare
associates this pain of the world with its
finiteness. For all the struggle and unrest
there can be no end till it be eased "with being
nothing." Finiteness implies change. In the
ceaseless flux of a finite world nothing remains steadfastly the same. This idea, which
is as old as Heraclitus and Empedocles, becomes a prominent motif in Renaissance
thought. Spenser in his "Cantos of Mutability"
gives it perhaps its most perfect and pessimistic expression. Mutability has broken, not
only the laws of nature,

But eke of Justice, and of Policie;
And wrong of right, and bad of good did make,
And death for life exchanged foolishlie;
   Since which, all living wights have learn'd to
      die,
And all this world is woxen daily worse.[3]

The theme of mutability runs through the
entire *Mirrour for Magistrates* and appears in
countless poems.[4] It enters also into the popular descriptions of "the ages of man," which
pictures life from the cradle to the grave as a

continuous change, usually from bad to worse.[5] Shakespeare's own "Seven Ages," despite its humor, has the usual touch of pessimism at the vanity and final nothingness of life: "Sans teeth, sans eyes, sans taste, sans everything."[6]

Lipsius pictures the world as a universe of mutation and death: the earth shaken by palsy fits from the vapors within her bowels, or corrupted by waters, and her shores daily fretted away. "For that great Architect pulls down and sets up, and (if vve may say it) doth even sport himself in the affairs of this world."[7]

Connected with the ceaseless flux of things and the notion of their rapid transcience was the element of time. Time became the great Destroyer. It is the enemy of all permanence, the foe of life, the instrument of decay and death.[8]

No one has presented more touchingly than Shakespeare the eternal pain of mutability and the pathetic yearning for an impossible permanence in the midst of change. Before the "wreckful siege of battering days" all things decay and finally become the "wastes of time."[9]

It is this finiteness of things, the change inevitable in a world of time, that is the metaphysical and first cause of suffering. Out of it arise the dissatisfaction with things as they are, the unrest and the conflict, the pain of the world. *Henry IV* is filled with dismay at the helplessness of the finite in the resistless flow of change:

> O God! that one might read the book of fate,
> And see the revolution of the times
> Make mountains level, and the continent,
> Weary of solid firmness, melt itself
> Into the sea . . . O, if this were seen,
> The happiest youth, viewing his progress
>   through,
> What perils past, what crosses to ensue,
> Would shut the book, and sit him down and
>   die.[10]

"How chances mock" introduces another phase of the problem. The basic question is whether to attribute pain and loss to mere chance and accident, to the providence of a supreme intelligence, or to fate. Out of the maze of thinking on this question, with its confusion of terms, we may roughly distinguish the two major tendencies in the Renaissance.

The first makes divine providence the director of the world and ranges from the extreme determinism of Calvin to the indefinite liberalism of Erasmus. Calvin denounces those who ascribe to God only the oversight of the middle region of the air and planets, and leave the world to the rule of chance and the will of men. He denounces as well those who ascribe to God only an uncertain and disordered oversight of the world, a kind of universal providence without direction of specific acts. For Calvin there is "neuer any winde doth rise or encrease but by the special commandment of God." He condemns the Stoic doctrine of fate as well as the idea of chance and fortune, for none of these have a place in a Christian system.

> Whereupon we affirm that not only the heaven and earth and other creatures without life, but also the purposes and willes of men are so governed by his Providence, that they be directly carried to the end that it appointeth. What then? Will one say, doth nothing happen by fortune or by chaunce? I answer that Basilius Magnus both truely sayd that fortune and chaunce are heathen mennes wordes, with the signification wherof the mindes of the Godly ought not to be occupied. For if every good successe be ye blessing of God, and every calamitie and adversitie be his curse, nowe is there in mennes matters no place left for fortune or chaunce.[11]

Nothing, therefore, happens without God's decree, and men have robbed God of his glory by attributing to chance what belongs to his providence. This absolutism of Calvin is found everywhere among the devout and religious minded.[12] Calvin realized the difficulties involved in it, but he faced them squarely. For if God's providence rules so absolutely every act of nature and of men, it is the cause of evil as well as good. Calvin agrees and is surprised at those who object. He points out that God caused Job to be tried, Christ to be slain, Absalom to commit incest with his father's wives, evil spirits to enter into Saul, the prophets to speak lies, and the sons of Eli to be disobedient, so that he might kill them. In fact, all the evil that happens is by his will.[13]

Over against Calvin's doctrine of absolute providence was the Stoic idea of absolute fate. Christians denounced this, because fate, as the Stoics conceived it, was a necessity that controlled even the gods themselves, while providence was a necessity God controlled. But there were attempts to identify providence with fate. Agostine Steuce, probably little known in England, contends in his *De Perreni philosophia* (1540) that Aristotle in his theory of Nature, Epicurus in his doctrine of Chance, and Seneca in his idea of Destiny are all merely describing the divine activity, and all really support the belief in providence.[14]

Justus Lipsius, however, gives the most interesting discussion. He accepts both providence and fate, and attempts to distinguish between them. Of providence he says:

> For (as you know) there is an eternal Mind which vve call God, vvich Rules, Orders, and Governs the lasting Orbs of heaven; the different courses of the Stars; the interchangeable variations of the Elements; and (in a word) all things whatsoever, as well above as below us.[15]

The "voice of nature," he says, proclaims this providence, and not chance or fortune, as the ruler of the universe. Every ebb and flow of human affairs, and the rise and fall of king-

doms depend upon it. For out of the First
Cause must come all later causes.

With this absolute providence, however,
Lipsius harmonizes a concept of fate. You cannot deny fate, he says,

> unless together with it, you deny the very
> Power and Being of Deity: For if God is,
> Providence is; if Providence, then a de-
> creed order of things; and if so then a firme
> and established necessity of events.[16]

This fate, however, is not an order of natural
causes which, by their own nature, work out
their results. It is rather an eternal decree of
providence "inherent in things moveable
which disposes every one of them in its own
Order, Place and Time." Providence is the
"faculty and power in God, by which he sees"
and destines events, but Fate is in regard to
things themselves. It is that necessity which is
decreed by God's providence and which disposes each thing to act in harmony with his
decree so that "all things vvhich are by Fate,
do necessarily come to pass."

The definition of Lipsius indicates the strong
influence of Stoicism on his thought. He is
much inclined toward Stoic fate, but finds it
somewhat too violent and coercive, allowing
no freedom of will. His own belief is that fate
is the subordinate working of God's providence through natural laws.

Others, however, were not as conservative
as Lipsius. Pomponazzi in his *De Fata* (1556)

distinguishes six views of fate and providence, which need not be discussed here, but he is strongly inclined toward the Stoic view because it has the advantage over Calvin's in that it makes God the author of evil only by the necessity of nature and not by his own will. This is a powerful swing toward a naturalistic voluntarism.

The Naturalistic View

Pliny and Cicero had perhaps the strongest influences on the growth of naturalism in the Renaissance. Pliny scoffs at the idea of divine providence as a "toy and vanity worthy to be laughed at."[17] If there are any gods other than the world itself, or nature, it would pollute their divinities to undergo so base a ministry as this catering to human needs. Cicero in Book II of *De Divinatione* contends that all that happens is the necessary result of natural causes. Prodigies which the superstitious point to as signs of the wrath of the gods are only rare events which have their causes in nature and are no more wonderful than other effects with which we are daily familiar. He deduced the dilemma that things are either naturally impossible, and therefore have not occurred, or they are naturally possible, and are therefore not extraordinary.

Etienne Dolet in his *De Imitatione Ciceriana* (cir. 1535) frankly accepts the view of Cicero. He omits all reference to providence, but in the article "Fatum" of his commentaries he ap-

pears to accept the idea of fate as the enchain-
ment of causes flowing from eternity. Nothing
has happened which has not had to happen,
and nothing will be of which nature does not
contain within itself the sufficient cause. Fate
is the eternal cause of things, not in the sense
of the superstitious, but as natural philosophers mean it, " the *raison d'etre* of that which
has been, of that which is, of that which will
be."[18] Significant is his confession that he was
compelled to believe in the power of destiny
because he had suffered misfortunes without
deserving them. The difficulty of reconciling
undeserved suffering with the justice expected
in a divine providence forced him to a naturalistic fatalism. For the same reason Pomponazzi favored Stoic fate.

Vicomercato denounces the belief in providence and miracles as superstitions of the
ancients.[19] God is an intelligent, unmoral ab-
straction who presides over the world, but
exercises his influence through the stars by
natural means. Nature is the cause of everything. To those theologians who distinguish
between the regular laws of nature and the
laws of nature extraordinary, which they call
providence, he replies that these extraordinary
events are merely infrequent happenings, but
are equally the result of natural law.[20]

The tendency to naturalism is shown in
Giordano Bruno, who satirizes the belief in
particular interventions of divine providence,
and says:

God, considered absolutely, has nothing to do with us, but only as to communicate himself by the effects of Nature, to which he is more nearly allied than Nature itself; so that if he is not Nature itself, certainly he is the Nature of Nature and the Soul of the world, if he is not the very Soul itself.[21]

One recognizes immediately the Neoplatonic concept underlying Bruno's naturalism, but the pertinent idea is that God influences men only through natural means, and by no miraculous or particular interventions.

The extreme which would make every event, even the puff of wind or an April shower, the immediate act of God's providence was often ridiculed by the opposite extreme which made everything the results of fixed natural laws. Des Periers, in his *Cymnalu Mundi* (1537) satirizes providence by representing Jupiter as looking each day at his book to decide what weather to make and worrying greatly for fear of losing his weather directory. Rabelais' first two books are a satire on providential miracles, praying for rain and against drouth, famine, war, and other calamities; and in a passage at first suppressed he used the arguments employed by the Sorbonne in defense of miracles to prove that the impossible is possible because it is impossible.

All of this indicates the restlessness of Renaissance thought. In spite of the extreme faith in providential intervention there was a growth toward pure naturalism. This was

probably induced in many instances, as it was
in Pomponazzi and Etienne Dolet, by the very
problem of suffering. Naturalism freed God
from the apparent injustice of inflicting or
permitting undeserved suffering. It put him
farther away from his universe, so that he no
longer influenced its working except through
natural laws. In the extreme of Vicomercato
the universe was completely unintelligent and
unmoral.[22]

Even among the more conservative the
tendency was to sweep aside superstitions.
The distinction between fortune and chance
was being lost, and chance was regarded
either as providential or the working of
natural laws which we do not understand.

The same tendency was sweeping away the
superstitions about the stars. This fight, to be
sure, was as old as Plutarch, who denounced
that ignorance which regarded natural eclipses
of sun or moon as signs of anger from the
gods. Such superstition, he declared, makes
men fear the gods and drives them to atheism.
Church leaders denounced it because it de-
tracted from God's providence, or encouraged
a fatalistic attitude toward sin.[23]

But many, like Aquinas, believed in a providential influence from the stars as part of the
natural means by which God governs the
world. The naturalists likewise accepted the
influence of stars as a regular law of nature.
Few, if any others, went so far as Pontus de
Tyard in his *Mantice* (1558) in practically

denying all celestial influence.[24] The main
tendency among the naturalists was apparently that of Pomponazzi, who denied the miraculous and explained such extraordinary events
as would foster superstitions as merely natural effects of the stars.[25]

The tendency, therefore, in the Renaissance
was to ascribe a more or less determining influence to the stars as a part of the natural
order of the world, but to regard as superstitious, those who believe in omens and prodigies as unnatural harbingers of evil and
disaster.[26]

Fate and Providence in Shakespeare

A study of Shakespeare's own reflections on
this background of changing thought through
the period of the tragedies reveals the disturbing influence of the newer naturalism. In
Venus and Adonis he speaks of how "the
world's poor people" are amazed at appari-
tions, signs, and prodigies, "infusing them
with dreadful prophecies,"[27] and of how the
wind imprisoned in the ground shakes the
earth and fills men's minds with terror.[28]
Likewise when Glendower boasts of the prodigies at his birth, Hotspur replies with scorn,
but in the spirit of the new naturalism, that

> oft the teeming earth
> Is with a kind of colic pinched and vexed
> By the imprisoning of unruly wind
> Within her womb, which, for enlargement
>   striving,

Shakes the old beldam earth and topples down
Steeples and moss-grown towers. At your birth
Our grandam earth, having this
   distemperature,
In passion shook.

But so it would have done at the same season
"if his mother's cat had but kittened."[29]

Friar Pandulph also describes the way the
ignorant misconstrue natural events and call
them "tongues of heaven."[30] Casca is terrified
at the electrical storm preceding the death of
Caesar and condemns those who would explain
it as merely natural, but the calm Cicero replies that

Men may construe things after their fashion
Clean from the purpose of the things
themselves.[31]

In *Lear* Gloucester's superstitious belief in
prodigies is met by the scornful naturalism of
Edmund.[32]

These instances indicate a skeptical attitude toward the interpretation of unusual dis-
turbances as supernatural portents. On the
other hand, there are numerous references to
the influence of the stars at birth,[33] and upon
the fortunes of men and nations, but it is an
influence exerted in a natural way.

Ulysses ascribes to the heavenly bodies
power to shake the earth, fill it with tempests,
and rend the married calm of states. The
naturalists explained these influences as
changes produced by the planets in the earth's

atmosphere, which in turn produced storms and calms in the elements and thus affected the lives of men. This naturalistic explanation runs through Timon's curse:

> Be as some planetary plague, when Jove
> Will o'er some high-vic'd city hang his poison
> In the sick air.[34]

But the question of human freedom in opposition to these mighty cosmic forces was a troublesome one. Helena, so tortured by unattainable desire that she feels her wishes all shut up within her baser stars, attempts with a fatalistic hope to define the limits of her freedom:

> Our remedies oft in ourselves do lie,
> Which we ascribe to heaven. The fatal sky
> Gives us free scope, only doth backward pull
> Our slow designs when we ourselves are dull.[35]

This is apparently Shakespeare's reconcilement of freedom and necessity. It voices both the independence of Edmund and the fatalism of Gloucester, but without the irreverance of the one or the superstition of the other. All our misfortunes cannot be blamed upon the heavens, for we are given a measure of freedom by which we may cooperate with the forces of destiny; but indecision may bring destruction. It is the same doctrine as Brutus's Stoic belief:

> There is a tide in the affairs of men
> Which taken at the flood leads on to fortune;

> Omitted, all the voyage of their life
> Is bound in shallows and in miseries.[36]

Brutus, a Stoic fatalist, is here emphasizing the necessity of acting with fate, or becoming its victim. Cassius, an Epicurean who has no belief in fate but only in chance, places the emphasis on the human will:

> Men at some time are masters of their fates:
> The fault, dear Brutus, is not in our stars,
> But in ourselves, that we are underlings.[37]

Both, however, know the importance of "time." It is the time element also which is important to the atheistic Machiavelli and other opportunists. Our limited freedom, declares Machiavelli, will always be successful if it hits with fortune, and will inevitably fail if it runs counter to it. But Machiavelli urged the adventurous spirit, because Fortune was a woman and was best kept under by beating and hard use![38]

But after all, the stars are only superficial aspects of the problem. They are merely natural instruments by which men would explain the supernatural. Back of them lies the eternal question of providence, chance, or fate. One who denied completely the influence of the stars, as Edmund and as Chapman's Byron did, denied also the power of the supernatural. He opposed himself to determinism in the universe, and became the supposed master of his own fate. Byron says:

> I am a nobler substance than the stars,
> And shall the baser overrule the better
> Or are they better since they are the bigger?
> I have a will, and faculties of choice
> To do or not to do: and reason why
> I do, or not do this; the stars have none.
> I'll wear those golden spurs upon my heels,
> And kick at fate; be free, all worthy spirits,
> And stretch yourselves, for greatness and for
>   heights.
> Untruss your slaveries; you have height
>   enough
> Beneath this steep heaven to use all your
>   reaches;
> 'Tis too far off to let you or respect you.[39]

This is the voice of absolute freedom, irreconcilable with necessity. It is surpassed only by the aspirations of Tamburlaine, who, confident in human strength, would "hold the fates bound fast in iron chains,"[40]

> march against the powers of heaven,
> And set black streamers in the firmament,
> To signify the slaughter of the gods.[41]

Marlowe evidently found it hard, as Tamburlaine did, to harmonize freedom with necessity, and the hopeless antinomy fills his tragedies with poignant suffering. Shakespeare, however, reaches a harmony, but with increasing emphasis on necessity.

The nature of this necessity, however, is interesting to know. There is no doubt about Shakespeare's faith in providence, which is especially clear in the first period and the last, but there is a strong swing toward sheer fatalism in the period of the tragedies, with a growing recognition of chance as the unexpected external cause beyond our control.

In Shakespeare's histories God is almost as common to the characters as their next door neighbor; both sides call upon him freely to curse the other, and even the darkest villains . keep him on their side and attribute all their victories to him. Probably such references are mere conventions and are insignificant as to Shakespeare's own belief. Henry V's pious speech after the victory of Agincourt, "Praised be God, and not our strength, for it,"[42] was considered a fact of history. Richard II is only voicing the conventional belief in the divinity of kings when he declares that not all the water in the seas can wash the balm from God's anointed king, and that for every soldier Bolingbroke has impressed against the crown

> God for his Richard hath in heavenly pay
> A glorious angel; then, if angels fight,
> Weak men must fall, for heaven still guards
>   the right.[43]

Notwithstanding the conventional element throughout these histories, however, God is more or less close and personal, a good friend, helper, and avenger, often disappointing the hopes of men and allowing the wrong to prosper, but never questioned as the untiring arbiter of human affairs. But with the coming of the great tragedies, a perceptible change takes place. There is a growing recognition of necessity, a sense of overpowering fate which thwarts the human will and takes the rudder out of man's control. It is not enough to say that this is merely the nature of tragedy, whose very essence is this frustration of the will. There might still be frustration, suffering, and blood, as in the histories, without the pervading sense of irresistible necessity.

In the tragedies, moreover, this necessity loses much of its Christian coloring and becomes more nearly Stoic fate. The sense of destiny as taking charge of life, and even against our expectations bending it to its own ends, is everywhere present. Under its direction, as Hamlet declares, mistakes may prove advantages, and deepest wisdom fail:

> Our indiscretions sometimes serve us well
> When our deep plots do pall; and that should
>   teach us
> There is a divinity that shapes our ends
> Rough hew them how we will,[44]

The thought is in complete harmony with Christian providence, but it lacks something of its intimate personal tone, the tone found in old Adam's prayer that he that feeds the ravens and "providentially caters for the sparrows" be comfort to his age.[45] But the chief difference between Christian providence and the Stoic, by which it was later colored, is exactly this lack of personal tone. Stoic provi-

dence was a divine necessity controlling every
detail, even the death of sparrows, but it acted
impersonally, and it could not be changed by
circumstance and prayer. It fixed the date of
death and none could alter it. The only part
for man was resignation and readiness.[46]

It is not to be inferred that Shakespeare does
not believe in Christian providence. Old Lafeu
is almost ready to believe in miracles when
the king is healed:

> They say miracles are past; and we have
> our philosophical persons, to make modern
> and familiar, things supernatural and
> causeless. Hence is it that we make trifles
> of terrors, ensconsing ourselves into seem-
> ing knowledge, when we should submit
> ourselves to an unknown fear.[47]

This is a deprecation of the extreme naturalism that would do away with all supernatural
intervention. But the "unknown fear" contains
the same indefiniteness as the "divinity that
shapes our ends." Providence has undergone
an ethnic coloring; it is no longer intimate
and personal. Banquo still says, "In the great
hand of God I stand," but the directing force in
Macbeth is deeply fatalistic. In *Lear* it is almost purely naturalistic.

There is greater insistence on accident or
chance, not as interventions of providence, but
as part of those common causes which control
the destinies of men without their wills. Even

the full Caesar is "but Fortune's knave, A minister of her will."[48]

With the tragedies, therefore, there is a deepening consciousness of human frailty, a lessening sense of the personal intervention of the heavens, and a greater insistence on the sway of necessity—inshort a tendency toward Stoic naturalism, perhaps no more extreme than that of Justus Lipsius, but emphasizing like his, the inherency of fate in natural things.

Universal Justice

The question of providence and fate is important chiefly because of its bearing upon the final problem of suffering and justice. The more personal and intimate providence is thought to be, the more difficult it is to explain unmerited suffering. Lucrece goes to the heart of the difficulty as she thinks of the Trojans slaughtered because of the love of Paris and Helen.

> Why should the private pleasure of some one
> Become the public plague of many more?
> Let sin, alone committed, light alone
> Upon his head that hath transgressed so;
> Let guiltless souls be freed from guilty woe;
>   For one's offence why should so many fall,
>   To plague a private sin in general?[49]

In seeking to establish a justice in the universe and explain the discrepancies between "ought" and "is," the Renaissance uses all the age-old arguments from Christian and

Stoic thought. From the Christian point of view Justus Lipsius declares that all calamities and suffering come from God himself to exercise us, to chasten us, or to punish us.[50] Other explanations are that the good must suffer as a trial of their loyalty, and as an exercise to make them stronger,[51] as a bridle to prevent their sinning,[52] or as a purgatorial expiation to prevent their having to suffer hereafter.[53] The wicked are allowed to prosper as a snare to heap damnation on their souls.[54] They are given long life that they may repent.[55] Yet their prosperity is only for a time because God moves in the affairs of men and will give each sinner his appropriate reward.[56] War, pestilence, and hunger,[57] lightning, hail, darkness, poverty, venereal disease,[58] and death are sent directly by God as punishments of sin or as trials and warnings.

Thomas Beard says, "God's quiver is full of venomed arrows, and his bow always bent, and when he shooteth there is no way to escape."[59] But since, for reasons we cannot understand, this punishment is not always meted out in the present life, all odds are evened in the time to come. Those who suffer here will be recompensed with pleasure over there. Lipsius says this life is only the first act of the play, and that our Master is a good poet who will not exceed the laws of his tragedy, but every crime will bring its own punishment and nemesis.[60]

The last phrase, however, introduces the

Stoic explanation. In conventional thought God personally distributes the punishments and rewards. Stoicism, however, places the arrangement of justice in nature itself. The universe is a whole, in which all parts have their uses, and what we may consider evil is for the good of all. Hutchinson in *The Image of God* says the "crocodrile, the little fly, and the small flea, have their commodity, albeit we know it not," for God has made all things "in measure, and number, and weight."[61] This absolute justice in all the proportions and measures of the universe is imaginatively set forth by Spenser as the only standard by which present justice can be measured.[62] Chapman also declares that each thing has its measured sphere of good, and all the goodness of the gods shall fail as soon as any one good to a good man.[63] The evil man, on the other hand, inevitably receives the just punishment for his crime. For everything is ordered for the good of the whole, but since sin and crime break the law of universal unity, they are crushed in their rebellion against the whole:

> He that strives t'invert
> The Universal's course with his poor way,
> Not only dust-like shivers with the sway,
> But, crossing God in his great work, all earth
> Bears not so cursed and so damn'd a birth.[64]

This is a Christian acceptance of the Stoic concept of world order in which each thing has its particular place and its relation to the whole, and every violation of this relation brings inevitable suffering.[65] For when one plucks from the whole his wretched part, and would reduce the universe to "such a rag as he," necessity itself reduces him to nought.[66] From the consequences of one's act there is no escape. Reward and punishment are not deferred till later years, or even to a future life, but are included in the act itself. They are chained together as thunder to the lightning.[67]

To explain apparent discrepancies between merit and reward, the Stoic fell back upon spiritual values as the only essential ones. The rewards and punishments are within. Virtue is rewarded by a greater capacity for virtue; vice is punished by greater viciousness. *"A good conscience,"* says the conservative Lipsius, *"is a sufficient praise and reward of virtue."*[68] Pomponazzi, who represents the extreme naturalists and who doubted immortality, says,

One must not forget that there is only one essential punishment and only one essential reward of vice and virtue: vice and virtue themselves. All vice bears its own punishment; all virtue its own recompense. All other sanction, even that of *d'outre-tombe*, is accidental.[69]

One must not suppose that the theocratic and the naturalistic concepts of suffering and justice are separate in the Renaissance. They are constantly mingled. The significance of the latter, however, is that it is an effort to arrive at an explanation of the problem based on pure reason. Those who found it impossible to reconcile the suffering and injustice of the world with faith in a just God who personally administers its least details sought a refuge for faith by recognizing a necessity in the universe implanted in the nature of things themselves and not needing the constant supervision of the Deity. This tendency to naturalism had two results. In its extreme form it led to atheism; in its conservative form it gave rise later to deism, which accepted God but separated him from the world.

Suffering and Justice in KING LEAR

The problem of suffering and universal justice, which first struck the deep tones of tragedy in *Hamlet*, reaches its greatest intensity in the insane dissonance of *Lear*. At the same time, significantly enough, the tendency toward naturalism, which also began in the fatalistic and skeptical searchings of Hamlet, here too reaches its climax. For *Lear* is almost a pure nature tragedy.

In the first place it is stripped almost completely of the veneer of civilization. While we are strangely given the impression of great numbers of characters, as if the world were moving before our eyes, this movement of life is at the same time reduced to its simple and elemental qualities. In *Hamlet* the court with its gaiety, its wassails and dance, is always in the background. In *Othello* we are moving in cities and fighting commercial wars. Even in *Macbeth* we have the courts of Scotland and England, with feasting and ceremony and the giving of largess.

In *Lear*, however, the indefinite view of the court, except for a brief glimpse, fades out after the first scene. The critical action takes place "from our home," in temporary quarters, caves, hovels, tents, or open fields. We have no life of cities, but only low farms, sheepcotes, and poor pelting villages. There is barren country where for many miles about is scarce a bush. The king must sleep in short and musty straw, and instead of gold and jewels he decks himself with fumiter and furrow weeds. We hear of wolves howling at thresholds, and we have talk of tadpoles, rats, and ditch-dogs and the killing of vermin.

We are carried back to the primitive and elemental also in motives and emotions—back to natural man. The gloss of good breeding is lacking. Gloucester can joke before his illegitimate son about the good sport at his making. In the presence of her own husband, Goneril contends for the love of Edmund, and Albany must contradict her banns. The passions here are natural, unrestrained, brutelike, knowing no law of decency. The emotions of parental and filial love are lacking, and anger at frustration and disappointment is elemental, almost without restraint. The cruelty that gloats over torture as the cat plays with the mouse is a part of the heartlessness of nature. And the titanic rage and grief of *Lear* is akin to whirlwinds and thunder.

Especially marked in *Lear* is the absence of all Christian coloring. The religion of *Lear* is a religion of nature. Christian terminology has completely disappeared,[70] and we are living in a pagan world whose gods are largely personifications of natural forces. When Bolingbroke in *Richard II* challenges Mowbray to the sacred trial by combat, both champions take oath "by God's grace" to prove the other a traitor to "the God of heaven,"[71] to himself, and to the king. In the identical situation here, Edgar merely "protests" that he will prove Edmund false to his "gods," his father, and his brother. Cordelia prays, "O you kind gods." Albany speaks of "the heavens" and "you justicers." Lear's prayer is addressed to no gods but is a meditation on the suffering of the poor.[72] In his curses he calls upon all the terrors of nature:

> Hear, Nature, hear; dear goddess, hear!
> Suspend thy purpose, if thou didst intend
> To make this creature fruitful![73]

"Blasts and fogs" are called to do their work, "nimble lightnings," all "the stor'd vengeances of heaven," the "taking airs," and "fen-suck'd fogs." These natural elements are vital forces in the *Lear* universe. Edmund is not different from Lear in choosing Nature for his goddess, but his interpretation of nature is intentionally

in harmony with the baseness of his birth. He
would follow the baser impulses and disregard
that phase of nature which is crystallized in
human law and custom.

Throughout the *Lear* world we have, then, a
dominance of natural forces. A personal God
has disappeared. Life and emotions are close
to the fields and sky. Cordelia's tears and
smiles are sisters of the rain and sun, and
Lear's passions are as unrestrained as "cataracts and hurricanoes." The question of suffering and justice is here interpreted in a
world in its natural state, untouched by
Christian ideals. It is as if Shakespeare is
asking and answering the question: In such
an utterly pagan world, devoid of Christian
influence, is there evidence of a Justice in the
universe to distribute appropriate punishments and rewards, or are the sufferings and
hopes of humanity subject only to blind and
pitiless Chance?

The underlying cause of the suffering in
Lear is twofold: the combined effects of natural
change and of human injustice. At bottom is
the eternal struggle against age and decay
which belongs to the finiteness of things. The
weariness of years compels Lear to surrender
his active duties and cares. He would divest
himself of "interest of territory, cares of state,"
and devote the remnant of his age to rest. Yet
he would retain "the name, and all the addi-
tions to a king," an independent retinue of a
hundred knights, and an income sufficient for
his and their support.

For one who has borne the burden of rule to the ripe age of eighty this seems a reasonable demand. The selfishness in retaining his kingly titles and honors seems entirely pardonable. But a natural world without Christian ideals can also be a world without gratitude and kindness. For one to expect honors without bearing the burdens out of which honors grow may be expecting more than nature will allow. One far wiser than Lear once pointed out that greatness is measured by the service it gives or the burdens it bears. Lear's dream of retaining his honors when age forces the surrender of his responsibilities, illustrates the reluctance of age in adjusting to change. In a fundamental sense the whole tragedy of Lear takes its rise from his dotage—the decay of his judgment and mental powers—a process of nature which is resistless.

To what extent Lear was responsible for his selfishness is also a question. Goneril and Regan had often discussed, no doubt with exaggeration, "how full of changes" Lear's age had become, and in the casting off of Cordelia the poverty of his judgment appeared too grossly. "'Tis the infirmity of his age," says Regan; "yet he hath ever but slenderly known himself." To which Goneril replies:

The best and soundest of his time hath been rash; then must we look from his age to receive not alone the imperfections of long-engraffed condition, but therewithal the unruly waywardness that infirm and choleric years bring with them.[74]

Forgetting the heartlessness of these two, we must recognize, nevertheless, the clearness of their judgment. Lear has been a man of Herculean powers and titanic emotions. His best years had been ruled more by passion than by judgment. In his position as king his imperious will had hardly known a check, and through the years it had engrafted in him a selfishness that demanded flattery and obedience. Both women understood that this "last surrender" was not at heart a surrender of authority, but only of the cares and inconveniences of rule. His first words under the new regime are as brusquely demanding as if he were in his own court: "Let me not stay a jot for dinner; go get it ready." Goneril was right in her surmise:

> Idle old man,
> That still would manage those authorities
> That he hath given away! Now, by my life,
> Old fools are babes again, and must be us'd
> With checks as flatteries, when they are seen
>   abus'd.[75]

But to check the will of Lear is not an easy task. He has never learned restraint. To call in his failing powers, recognize his decay of judgment, and learn obedience to the necessity of time and change are lessons he could learn only through tragic suffering. He rebels at the first pinch of the reins. "As you are old and reverend, you should be wise," says Goneril.[76] But he responds with a torrent of curses and the futile threat to resume his former shape. Regan's remonstrance is no better:

> O, sir, you are old;
> Nature in you stands on the very verge
> of her confine. You should be rul'l and led
> By some discretion that discerns your state
> Better than you yourself.[77]

But Lear is unaccustomed to "be ruled." Regan's malicious taunt, "I pray you, father, being weak, seem so," only drives him to fury. He refuses to see his helplessness. In irony he falls upon his knees to show the unnatural beggery to which they both would drive him:

> Do you but mark how this becomes the house:
> "Dear daughter, I confess that I am old;
> Age is unnecessary. On my knees I beg
> That you'll vouch safe me raiment, bed, and
>   food.[78]

The constantly repeated taunts of "age," weakness, dotage, and decay—the tragic, inevitable results of a finite world—are made more bitter by the unfeeling aggressiveness of youth. Goneril and Regan are as pitiless as fate. They are greedy to seize the rule and powers of state more rapidly than age can lay them by. In their determination to exercise the prerogatives of rule they forget all filial duty and respect. Lear is no longer a father, but a rival and a foe. "This man hath had good counsel," says Goneril. When Albany remonstrates with her about the treatment of her father and reminds her of his kindness, he is no longer a father but a villainous enemy. She replies scornfully:

> Fools do those villains pity who are punish'd
> Ere they have done their mischief.[79]

She has set herself deliberately to break his power, crush his will, and reduce him to "an obedient father." If his knights displease her, the fault will not escape "censure, nor the redresses sleep."

But the theme of *Lear* is strangely broadened by a subplot which duplicates and strengthens at almost every point the ideas of the central action. Gloucester is old like Lear and in his dotage. His injustice to Edgar is more severe than Lear's to Cordelia. He is destined to suffer even more cruelly than the king, and his treatment at the hands of his son Edmund is more cunningly planned and aggressively pursued than the relentless cruelty to Lear. Here again in even a more marked degree is the aggression of "younger strengths" against the failing impotence of age and dotage. The antipathy of youth and age was a recurrent theme in Elizabethan poetry and had been satirically dramatized in *The Old Law*. Here Edmund's letter states the case of youth: "The policy and reverence of age makes the world bitter to the best of our time; keeps our fortune from us till our oldness cannot relish them."

Just as Regan tells Lear his age should "be ruled and led" by some one younger, so Edmund says, "Sons at perfect age, and fathers declin'd, the father should be as ward to the son, and the son manage his revenue." As he plans to betray his father to the Duke, he says,

> This seems a fair deserving, and must draw me
> That which my father loses,—no less than all;
> The younger rises when the old doth fall.[80]

The duplication and varied treatment of this theme give it significance. We are looking, not at a single isolated incident, but at the whole movement of life, the struggle of the new against the old, youth against age, change against fixedness. It is the eternal flow of things, each wave driven onward by successive waves to its final rest when movement stops. Edmund, Goneril, and Regan are only parts of the resistless surge against which the frailty of decaying strength is beaten out in hopeless struggle. The individual life is caught up and borne onward helplessly in the cosmic sway. For all things change and cease. Lear and Gloucester are only microcosms in the great cosmic struggle. They are of a piece with nature, threads in the vast pattern of suffering and change which is the universe. The smell of mortality is already on Lear's hand, and Gloucester exclaims:

> O ruined piece of nature! this great world
> Shall so wear out to nought.[81]

Coupled with the inevitability of natural change and decay, which humbles the will and crushes vitality, even more tragic in *Lear* is the cruelty of humanity itself. In no other play has Shakespeare so emphasized this aspect of mankind. The evil in *Hamlet* is of a different nature. Lady Macbeth's cruelty is somewhat modified by the remembrance of her father. In Macbeth himself it requires time to grow to brutal callousness. Iago possesses it in greater measure. But *Lear* is throughout a play of heartless torture. Ingratitude, which runs through nearly all the plays from *As You Like It* to *Timon* as the worst of evils because it repays benefits with injustice, is shown here in its basest form and connected with the utmost cruelty.

Goneril's adamantine will is as heartless and inexorable as destiny. She is aggressive, determined.

> Be then desir'd
> By her, that else will take the thing she begs,[82]

is a threat that reveals the steel beneath the calm exterior. It is a hardness that can torture deliberately without emotion, pitilessly, persistently, relentlessly. It tears like a vulture at the heart of Lear.

Regan is even more malicious in her cruelty, more biting, sharp, and eager. She strikes with the quick stab of a stiletto. "I gave you all," cries Lear. "And in good time you gave it," comes the quick retort. Both

Regan and Goneril are impervious as stone to grief and tears. As Lear rushes out into the night and storm and they lock the door against him, Goneril exclaims,

> 'Tis his own blame; hath put himself from rest,
> And must needs taste his folly.[83]

Torture in *Lear* knows no bounds. The bodies and souls of men are stretched and broken upon the rack. Lear exclaims in utter anguish,

> I am bound
> Upon a wheel of fire, that mine own tears
> Do scald like molten lead.[84]

Continually in *Lear* the cruelty of humanity is emphasized by references to the savagery of nature. Goneril and Regan are "dog-hearted daughters," "pelican daughters" that feed upon their parent's blood, "tigers, not daughters," more savage than the "head-lugg'd bear." Gloucester, speaking to Regan about Lear, says,

> I would not see thy cruel nails
> Pluck out his poor old eyes, nor they fierce
>   sister
> In his anointed flesh stick boarish fangs.[85]

In this torture scene where Gloucester loses his eyes we have all the unnatural cruelty of unmeasured rage, the fierce joy of seeing an enemy writhe in pain. No courtesies of custom, nor the respect of guests for the kindness of their host, can prevail against it.

Perhaps no scene in literature surpasses its brutality. In preparation Cornwall sends Edmund away, because "the revenges we are bound to take upon your traitorous father are not fit for your beholding." Regan even surpasses Cornwall in her hate. It is she that plucks the whitehaired Gloucester by the beard—an act of indignity and contempt—and she cries, "Hard, hard," as they bind his aged and withered arms. And after his eyes are gouged out, hers are the final words that reach the climax of exultant malice:

> Go thrust him out at gates, and let him smell
> His way to Dover.[86]

This scene has often been condemned for its unbearable brutality. No other play has had such complete revision to adapt it to the later stage. Not only has this scene been omitted but the brutality and fierce passions in other scenes have been toned down, the insanity of the fool has been left out, and a happy ending introduced.

But no matter how much we may shrink from the extreme cruelty everywhere present in *Lear* and reaching its climax of horror in this scene, we must remember that it is nevertheless Shakespeare's picture of the world. He could himself have suppressed the scene. In his sources it is barely and very indefinitely suggested: "This old man . . . was lately . . . by the dog-hearted ungratefulness of a sonne of his, deprived, not onely of his kingdom . . .

but of his sight, the riches of which Nature grants to the poorest creatures."[87] Shakespeare turns this meager suggestion into a vivid and brutal reality. But not only that, he introduces a further touch of almost unbelievable cruelty not even hinted at in the sources, when he has Edmund personally pursue his father to murder him in his blindness.

Shakespeare has apparently pressed his art to the utmost limits, and some think even beyond, in his effort to present the ruthlessness of life. The human struggle is far more pitiless and cruel than the irresistible ravages of time. Between opposing wills the relationship of parents and children changes to enmity and hate. We must not forget that Lear himself calls down upon his daughters "All the stored vengeances of heaven," and vows such revenges on them both as shall be the terrors of the earth. Gloucester also sends out everywhere to apprehend his son and bring him to "the stake." Strange as it may seem, the sacred bond is indeed "crack'd 'twixt son and father," and between father and child.

There is another strangeness, however, that we must now consider. We must not be misled into thinking that Shakespeare is presenting merely the exceptional brutality of some barbarous age in which torture like that of Gloucester was not considered so horrible. As has been pointed out by others, he himself does not explain the torture of Gloucester on these grounds. He is rather, in this primitive natural setting, where emotions are as unrestrained as the forces of nature, presenting the basic and universal qualities of life. The finer emotions were present in Lear's world as well as the brutal passions. For the torture of Gloucester was not so common, but that even Cornwall's servant "thrill'd with remorse, oppos'd against the act" and laid down his life to prevent it. The pity of the common servant was as noble as that of any age. It relieves the horror of the scene by releasing the emotions through an act of sympathy. But at the same time it intensifies the sense of unbearable cruelty by its contrast with desperate pity. In the same scene where cruelty reaches its utmost extreme pity is present in its purest form. They are alike elements in this natural life.

This is the strangeness that makes the world almost unintelligible and insane. Alongside Edmund there is an Edgar. In contrast with Goneril and Regan there is Cordelia, who in her loveliness

> . . . redeems nature from the general curse
> Which twain have brought her to.[88]

Regan can pitilessly lock the doors against her father and forbid all aid and comfort. But Cordelia is the personification of love and pity as she bends above his worn and broken form:

> Was this a face
> To be oppos'd against the warring winds?

To stand against the deep dread-bolted
      thunder?
In the most terrible and nimble stroke
Of quick, cross lightning? to watch—
      poor perdu—
With this thin helm? Mine enemy's dog,
Though he had bit me, should have stood that
      night
Against my fire; and wast thou fain, poor
      father,
To hovel thee with swine and rogues forlorn
In short and musty straw? Alack, alack!
'Tis wonder that thy life and wits at once
Had not concluded all.[89]

Unbearable cruelty that destroys with relentless hate is here side by side with a pity that
pierces the heart and soothes and heals. Yet
both are parts of the nature of things. In no
other play has Shakespeare drawn such vivid
contrasts between good and evil. In no other
are characters so extremely cruel as Goneril,
Regan, and Edmund or so completely filled
with pity and love as Cordelia, Edgar, and Kent.
It is impossible that such complete differences
should exist together, and they draw apart as
inevitably as positive and negative ions fly
to the opposite poles. They are the extremes
of antagonism, mutually self-exclusive. Yet,
senseless as it may seem, they are both
products of nature. Utter cruelty and utter
pity, utter hate and utter love, are inexplicably
united in the natural process. It sounds un-

intelligible, insane, but the *Lear* universe emphasizes this element of insanity.

It is no mere accident, therefore, that insanity enters so completely into the warp and woof of the play. It seems to be as much an integral part of the concept as the plot itself. The *Macbeth* universe is filled with fear and a nameless necessity that drives men onward in spite of terror, but the universe of *Lear* is filled with unreason and ruled by violence. Mr. Knight has admirably traced the incongruity that lies at the heart of the action. All the tragic consequences flow out of merest trifles. There is Lear's childish testing of his daughters' love, and Gloucester's almost imbecilic credulity at Edmund's plot. Equally childish and unreasonable is Cordelia's petulant stubbornness and Edgar's gullibility. But more insane than anything is Lear's tempestuous anger. Lear is endowed with almost superhuman strength. His emotions are like tempests and cataracts, and in his "little world of man" he strives to out-scorn "the to-and-fro-conflicting wind and rain." He is a microcosm that would rival the greater universe in power, and yet to direct this almost cosmic force he has the intelligence of a child. This is the incongruity of things—unmeasured power without a guiding intellect.

The Fool in *Lear* is unlike any other creation in Shakespeare. He also is a part of the incongruity. In the stark tragedy that suddenly envelops the action, in the darkness and

storm, his pitiful, shivering figure, dogging
his master's steps, looks strangely pathetic
and out of place. It adds to the hideous medley
of unreason that turns the night into a bed-
lam. It is a part of the incongruity also that it is
the Fool who sees most clearly the nature of
things, and who tries persistently to open his
master's eyes. To Kent's call through the storm
he answers, "Marry, here's a wise man and a
fool." But the irony is too bitter for laughter.
For had Lear possessed half the brains of his
Fool, he would have kept a "house to put's
head in."

The office of the Fool is not only to unmask
Goneril and Regan and to beat like conscience
at his master's mind; it is also to point out this
very incongruity of things. He turns everything the wrong side out, and instantly it fits
the crazy world. "Why, this fellow has banish'd
two on's daughters, and did the third a blessing
against his will." "When were you so full of
songs, sirrah?" asks Lear. "I have used it,
nuncle, e'er since thou mad'st thy daughters
thy mothers; for when thou gav'st them the
rod, and putt's down thine own breeches,"

> Then they for sudden joy did weep,
> And I for sorrow sang.[90]

The grotesqueness of the suggestion reveals with biting irony the unreason of the
truth. But the same unreason is suggested by
the savage cruelty of the hedge sparrow's feed-
ing the cuckoo and getting its head bitten off
for its kindness.

It is this incongruity in the world that keeps beating persistently upon the mind of Lear. He cannot reconcile his daughters' cruelty with his own kindness. It is as unreasonable as the mouth's biting the hand for lifting food to it. The unnatural injustice overwhelms him.

In reality irreconcilable incongruities may be emotionally reconciled either through laughter, as Mr. Knight has also pointed out,[91] or through tears. Both emotions are based upon incongruity, and grow naturally out of it. They are the necessary release for the breaking mind, turning it away from the unbearable reality and healing its division through the soothing relief of an emotional act. But Lear can neither laugh nor weep.

The Fool tries to out jest his heart-struck injuries and bring the balm of humor to his bleeding mind. He would not deny the unreason of cruelty and kindness in the world, but would point it out, reduce it to absurdity, and dissolve its incongruity in laughter. As Lear cries, "O me, my heart, my rising heart! But, down!" the Fool answers, "Cry to it, nuncle, as the cockney did to the eels when she put 'em i' th' paste alive; she knapp'd 'em o' th' coxcombs with a stick, and cried 'Down, wantons, down' 'Twas her brother that, in pure kindness to his horse butter'd his hay."

Here in a lightning flash is the *reductio ad absurdum* of cruelty and kindness. For a woman so ridiculously cruel as to bake live, squirming eels in a pie and when they objected, knocking them on the head, to have a brother of such imbecilic kindness as to butter his horse's hay, suddenly reduces the incongruity of the world to utter absurdity, and the pain of it is swallowed up in laughter.

But Lear is unable to laugh at the cruelty of the world. Instead it beats persistently upon his mind, and added to human injustice, the storm thunders it in his ears. Edgar's naked, shivering form holds it before his eyes until his incoherent, insane chatter suddenly becomes the philosophy of the universe. The mind of Lear, already undermined by the inevitable changes of age and decay, breaks at last and surrenders to the unreason of the world.

But Lear is not alone in feeling the pressure of incongruity. The sudden and unbelieveable events that have driven him out, the pitiless cruelty of the night and storm, and the insane irrelevance of Edgar's "philosophy" jangle discordantly in a wild medley that even the Fool with his natural humor can hardly resist. "This cold night," he cries, "will turn us all to fools and madmen." And Gloucester says, "I'll tell thee, friends, I am almost mad myself."

Justice in Lear's Universe and Ours

Where extreme cruelty is as natural as extreme pity, where unreason seems to rule, need we look at all for justice? Shakespeare seems to say in *Lear*, it depends upon what kind of justice. If, like the world in general, we look

for the measured justice which dispenses to
each his appropriate *material* reward, we shall
look in vain. That is more nearly the design of
the histories, though even there imperfectly
fulfilled. One who reads the series from *Richard II* through *Richard III* is impressed by the
inevitable exactness with which each crime is
punished, if not each virtue rewarded. It is
especially evident in *Richard III*, where all the
crimes of the long civil wars finally culminate
and are avenged one by one with their appropriate punishments. This is highly satisfactory. It impresses one almost with the accuracy of bookkeeping when a perfect balance is
struck at the close of each account. Everywhere is the evidence of an intelligence
guiding the distribution of justice. God is moving personally among men, supervising his
universe. Buckingham is skeptical of the power of curses. But Margaret says,

> I will not think but they ascend the sky,
> And there awake God's gentle-sleeping
>   peace.[92]

One by one her curses are executed in full
detail, and Buckingham awakes to find his own
curse fallen upon his head:

> That high All-seer, which I dallied with,
> Hath turn'd my feigned prayer on my head
> And given in earnest what I begg'd in jest.
> Thus does He force the swords of wicked men
> To turn their own points in their master's
>   bosoms.[93]

All of this indicates the care and thought which Shakespeare gave to the question of justice. As Lipsius says of God, Shakespeare himself was "a good poet" and would "not exceed the laws of tragedy" which called for each crime to bring its own nemesis.

With this early attention and his constant brooding upon justice in nearly all the plays from *Hamlet* to *Timon* we should naturally expect him to give it equal attention in *Lear*. In this we are not mistaken. The problems of justice and injustice are interwoven into the texture of the play throughout, but the results are startlingly different from those of the earlier histories. The personal element has largely disappeared. God is no longer pictured as directing each step of the action; nature has intervened. Personal vengeance and reward has given place to a working out of natural laws and forces. We have a natural justice, which is as inexorable and pitiless as nature itself, and as inexplicable.

After Goneril and Regan lock their father out of the house at night in the storm, Albany exclaims,

O Goneril
You are not worth the dust which the rude wind
Blows in your face. I fear your disposition.
That nature which contemns its origin
Cannot be bordered certain in itself.
She that herself will sliver and disbranch
From her material sap, perforce must wither
And come to deadly use.[94]

Goneril retorts, "No more; the text is foolish."
Albany is "preaching" a natural retribution
which she scorns. Again he says,

> If that the heavens do not their visible spirits
> Send quickly down to tame these vile offenses,
> It will come,
> Humanity must perforce prey on itself,
> Like monsters of the deep.[95]

Here are contrasted the two ideas of divine
punishment and natural retribution. If the
heavens do not visibly tame the offenses,
humanity will inevitably work out its own
punishment by a universal self-destruction. It
is the same natural chaos which Ulysses
describes when men forget all justice and law.
They at last "eat up" themselves, the doom of
universal justice.

In *Lear* Shakespeare shows this natural retribution working itself out. At the height of
Gloucester's torture, a servant that Cornwall
himself had bred, "thrill'd with remorse," became the avenger, though he himself is slain
in turn. The suddenness of the punishment
makes Albany exclaim,

> This shows you are above
> You Justicers, that these our nether crimes
> So speedily can venge![96]

But the Justicers above, it must be noted,
execute their vengeance through natural
means. The cruelty of Cornwall arouses the
natural pity that brings its own destruction.

Humanity preys on itself. In a similar way the unnatural wickedness of Goneril and Regan, through their mutual jealousy and hate, brings their self-destruction. Albany, who is saved the distasteful task of punishing his own wife, again pronounces it a "judgment of the heavens." Gloucester also and Edmund, through natural means, must each suffer the Nemesis of his own crime:

> The gods above are just, and of our pleasant vices
> Make instruments to plague us.
> The dark and vicious place where thee he got
> Cost him his eyes.[97]

All this is quite logical and intelligible. But there is much that is not so intelligible in the justice of *Lear*, much that is as unreasonable as the unreason of nature. For the course of justice moves with the impassive, pitiless sway of natural forces against which even prayer itself seems futile. The aged Gloucester in pure pity for the suffering king risks his own life to give him food and shelter. "The gods reward your kindness!" prays the faithful Kent. The reward is torture and total blindness! He is tied to the stake and must stand the course. "He that will think to live till he be old," he cries, "give me some help! O cruel! O you gods!" Whatever the gods were feeling, a common menial rebelled at the unspeakable cruelty, and for his kindness of heart was instantly slain. It was the impassioned protest of hu-

manity against injustice, but of no avail. "Lost
he his other eye?" asked Albany. "Both, both,
my lord."

There is unforgettable pathos in Lear's prayer to the aged heavens for sympathy and aid:

> O heavens,
> If you do love old men, if your sweet sway
> Allow obedience, if you yourself are old,
> Make it your cause; send down, and take my
>   part.[98]

But the answer is the closed door, the darkness, and the storm. There seems no more
pity in the skies than within the stone walls of
the castle itself. The storm rages with unabated
fury, and, as it adds its pitiless force to his
daughters' cruelty, Lear feels suddenly helpless:

> Here I stand, your slave,
> A poor, infirm, weak, and despis'd old man;
> But yet I call you servile ministers,
> That will with two pernicious daughters join
> Your high engender'd battles 'gainst a head
> So old and white as this.[99]

To Lear it seemed as if the heavens themselves had turned against him. Gloucester too
has the same reaction to his suffering. The
world had become an unintelligible place,
where eyes are of no use, where men stumble
when they see, where our very means destroy
us and our defects prove commodities. It is a
place where kindness is met with cruelty,

where one's own flesh and blood grows vile
and hates what gets it, where prayer is an-
swered by torture and men are bound to the
stake and must stand the course. Against this
universe of torture Gloucester cries,

> As flies to wanton boys are we to the gods;
> They kill us for their sport.[100]

Edgar, too, who has been utterly clear of any
fault, is subjected to the same torture of the
elements and of humanity. Forced to shift
into a madman's rags, and assume a sem-
blance that the very dogs disdained, he is reduced to the depths of human baseness. Kent,
who is the soul of honesty and faithfulness,
and who humbles himself to do service im-
proper for a slave, is not even permitted the
reward of his master's thanks.

But perhaps the cruelest irony of all is the
death of Cordelia, the one soul who is the
personification of pity and love in a world
of cruelty. The disgrace of her death is itself
revolting. Edmund is permitted to die like a
knight, in armor, and even Goneril and Regan
with a degree of dignity. Suicide, which was a
suggestion of the sources, would have had a
Roman dignity. But hanging was reserved for
common criminals. Cordelia must undergo
even worse indignity than Kent endured in the
stocks and Lear with swine in short and musty
straw. But added to the disgrace of her death
is the irony of its needlessness. Outside are
friends anxious to protect, and already aveng-

ing the injuries of her father. But at the instant
when "the heavens" outside are executing
"judgment," the hangman within is going
about his task. Someone's memory has slipped.
"Great thing of us forgot!" cries Albany. "The
gods defend her!" His prayer is instantly an-
swered by Lear, bearing the dead Cordelia in
his arms.

The bitter irony of the thing seems too
pointed to be accidental. Shakespeare has
deliberately changed his sources, which ended
the battle happily with Cordelia victorious
and her father restored to his throne. Instead
he has substituted a needless cruelty. He has
furthermore deliberately emphasized its cruelty with all the resources of his art. He has
tortured his audience throughout the scene
by letting them know beforehand the murder
that is taking place, and reminding them of it
persistently. Edmund confesses that he has
done all he is charged with and more; "the
time will bring it out." One enters with a
bloody knife and the cry: "It came from the
heart of—O, she'd dead!" To the suffering of the
spectator how ironical seems the talk of "the
gods are just" and the "judgment of the heavens." He is seeing before his eyes an unspeakable crime, which might easily be pre-
vented and which all would want to prevent,
but which goes steadily on while the heavens
stand by and earth forgets!

That *Lear* has ruthlessly emphasized the
cruelty and injustice in the world is evidenced

by the reaction against it and the attempts to soften and change it. Tate's version indicates the feeling, and Dr. Jonson voices it emphatically:

> Shakespeare has suffered the virtue of Cordelia to perish in a just cause, contrary to the natural ideas of justice, to the hopes of the reader, and, what is yet more strange, to the faith of chronicles. . . . . A play in which the wicked prosper, and the virtuous miscarry, may doubtless be good, because it is a just representation of the common events of human life; but, since all reasonable beings naturally love justice, I cannot easily be persuaded that the observation of justice makes a play worse . . . And, if sensations could add anything to the general suffrage, I might relate, that I was many years ago so shocked by Cordelia's death, that I know not whether I ever endured to read again the last scenes of the play till I undertook to revise them as an editor.[101]

That Shakespeare understood perfectly the type of sensibility represented by Tate and Dr. Jonson is suggested by a passage in *Pericles*. Dionyza, whose husband is shocked at her supposed murder of Marina, turns on him with scorn:

> You are like one that superstitiously
> Do swear to the gods that winter kills the
>   flies.[102]

She is contemptuous of those too tender-hearted to face the fact of cruelty even to flies, but would superstitiously clear the gods by blaming nature. Shakespeare must have understood the revulsion of his audience; yet he faces the fact of cruelty and evil, both in humanity and in nature, with a fearlessness unequalled outside the Book of Job. And his answer is ultimately similar.

It is both fideistic and stoic. Unable to fathom the unintelligible tortures of the world, yet confronted by the vision of omnipotent Majesty, Job abhors himself for his questioning of God and finds healing in humble submission. To Shakespeare suffering is equally unintelligible; yet in *Lear* he neither sets aside the gods nor denies their responsibility. They have created the forces of nature, and in these forces have implanted both a capacity for unrestrained cruelty and a justice that works out inevitably its rewards and punishments.

But these are apparently punishments and rewards in kind. "Virtue is its own reward," said Lipsius. Each virtuous act enlarges the capacity for greater and greater virtue. Likewise, each evil act leads to deeper and deeper evil, until, through its very excess, it arouses the sense of justice implanted in the nature of men and brings its own destruction. Before this resistless justice of the universe it is the wisdom of man to humble himself and submit.

Such wisdom, however, must often be learned through suffering. Upon this there is continual emphasis. The world in *Lear* is like a purgatory where each must learn obedience through the things which he suffers, and where selfishness is purged by the fires of torture. The old king cannot lay aside authority and submit with patience to necessity, nor does he recognize his selfishness. Though he had disinherited and cursed the one daughter who loved him, he cries in self-pity to the dreadful summoners of the sky,

> I am a man
> More sinned against than sinning.

The ceaseless pelting of the storm, however, brings with it a sense of helplessness, and he resolves to be the "pattern of all patience." The passion of revenge slowly bows before a growing humility and unselfishness. He turns with pathetic solicitude to the Fool: "How dost, my boy? art cold? I'm cold myself." Outside the hovel of musty straw, whose vileness is made precious by necessity, he utters his strange, new prayer:

> Poor naked wretches, wheresoe'er you are,
> That bide the pelting of this pitiless storm,
> How shall your houseless heads and unfed
>   sides,
> Your loop'd and window'd raggedness, defend
>   you
> From seasons such as these? O, I have ta'en
> Too little care of this! Take physic, pomp;

Expose thyself to feel what wretches feel
That thou mayst shake the superflux to them,
And show the heavens more just.[103]

Here is indeed a growth through suffering! It has burned out the pride of kingship and authority and made him one with suffering humanity. To all who weep he is united by the common bond of pain, and he feels responsible with all those in power for piecing out the justice of the heavens.

Unrelieved suffering breaks false pride. It feelingly persuades us what we are. The storm and the suffering in Lear's mind have done their work. As he sees the naked Edgar, the humiliation toward which his mind is driven suddenly becomes complete. By a flash of intuition he recognizes at last the essence of *Man*, and is ready to take his honest place in the world:

Is man no more than this? Consider him well.
Thou ow'st the worm no silk, the beast no
hide, the sheep no wool, the cat no perfume
. . . Thou art the thing itself; unaccommo-
dated man is no more but such a poor, forked
animal as thou art.[104]

With a recognition of the insignificance of man in the presence of the necessity that sways the world, Lear is ready to preach patience to Gloucester also. But Gloucester has already learned the lesson. The impatience which had driven him to the verge of suicide has been succeeded by a Stoic calm. He has learned that

> Men must endure
> Their going hence, even as their coming
>   hither;
> Ripeness is all.[105]

So through suffering both men have learned humble submission. Lear, who had knelt in bitter mockery before Regan, would now kneel in humble penitence to Cordelia. Pride in his kingdom and his hundred knights is utterly forgotten. With Cordelia alone he can now "pray, and sing, and tell old tales, and laugh" even in a prison cell. His selfishness has given way to a great love and tenderness. He is no longer concerned for himself but only for the child who has borne so much for him. His soul has been so transformed through his suffering that he can now understand for the first time the meaning and beauty of her sacrifice:

> Upon such sacrifices, my Cordelia,
> The gods themselves throw incense.[106]

But this touching tribute reveals also the transformation in Cordelia. It seemed such a petty thing that drew down her father's wrath and curses upon her in that first tragic scene. She should have known his craving for affection in his old age, and his love of petting and flattery. She could have humored his childishness and been perfectly sincere. But when the

king asked an expression of love surpassing
the extravagant flattery of her sisters, she was
speechless. Indignation at her sisters' brazen
hypocrisy drove her to the opposite extreme
of an honesty so blunt as to misrepresent her
love completely.

To her father her answer was like a blow in
the face—an unexpected, incomprehensible
shock from the one he loved the most and on
whom he had set his hopes. Incredulous, he
asked again. But Cordelia had inherited a
measure of her father's stubborn pride, and her
speech once made she could not change. The
fury of Lear's disappointed love is equalled
only by the depths of his penitence, as, her
"most small fault" now completely forgotten,
he falls on his knees to ask her forgiveness.

But Cordelia's pride and stubbornness are
also gone. As she sees the suffering of Lear,
for which she was in a measure unintentionally responsible, her love overflows. She is
the soul of pity and gentleness, and her tears
are a balm to his tortured soul.

But this breaking down of pride, this growth
in humility, love, concern for others, and consciousness of responsibility has been a tragic
process. In *Lear* it seems to be the mission of
the universe. For even in pagan times there
was evidence that, implanted in the very
nature of men and of all living things, as
Aquinas has said, is the eternal law "that
good is to be done and gone after and evil is to
be avoided."[107] Those who bow in subjection,

as Lipsius has said, find immeasurable reward in the enlargement of their souls in richness and beauty. But this enrichment often comes through suffering. Kent voices the torture of the world and the pity of the tragic struggle when he exclaims over the dying king:

> Break, break, I prithee, break! . . .
> O, let him pass! He hates him
> That would upon the rack of this tough world
> Stretch him out longer.[108]

Painful as the suffering has been, it can leave upon the reader a far different impression from that recorded by Dr. Johnson. For Shakespeare has pictured, even in a pagan world, a natural justice that exacts inexorable punishment for every wrong and confers lasting rewards on those who have merited its favor. As demonstrated by the nameless servant this innate justice finally rises in revolt against unbearable cruelty and evil and rights the wrongs of humanity. In attributing this retribution to the Justicers above, Albany is not ignoring the servant, but considers him the instrument of Supreme Justice.

Just as equitably, Lear and Cordelia, Kent and Edgar, though all suffer, partly from their own faults, partly from the injustice of others, yet all acquire an enrichment of soul that far outweighs the suffering. Shakespeare, therefore, leaves us with the feeling that they have attained a greatness which triumphs over tragedy, and our sense of pity is mingled with admiration.

FOOTNOTES AND REFERENCES

1. *Lucrece*, 848-854.
2. *Richard II*, V, v, 1-41.
3. *The Faerie Queene*, VII, vi, 6. See also "Daphnaida," 428ff.
4. Farr, *op. cit.*, I, 203ff, 226ff; II, 400.
5. See Kerton, *op. cit.*, and Batman, *op. cit.*, Bk. VI, ch. i.
6. *As You Like It*, II, vii, 39-166.
7. Lipsius, *A Discourse of Constancy*, Bk. I, ch. xvi.
8. See *The Faerie Queene* III, vi, 39-41; "Cantos of Mutability," VII, 47; "The Ruins of Time,"; "Visions of the World's Vanities," "Visions of Petrarch."
9. See *Sonnets* 12, 60, 64, 65.
10. *II Henry IV*, III, i, 45-56.
11. Calvin, *op. cit.*, Bk. I, ch. xvi.
12. See Nicholas Ridley, *Works*, ed. for The Parker Society (Cambridge, England: University Press), p. 79; Beard, *op. cit.*, Preface; Thomas Beacon, *Works*, ed. for The Parker Society (Cambridge, England: University Press, 1843), III, 808-616.
13. Calvin, *op. cit.*, Bk. I, ch. xvi.
14. Busson, *op. cit.*, p. 146f.
15. Lipsius, *Of Constancy*, p. 74f.
16. *Ibid.*, p. 99ff.
17. C. Secundus Plinius, *The Historie of the World* (London: Adam Islip, 1634), Bk. II, ch. vii.
18. Busson, *op. cit.*, pp. 125f.
19. *Ibid.*, p. 229.
20. *Ibid.*, p. 223.

21. Boulting, *op. cit.*, p. 154.

22. It is a question of course, as to how many of the French naturalists were known in England. It is quite certain that Shakespeare was acquainted with the conservative work of Justus Lipsius and Gelli, and from references to Gargantua's mouth in *As You Like It*, he must have been familiar with Rabelais. But ideas were widely circulated in the Renaissance and could have come to him from various sources.

23. See Hutchinson, *op. cit.*, p. 77.

24. Busson, *op. cit.*, p. 412.

25. For Vicomercato's denial of the supernatural see Busson, *op. cit.*, pp. 225-227.

26. See Montaigne, *op. cit.*, Bk. I, ch. xi.

27. *Venus and Adonis*, 925-928.

28. *Ibid.*, 1045-1050.

29. *I Henry IV*, III, i, 20-34.

30. *King John*, III, iv, 158.

31. *Julius Caesar*, I, iii, 34f.

32. *King Lear*, I, ii, 128-145.

33. *Richard III*, IV, iv, 215; *Much Ado about Nothing*, II, i, 349; *All's Well That Ends Well*, I, i, 197; 205f; *King Lear*, IV, iii, 34-37; *Two Gentlemen of Verona*, II, vii, 74.

34. *Timon of Athens*, IV, iii, 108-110.

35. *All's Well That Ends Well*, I, i, 197-234.

36. *Julius Caesar*, IV, iii, 218-221.

37. *Ibid.*, I, ii, 139-141.

38. Machiavelli, *op. cit.*, p. 207.

39. Chapman, *The Conspiracy of Charles, Duke of Byron*, III, i.

40. Marlowe, *I Tamburlaine*, I, ii, 173-176.

41. Marlowe, *II Tamburlaine*, V, iii, 48-51.

42. *Henry V*, IV, viii, 80.

43. *Richard II*, III, ii, 60-62.

44. *Hamlet*, V, ii, 8-11.

45. *As You Like It*, II, iii, 43-45.

46. See *Hamlet*, V, ii, 232ff.

47. *All's Well That Ends Well*, II, iii, 1-6.

48. *Antony and Cleopatra*, V, ii, 3f.

49. *Lucrece*, 1478-1484.

50. Lipsius, *Of Constancy*, Bk. II, ch. viii. See also Hutchinson, *op. cit.*, p. 72; and Pilkington, *op. cit.*, p. 178, who gives the devil his due in cooperating with God in causing human suffering.

51. Bradford, *op. cit.*, I, 210.

52. Spenser, *The Faerie Queene*, Bk. II, canto III, st. xi.

53. Hutchinson, *op. cit.*, pp. 58-60; Philpot, *op. cit.*, p. 270.

54. *Ibid.*, pp. 73f; Rogers, *The General Session*, ch. XII, Spenser, "Daphnaida," 358-364.

55. Spenser, *The Shepherdes Calender*, 15.

56. Spenser, *The Faerie Queene*, V, canto xi, st. 1.

57. Beacon, *op. cit.*, 240.

58. Harkness, *op. cit.*, p. 132.

59. Thomas Beard, *op. cit.*, A iii.

60. Lipsius, *Of Constancy*, Bk. II, ch. xiii.

61. Hutchinson, *op. cit.*, p. 67.

62. Spenser, *The Faerie Queene*, Bk. v, canto II, st. 23-26.

63. Chapman, *The Tragedy of Caesar and Pompey*, I, i, See also *The Revenge of Bussy D'Ambois*, V, i, 27-32.

64. Chapman, *The Revenge of Bussy D'Ambois*, III, i, 435-452.

65. Chapman, *The Conspiracy of Charles, Duke of Byron*, I, i, 374-384.

66. Chapman, *The Revenge of Bussy D'Ambois*, IV, i, 138-156.

67. *Ibid.*, V, i, 7-14.

68. Lipsius, *Sixe bookes of politickes and civil doctrine*, p. 10. Yet Lipsius is too Christian to disregard the need of a future life to adjust discrepancies that still remain. (See *Of Constancy*, Bk. II, ch. xiii, p. 206). He is also thoroughly Christian in discouraging curiosity about God's justice: "God strikes, and God passes by; what would you more?" Bk. II, ch. xii, p. 204.

69. Busson, *op. cit.*, p. 37.

70. How much this may be due to the law of James I against using God's name in vain on the stage is a question. But aside from allusions to deity the tone is definitely pagan.

71. *Richard II*, I, iii, 22-40.

72. *King Lear*, III, iv, 27-36.

73. *Ibid.*, I, iv, 297-299.

74. *Ibid.*, I, i, 298-310.

75. *Ibid.*, I, iii, 16-20.

76. *Ibid.*, I, iv, 261f.

77. *Ibid.*, II, iv, 149-153.

78. *Ibid.*, II, iv, 155-158.

79. *Ibid.*, IV, ii, 54f.

80. *Ibid.*, III, iii, 24-26.

81. *Ibid.*, IV, vi, 137f.

82. *Ibid.*, I, iv, 268f.

83. *Ibid.*, II, iv, 293f.

84. *Ibid.*, IV, vii, 46ff.

85. *Ibid.*, III, vii, 55-57.

86. *Ibid.*, III, vii, 92f.

87. Sir Philip Sidney, *The Countess of Pembrokes Arcadia*, (Cambridge, England: University Press, 1922), p. 208.

88. *King Lear*, IV, vi, 210f.

89. *Ibid.*, IV, vii, 31-42.

90. *Ibid.*, I, IV, 187-190.

91. Knight, *The Wheel of Fire*, (London: Oxford University Press, 1930), pp. 175-193.

92. *Richard III*, I, iii, 287f.

93. *Ibid.*, V, i, 20-24.

94. *King Lear*, IV, ii, 29-36.

95. *Ibid.*, IV, ii, 46-49.

96. *Ibid.*, IV, ii, 78-80.

97. *Ibid.*, V, iii, 170-173.

98. *Ibid.*, II, iv, 192-195.

99. *Ibid.*, III, ii, 19-24.

100. *Ibid.*, IV, i, 38f.

101. Horace Howard Furness, ed. *King Lear* (Variorum, 11th Edition, Philadelphia: J. B. Lippincott, 1908), p. 419.

102. *Pericles*, IV, iii, 49f.

103. *King Lear*, III, iv, 28-36.

104. *Ibid.*, III, iv, 108-113.

105. *Ibid.*, V, ii, 9-11.

106. *Ibid.*, V, iii, 20f.

107. Etienne Gilson, *The Philosophy of St. Thomas Aquinas*, (St. Louis: B. Herder Book Co., 1929), p. 328.

108. *King Lear*, V, iii, 312-315.

Chapter 6

MACBETH AND ABSOLUTE EVIL

From the profound pessimism and doubts of *Hamlet*, Shakespeare has concluded in *Troilus and Cressida* that good and evil are not a mental mirage based on personal likes and dislikes, but are reflections of a universal moral law implanted in the natures of men. He has also shown how difficult it is to attain the right standard of conduct and even the impossibility of expecting perfect justice in human affairs. He has further revealed the tragic results of the moral insurrection which moves men, against the warnings of reason and conscience, to choose the "heaven" that leads them to their hell. In *Lear*, too, he has shown with almost brutal honesty that for the evil that sometimes tortures human lives as on a wheel of fire there is a justice in the universe which ultimately distributes appropriate rewards and punishments.

But the nature of this mystery of evil which can overthrow reason, corrupt the soul in its supposedly impregnable fortress, and bring suffering and destruction to men is the particular problem of *Macbeth*.

Macbeth's "Fate and Metaphysical Aid"

In *Macbeth* Shakespeare searches the heart of this mystery. Here evil is the primary fact. It is the dominant force which sways the purposes and controls the actions of the characters. Out of it grow the nameless terrors which paralyze resistance and freeze up the fountains of the will, and by it are wrought the subtle changes in heart and mind that mark the fatal disintegration of the human soul.

Here for the first time Shakespeare gives prominence to the supernatural, or as Macbeth terms it, the "metaphysical." Psychological explanations based entirely upon physical stimuli may satisfy the materialist, but are hardly adequate for one who believes in a spiritual world, and who makes a distinction between soul and body, as Shakespeare does. The thing which is by nature inclined to the good and chooses evil is not the flesh, but ultimately the spirit. Flesh could have no powers within itself. Behind the physical stimuli, therefore, is felt to lie the unseen—a world or force or influence, however variously conceived—which is essentially evil and which affects the soul both through and in connection with the physical.

To Aristotle, the Neoplatonists, Augustine, and Aquinas, this realm of evil was privation, or Nothingness. The world with all its forms was created, or called into being, from nothing, and Augustine explains that evil is the tendency of the will or of Being to slip back into Nothingness again. Evil, therefore, is Non-being as opposed to Being, chaos as opposed to cosmos, dark as opposed to light, utter nothing as opposed to something.

But this concept, which laid the metaphysical basis for the dissolution of the soul through moral evil, did not prevent the further concept of a malignancy in the universe whose sole business was to disrupt the order, bring in chaos, or tempt the soul to nothingness again. This malignancy was conceived in various ways, and pagan and Christian thought was often interwoven with strange results. The idea of good and evil demons or genii among the pagans was similar to the good and evil angels, or angels and devils, of Christianity.[1]

The idea of a tutelary spirit for each person, which is at least as old as Hesiod, Socrates, and Plato, and is repeated by Plotinus,[2] is referred to by Shakespeare in reference to Antony, Caesar, and Macbeth.[3] But to this good genius, Servius in the fourth century added an evil one, as Professor Knowlton points out.[4] Bartholomaeus says that an evil angel is given each man for the purpose of "assailing and tempting" him.[5] Agrippa gives to each person three genii: one holy and coming from God, the next from the stars and characterized by the disposition of the planets at each man's birth, and the third a genius of "profession," which men choose as they select a good or evil course.[6] Spenser postulates a good and

evil genius, not given to each person indi-
vidually, but controlling life at its source.[7]

While no doubt many in Shakespeare's time
still believed in a personal good and evil
angel who aided and tempted men, this belief,
Chapman says, had come to be discredited
among men.[8] Faustus is tempted by his evil
angel rather than by Mephistopheles, but this
is probably no more than a convention under
which Marlowe presents the psychological
struggle. On the basis of Chapman's statement
it is probable that many references to evil
genii may have been only figurative speech to
describe the baser fleshly nature.[9] Shakespeare's reference to his friend and the Dark
Woman as his good and evil angels is of
course figurative. But Gloucester's statement,

> Let not my worser spirit tempt me again
> To die before you please![10]

may indicate the speaker's belief in an evil
angel, whatever might be Shakespeare's own
belief.

But apart from the idea of personal angels
and tutelary spirits there was the most widespread belief in devils and evil spirits in
general. Bartholemaeus says these evil spirits
take upon them any shape they desire, that
they molest and disquiet men, trouble the elements, make tempests in the sea and air, corrupt and destroy the fruits of the earth, tempt
men to discord and strife and vain-hope, and
that "all malice and vncleane thoughts come

of their doeing, the which they may put in mens thoughts."[11] It is only the lowest order of good angels, the Potestates, that prevent these evil spirits from violently overcoming men and doing much more harm than they now do.[12]

Nothing was more devoutly believed than the existence of the devil, and his eternal vigilance in drawing men into sin. Latimer calls him the most diligent prelate in England, never out of his pulpit.[13] His evil spirits were present everywhere, always ready to tempt the souls of men. Gabriel Harvey suggests that the air itself may be a "compound of aierye, wyndie, raynie, snowe, frostye, coulde, whott, fayre, fowle, hwolsum, contagious, caulme, and blustering tempestuous spirites . . . whirling into every mans eares infinite blastes of aierye conceptes, and levityes, sutch as light women and fantasticall heddes ar puffed upp withall; and specially diverse franticke herritiques that ar the fonders and ringleaders of newfanglid opinions and vayne ridiculous sectes?[4] Likewise he asks,

Why may not that which they call fyer for anythinge that is certainely knowne to the contrarye be the very local place and seate of Hell, where is sutch continual burninge flames as both the formiddiste Catholique divines and most excellent profane writers threaten against the wicked? Or at leastwise why maye it not be a certayne excessive and everlastinge heate, proceed-

inge from the whott breathes of so many
divelish sprites and scalding fiendes, as
ar ther inhabitinge, and by a forcible burninge influence inflaminge the alreadye
furious and boylinge minds of tyrants and
whott impatient divellish fellows . . .[15]

Harvey is sure that "fierye, aierye, water-
ishe, and earthely divels are ye onlye absolute
monarches of ye worlde, if they be not ye
worlde itself," and that they control all the
elements, and know their own advantage and
"where the shoe pinches us most," as well as
the beggar knows his dish.[16] While Harvey is
attempting to be humorous, he probably does
not greatly exaggerate the popular belief
around 1579 in the number and the ubiquitous
nature of these evil spirits.

Yet many differed in opinion about them.
Roger Hutchinson says many "late-born Sa-
ducees" declared "that the devil is nothing
but *nolitum*, or a filthy affection coming of the
flesh," but would not argue the matter "stiffly"
for fear of the commonwealth. He denounces
these and the Libertines for holding that evil
spirits are only "beastly affections, evil
thoughts."[17]

There were at least three views concerning
the devils, which La Primaudaye sets forth at
some length. First, some believed that evil
spirits actually "in their very substance enter
into the bodies or soules, heartes or mindes of
men." Second, others held that "evil spirites
trouble the heartes and mindes of men onely

by provocations, temptations, and illusions," and third, some "referre all the madnesse of lunaticke folkes to natural causes, as if they proceeded either from melancholike or choler-ike humors, or some such like causes, as frensinesse, madnesse, and furie, or some such diseases whereby men are carried beside them-selves."[18]

Reginald Scott, who did much to uproot the superstitions about witchcraft, apparently held the second view but gave much credence to the third. On the basis of the distinction between spirit and flesh, he held that, since the devils have no bodily form but are merely spirits, their temptations can be only spiritual.[19] It is merely the will and mind of man which are vitiated and depraved by the temptations of the devil, but no one is possessed and given super-natural powers.[20]

This view was anathematized by King James, who commanded the book to be burned and re-plied to it himself in his *Demonology* (1597). James believed profoundly in witches and their supernatural powers, including their gifts of prophecy. He refutes the argument that "devil-possession" may be only a disease of the mind or imagination caused by too much melan-choly, but he believes also that the passions of the mind open the way for the devil to enter. Revenge and ambition, together with the despair which accompanies them are the two passions most susceptible to the wiles of the devil.

Macbeth with its witches and its passion of ambition, which prepares the way for the mystic union between the protagonist and the supernatural world, could have been interpreted by King James as in complete harmony with his views. But *Macbeth* is far more than a mere witch play. Under the garb of a popular superstition which would appeal most vividly to the imagination of his audience Shakespeare is presenting a universal problem. This becomes evident from a study of the wierd sisters themselves. They are not mere witches, nor does Shakespeare ever refer to them as such. The term "weird" suggests their power over the destinies or fates of men, and when they are not referred to as "weird sisters" they are called merely "sisters," "instruments of darkness," "imperfect speakers," "juggling fiends." Their immateriality is constantly suggested. They are unnatural, formless, sexless creatures

That look not like the inhabitants of the earth
And yet are on it.[21]

Their unreality suggests the creations of delirium, and as they vanish like bubbles into the air, they leave a doubt of whether they have ever been:

Were such things here as we do speak about?
Or have we eaten on the insane root
That takes the reason prisoner.[22]

In their dancing around the cauldron, their

love of darkness, storm, and rain they have the qualities of popular witches; in their prophetic vision they suggest the gloomy superstition of the Scottish Highlands; and in their control over destiny and their blinding of the judgments of men they are like the Fates and Furies.

The perfect artistry of Shakespeare is shown in leaving their outlines vague and uncertain. Were they definitely witches and no more, they would belong to the earth and the wonder would cease, for their supernatural power would be mere superstition. Were they definitely "devils," the whole problem of evil would fall into the stereotyped theological explanation of Satanic suggestion. But with fatalism added, the concept is lifted into another realm. In these intangible, fleshless, elusive phantoms is personified the principle of evil, the malignancy in the universe, in whatever form it takes hold upon the imaginations of men.

The artistry of Shakespeare is further shown in his keeping these spectral figures in the background. Only twice do they make actual contact with Macbeth, and then in such weird and unnatural surroundings as to suggest unreality and illusion. They have no "local habitation and a name," but haunt the "fog and filthy air," control the winds, raise tempests, and are companions of the lightning and the rain. They could no more be given material form than one can explain and make visible the mystery of evil in the world, but their shadowy forms, from the obscurity, direct the course of events and throw over the action a sinister, tragic gloom. They symbolize not only the evil which pervades the Macbeth universe, but all the subtle, intangible forces, of whatever form, that disrupt the "married calm" of states and individuals and bring destruction to the world.

"Fair is Foul and Foul is Fair"

The first characteristic of this malignancy is its disorderliness, its antagonism against rule and nature, its tendency toward utter chaos both in the physical world and in the human soul. That this is Shakespeare's concept of Absolute Evil is indicated by a number of passages in which he has attempted to express in language the ultimate antithesis of the Good. Traveling rapidly from the ideal of "right" and "justice" to the opposite extreme, the mind of Ulysses pictures the state of Absolute Evil as one of utter disorder, lack of restraint, chaos, and finally Nothingness, when appetite, "an universal wolf,"

> Must make perforce a universal prey,
> And last eat up himself.[23]

When Albany pictures the extreme evil to which the viciousness of Goneril and Regan, if unchecked, will grow, he uses the same idea of self-destruction and oblivion, for

> Humanity must perforce prey on itself
> Like monsters of the deep.[24]

When Timon would pray for ultimate evil to envelop the world, he would have all order, law, justice, truth, and respect,

> Decline to your confounding contraries,
> And let confusion live.[25]

Macbeth thinks of evil as the absolute disorder where "nature's germans tumble all together," even till destruction sickens.[26] And when Malcolm expresses the absoluteness of his evil, beyond which he could envision no other concept, the image is also one of utter chaos and discord, for he would

> Uproar the universal peace, confound
> All unity on earth.[27]

The essence of Absolute Evil, in Shakespeare's mind, may therefore be identified with Absolute Disorder, Chaos, Oblivion, Nothingness. It is as personifications of the power of Disorder or Nothingness over the human soul that the Weird Sisters become significant. They themselves are utterly "unnatural"; they break the unity of kind; and where they move, disorder inevitably reigns. They dance in the confusion of rain and thunder, and they fill the land with the "hurlyburly" of rebellious war.

This topsy-turvy chaos is one of the marked features of the *Macbeth* world, from its tumultuous beginning till it passes into nothingness with the coming of concord. The opening battles are unnatural, bloody, and confused,

filled with strange images of death; and
scarcely is one dismal conflict ended when
another begins. The day itself is unnatural
and wild. The world is filled with misrule,
and things occur against the use of nature.
The Old Man, who has lived long, says,

> I have seen
> Hours dreadful and things strange; but this
>   sore night
> Hath trifl'd former knowings.[28]

Darkness entombs the earth when by the
clock the living light should kiss it. A falcon
is struck and killed by a mousing owl, and
Duncan's horses turn wild in nature and eat
each other.

This civil strife and cosmic discord, however, only reflect the deeper moral chaos. The
strange paradox of the weird sisters, "Fair is
foul and foul is fair,"[29] sounds the note of confusion at the first, and is startlingly echoed in
Macbeth's opening words. It is as if the unnatural events through which he has passed
have wrought upon his blood, as Professor
Dowden suggests, and there is already established a subconscious connection with
these spirits of Discord that prepares him for
his conscious and unnatural revolt. His own
amazing and bloody success perhaps has no
small part; for ambition, according to contemporary belief, opens the way to temptation, and his first words to Lady Macbeth are
strikingly significant: "They met me in the
day of success."[30]

The greeting of the Destinies apparently falls upon a heart already charged with secret dreams of power and leaves it speechless with a guilty fear. Banquo might well ask,

> Good sir, why do you start, and seem to fear
> Things that do sound so fair?[31]

To Banquo's mind, innocent of all guile, it was a greeting of "present grace and good prediction," and nothing to be feared. But to Macbeth it is like the dawning of a guilty thought, a sudden flood of light in secret, evil places, the startling exposure of ambitions he had never breathed or acknowledged even to himself, and his mind leaps instantly to that which holds him rapt in terror. No more artfully could Shakespeare have suggested the occult force of evil. The work of discord had already started, and the prophecy was like a self-revelation, setting before him clearly the hidden purpose of his heart.

The immediate effect is to fill his soul with discord and confusion. Banquo, still undisturbed, sees the danger to which the prophecy could lead:

> That trusted home
> Might yet enkindle you unto the crown.[32]

Banquo repels the temptation because he suspects the evil nature of the tempters:

> And sometimes, to win us to our harm,
> The instruments of darkness tell us truths,

> Win us with honest trifles, to betray's
> in deepest consequence.[33]

Macbeth, however, swayed by the passion of
ambition, undergoes the same blinding of the
moral judgment which Tarquin suffered and
which Antony feared. "Foul" has become
"fair." He cannot distinguish good from evil.
The truth of one prophecy is earnest of the
good of all; yet this imagined good is strangely
confused with images of evil.

> This supernatural soliciting
> Cannot be ill; cannot be good; if ill,
> Why hath it given me earnest of success,
> Commencing in a truth? I am thane of Cawdor:
> If good, why do I yield to that suggestion
> Whose horrid image doth unfix my hair
> And make my seated heart to knock at my ribs,
> Against the use of nature?[34]

Confusion, wrought by discord in his soul,
like the insurrection which Brutus faced, fills
him with nameless terror. His truly noble
mind recoils and yet is irresistibly fascinated
by the mystery of evil. It is a suggestion that
apparently comes from without, seizing first
upon his subconscious mind and preparing it
for the conscious temptation. It seems not of
his own choosing, nor of his own creating. It
is alien and dark and terrifying, filled with
forebodings and repugnant to his consciousness of good. Yet its strange, resistless power
takes hold upon his mind, excites his imagination with images that unfix his hair and
smother up the source of action. He is swept

helplessly beyond the world of fact and truth
into the realm of fanciful unreality, where
all bounds of good and evil are lost in spectral
shadows and the world of non-being becomes
the world of being.

> Present fears
> Are less than horrible imaginings.
> My thought, whose murder yet is but
>   fantastical,
> Shakes so my single state of man that function
> Is smother'd in surmise, and nothing is
> But what is not.[35]

It is a mistake, as Mr. G. Wilson Knight has
already insisted,[36] to interpret the Weird
Sisters as mere dramatic representations of
Macbeth's thinking, and his temptation the
outgrowth of his own suggestion. They are
rather personifications of external, alien
forces, antagonistic to his mind, but irresistible in their power—the malignancy in the
universe. It is this fact that makes them
terrible. Fear fills his soul, but evil draws
him on in spite of fear. So strangely is he
wrought that what he wills he even shudders
to think upon.[37]

Lady Macbeth's subtle analysis helps us to
understand the struggle in his soul. He is "too
full o' the milk of human kindness to catch the
nearest way." He lacks the "illness," the un-
scrupulousness, that should attend ambition.[38]
Lady Macbeth is speaking like a disciple of
Machiavelli. Whatever end is desired must
justify the means. But Macbeth lacks this

unity of mind. He desires an end which calls
for crime, and in desiring it he even wills the
crime itself—he would "wrongly win," would
not wish the means "undone"; yet would not
play false! Like Angelo, he would and he
would not.

But Lady Macbeth is unity itself. Her mind
and soul are entirely in accord with the suggestion of evil. She would shut out the eye of
heaven from her deed, and pray the spirits
that "tend on mortal thoughts" to make her
equal to her task, to unsex her, transform her
very nature to their own,

> And fill me from the crown to the toe top-full
> Of direst cruelty! make thick my blood;
> Stop up th' access and passage to remorse,
> That no compunctious visitings of nature
> Shake my fell purpose, nor keep peace between
> The effect and it![39]

With such complete accord she has the appearance of one possessed by the spirit of
evil. For the moment she identified herself
with the demonic forces and, like one of them,
she is ready to pour her spirits into her husband's ear.

Macbeth's temptation follows psychological-
ly the course of Tarquin's. The insurrection
within his soul awakens his conscience,
which instantly marshals all the resources
of reason against the deed.

Duncan is his guest, his kinsman, and his
king. As his guest he should shut the door
against his murderer, not bear the knife him-

self; as his kinsman and his king, both nature and loyalty oppose the deed. Besides the king has been so meek,

> So clear in his great office, that his virtues
> Will plead like angels trumpet tounged against
> The deep damnation of his taking off.[40]

Macbeth's soul is not unwarned. He realizes fully the extreme evil of the deed. His own reputation is at stake. He has bought "golden opinions from all sorts of people" that would be worn in their newest gloss, not cast aside so soon. He is aware of all the probable consequences, for in these cases

> We still have judgment here, that we but teach
> Bloody instructions, which, being taught,
>   return
> To plague th' inventor.[41]

This is the inevitable retribution of universal justice. But since justice so often miscarries in this present world, as Macbeth weighs the chance of failure against the glory of the crown, murder becomes no longer a question of right and wrong, but only of expedience.

>   If the assassination
> Could trammel up the consequence, and
>   catch,
> With his surcease, success, that but this blow
> Might be the be-all and the end-all here,
> But here, upon this bank and shoal of time,
> We'd jump the life to come.[42]

Conscience has finally given way, until with Machiavellian casuistry the success of the immediate end justifies even murder as the means. He has aligned himself fully with Lady Macbeth and the powers of evil.

This significant change prepares the way for the final step. With conscience stilled and expedience the only question, it becomes chiefly a matter of courage, which in itself is a virtue. But to whet his courage further for the deed, Lady Macbeth taunts him,

> Art thou afeard
> To be the same in thine own act and valour
> As thou art in desire?[43]

Macbeth replies,

> I dare do all that may become a man;
> Who dares do more is none.

Lady Macbeth's next attack beats down this last defence. What made him break the enterprise to her? Then he was a man, and then he had the courage to carry the venture through. She would rather pluck the baby from her breast and dash its brains out than break an oath so deeply sworn as his. This puts it squarely as a matter, not only of courage, but of honor and integrity, a solemn obligation. By subtle shifts of sophistry the complete inversion of good and evil has been attained, until a deed which represents the extremity of evil becomes a duty which he must perform or live perjured and a coward in his own esteem. He is won, but yet with trembling and fear:

> I am settled, and bend
> Each corporal agent to this terrible feat.[44]

The horror of the thing which he must do still grips his mind, and from his "heat-oppressed brain" come visions of terror that deceive his eyes. He is led like one under the spell of an hypnotic power.

"Life's Fitful Fever"

Evil does not end merely with temptation and the conquest of the mind; the after-process is as profound as its inception. Here most clearly is shown its essential meaning—as Augustine expressed it, its tendency to chaos and dissolution. With the death of Duncan the work of the powers of evil is only well begun; their ultimate goal is to work such charms,

> As by the strength of their illusion
> Shall draw him on to his confusion.[45]

The disintegrating power of evil pursues a different course in each of the protagonists, and yet its basis is essentially the same. Evil is conceived as containing within itself the germs of its own dissolution; it is self-punishing, self-destroying. La Primaudaye writes that the very instant evil is committed

> she frameth for and of hir selfe hir owne torment, and beginneth to suffer the pains of hir mischieuous deede through the remorse thereof. This is that worme that continually gnaweth the conscience of a

malefactor, and accompanieth his miserable life with shame and confusion, with frights, perturbations, anguish and continuall disquietness, euen to his very dreames.[46]

The torments of conscience were believed never to be completely extinguished as long as one lived.[47] It never let a wicked man rest in peace, and at its worst it drove men to despair. Richard III, though hardened by crime and unfeeling when awake, is more terrified in sleep by the phantoms of his conscience than by ten thousand foes.[48] Even the calloused murderer is represented by Shakespeare as being troubled by conscience:

A man cannot steal, but it accuseth him; a man cannot swear, but it checks him; a man cannot lie with his neighbor's wife, but it detects him . . . It beggars any man that keeps it. It is turn'd out of towns and cities for a dangerous thing; and every man that means to live well endeavors to trust to himself and live without it.[49]

In Lady Macbeth the disintegrating effects of evil are not immediately apparent. She is too completely under its sway, and there is no dissonance in her soul. For the time she has no conscience about the deed, but is concerned only about its success: "Th' attempt and not the deed confounds us."[50]

Her mind works clearly, efficiently; she returns the daggers and smears the faces of the grooms with blood. She upbraids Macbeth for his brainsick, childish fears; her hands are of his color, but she shames to wear a heart so white. When all is said,

> A little water clears us of this deed:
> How easy is it then![51]

Only three things indicate the incipient weakness beneath this superhuman strength, this will possessed and transformed by the power of evil. Fearing the weakness of her husband, she had planned to execute the murder by herself, but her courage failed and must be bolstered by the artificial means of drink. Then her heart failed again as she looked at Duncan; he resembled too much her father as he slept. And finally as she hears Macbeth's incoherent ravings, her mind leaps shudderingly to the thought of madness:

> These deeds must not be thought
> After these ways: so, it will make us mad.[52]

This is adequate preparation for the break in her mind which begins with her fainting. She had steeled herself for the ordeal of Duncan's death, and she faced it bravely out; but when, on top of this, came so suddenly the unexpected murder of the grooms, her power of endurance failed.[53]

The passing of the excitement of evil, which had increased her powers beyond their natural strength, leaves her again a woman. She is haunted by fears and can find no peace.[54] We learn of terrible dreams that shake her nightly. Awake, her will still dominates, but in sleep nothing checks the fear which gradually breaks her strength and drives her to despair. The ravages of conscience have never been presented with more terrible effect than in the sleep-walking scene, with its washing of hands and smell of blood. Her mind has become broken and helpless, until like a child she is even afraid of the dark. It is the disintegrating power of evil before which medical science is futile, and the doctor exclaims with mingled fear and compassion:

> More needs she the divine than the physician,
> God, God, forgive us all![55]

The effect of evil upon Macbeth is different. Unlike Lady Macbeth there is discord in his soul which even his bending up of each corporal agent could not remove, and the murder leaves him pitifully shaken and distraught. In the grip of evil he has been carried entirely beyond his own nature; he is in the presence of a power before which he trembles and is helpless. He cannot understand himself, nor why prayer dies in his throat:

> But wherefore could I not pronounce "Amen"?
> I had most need of blessing, and "Amen"
> Stuck in my throat.[56]

The natural goodness of his soul, struggling for expression even at the moment of his crime, is checked and smothered by this counterforce. Voices ring in his ear:

> Glamis hath murder'd sleep, and therefore
>   Cawdor
> Shall sleep no more; Macbeth shall sleep no
>   more![57]

Conscience, even in the instant of the act, has begun the course of "even-handed justice" which he feared. The blood upon his hands plucks out his eyes!

His ensuing course is a struggle of fear against fear, a desperate, losing battle, not for a crown, but merely for existence. While Lady Macbeth must suffer in silence from a "mind diseas'd," Macbeth by action now attains a hardening which brings a measure of peace.

This is achieved in two ways: first, as Charron put it, through "long familiarity" with crime, which gradually heals the discord in his soul until he is frankly at one with the powers of evil; and second, through fatalism.

The step which marks the beginning of this hardening, as well as of Lady Macbeth's decay, is the sudden slaughter of the grooms. This was an easy task, for it had the outward motive and appearance of an act of open justice:

> Here lay Duncan,
> His silver skin laced with his golden blood,
> And his gashed stabs looked like a breach in
>   nature

For ruin's wasteful entrance. There, the
  murderers,
Steeped in the colors of their trade, their
  daggers
Unmannerly breeched with gore. Who could
  refrain
That had a heart to love, and in his heart
  Courage to make's love known?[58]

Through the sophistry of emotion his passion for justice could achieve a double murder as if it were a good. The act is significant
because it indicates the progress of his mind.
He no longer needs the incitement of his wife;
in an hour he has outstripped her far in evil
and from now on takes the lead.

But it is no longer ambition which drives
him on. Ambition has given way to a growing conviction of inevitable doom. Instead of
joy the imperial crown has brought him haunting fears. The prophecy of the witches has
bound him to Banquo with a secret dread. Banquo is still free, he has not yielded to temptation, and Macbeth's Genius stands rebuked in
his presence. Yet it is not Macbeth's conscience which troubles him, but that he has
bartered his eternal jewel to make the seed of
Banquo, kings. Rather than that he is ready to
call Fate into the lists. It is a resolution born
of despair, but it nerves him for the extremity
of crime.

But let the frame of things disjoint, both the
  worlds suffer,

Ere we will eat our meal in fear, and sleep
In the affliction of these terrible dreams
That shake us nightly: better be with the dead,
Whom we, to gain our peace, have sent to
        peace,
Than on the torture of the mind to lie
In restless ecstacy. Duncan is in his grave;
After life's fitful fever he sleeps well;
Treason has done its worst; nor steel, nor
        poison,
Malice domestic, foreign levy, nothing,
Can touch him further.[59]

The tragic change in Macbeth, from the glorious days in which he had "bought golden opinions from all sorts of people" to this bitter envy of the dead, is the logical result of evil. Negation had set its mark upon his soul, and no amount of crime could bring back again the values of life for him. But he misunderstands his trouble. His torture is the fear of his own mind, which he imputes to those around him. Banquo's death, which follows, brings no relief, but rather fresh terrors to haunt his memory. He is obsessed with the fear of retribution. Murder now will not lie still as in the olden times before the "humane statute purged the gentle weal," but "blood will have blood."

"A Tale Told by an Idiot"

Such tortures of the soul cannot endlessly endure. They will either break the mind or harden it, and Macbeth's mind is hardened. He

has stepped in so far in blood there is no turning back. He arrives at that detachment from
the moral universe which characterized Edmund, Richard, and Iago, where all distinctions of good and evil are swept aside except
what centers around himself; self-interest is
now his only moral law.

> For mine own good,
> All causes shall give away . . .[60]

Heretofore the powers of evil had sought out
Macbeth; the contacts had been unexpected,
and he had followed their suggestions with
fear. Now he voluntarily seeks them and places
his fortunes under their direction; he would
know "by the worst means, the worst." He has
thrown himself irrevocably on the side of
evil. The division in his soul is almost
closed, and he can speak of strange things he
has in head

> that will to hand,
> Which must be acted ere they may be scann'd[61]

He is yet but "young in deed."

The sheer fiendishness of this last suggestion denotes a radically new Macbeth—one in
whom the strange alchemy of evil has changed
the "milk of human kindness" to virulent
poison.

But this radical change brings also a new
and definite relation to the world. While the
division within his own soul has been closed,
the breach between him and the whole universe of good has been infinitely widened. In

aligning himself with evil he has placed himself in opposition to all that is good, and henceforth there must be inevitable discord and strife between him and the world in which he lives.

It is the situation described by Aquinas when one sets himself against the moral order. He becomes a disrupting factor, a cause of disorder, and as a consequence inevitably destroys himself. For nothing can oppose the actual good. As we have seen in the Universal Justice of *Lear*, it is the Eternal Law, implanted in the very nature of things, "that good is to be done and gone after and evil is to be avoided." From this law nothing can withdraw itself, says Aquinas, "since everything which attempts to do so, destroys itself in proportion as it succeeds."[62]

Thus the more completely Macbeth violates the moral law, or withdraws himself from the good, the more completely does he destroy himself and pass into Nothingness. He gradually finds himself deserted by former friends, followed half-heartedly through fear by those under his command. He dares trust no one, but fills the homes of Scotland with his spies.

Against these external fears, however, Macbeth finds a second way to calmness—through fatalism. This is an attitude of mind born often of despair. It gives courage by blinding the judgment against reality. Antony, in harmony with Greek thought, describes it as the blinding of the gods, but connects it also with our own viciousness:

> But when we in our own viciousness grow
>   hard,—
> O misery on 't!—the wise gods seal our eyes;
> In our own filth dark our clear judgments:
>   make us
> Adore our errors: laugh at 's, while we strut
> To our confusion.[63]

Like Antony's "wise gods" Shakespeare here uses the powers of evil as Greek Furies to effect this fatalistic blinding of Macbeth. These "instruments of darkness" had already blinded his judgment until what is "fair" seemed "foul," and what is evil seemed good. This darkening of judgment also seems not entirely his own doing, for his inner desires are strengthened by external suggestions and opportunities, as in Duncan's unexpected announcement of his visit to Inverness. Now they darken his judgment further by convincing him that he is impregnable against all opposition. Macduff is identified as his chief enemy, but he need fear none "of woman born." The philosophy that "Things bad begun make strong themselves by ill,"[64] now becomes a settled conviction. His success in crime, and despair of any other means, make him cling desperately to the hope that with its aid he still can triumph:

> Be bloody, bold, and resolute; laugh to scorn
> The power of man, for none of woman born
> Shall harm Macbeth.[65]

With this ultimate blinding, he can "strut"

to his confusion. His course becomes careless in blood. His crimes have formerly been necessary to the attainment of his ends, but now he gives way to the rashness of his temper and lets the firstlings of his heart become the firstlings of his hand. His destruction of Macduff's family is an act of ruthless, unnecessary hate for which he must pay in even coin, but there is no longer any conscience or fear within to check his impulse, and with the thought he acts.

Against this overconfidence in evil and the forces of discord and destruction, finally arise the powers of good. It was more than a mere flattery of King James, who claimed the power of divine healing, that called out the brief but vivid picture of Edward the Confessor. This good king contrasts as sharply with Macbeth as light with darkness, or good with evil. Evil unchecked had turned Scotland into a shambles. Ross describes it as

> Almost afraid to know itself! It cannot
> Be call'd our mother, but our grave; where
>   nothing,
> But who knows nothing, is once seen to smile;
> Where sighs and groans and shrieks that rend
>   the air,
> Are made, not mark'd; where violent sorrow
>   seems
> A modern ecstasy: the dead man's knell
> Is there scarce asked for who: and good men's
>   lives

Expire before the flowers in their caps,
Dying or ere they sicken.[66]

In contrast to this state, which is fast near-
ing Shakespeare's concept of absolute evil,
is the image of the good Confessor with healing in his touch. Strange ills that even human
art cannot convince he heals with prayer and
grace divine, and sundry blessings hang about
his throne.[67]

The return of Malcolm and Macduff, the coming of the English, the rising of the Scottish
thanes, are like a marshalling of all the forces
of good against the hosts of evil. "The powers
above put on their instruments." It is the
eternal Armageddon, when the forces of evil
feel the pangs of dissolution come upon them
and flee before the light and dissolve into
nothingness.

Macbeth is aware of the coming doom, and it
fills him with fear again. Some say he is mad;
others call it fury. It is a terror rising from
the knowledge of himself, for all that is within
him condemns itself for being there.[68] His
heartsickness at the emptiness of life prepares him for its final dissolution:

I have liv'd long enough: my way of life
Is fall'n into the seer, the yellow leaf;
And that which should accompany old age,
As honor, love, obedience, troops of friends,
I must not look to have; but in their stead,
Curses, not loud but deep, mouth-honor,
    breath,

Which the poor heart would fain deny, and
    dare not.[69]

His desire that the doctor find out the malady
of the land and purge it again to sound and
pristine health is more than dramatic irony;
it is the pathetic, hopeless longing of a lost
soul for the good it once has known. But the
chance has passed. He has supped full with
horrors; the good within his soul has gradually died away, and with it his better emotions
and his sense of values. Even his wife's death
scarcely moves him; for life itself, and all the
things that are, have lost their meaning and
are only the ravings of imbecility.

Tomorrow, and to-morrow, and to-morrow,
Creeps in this petty pace from day to day,
To the last syllable of recorded time;
And all our yesterdays have lighted fools
The way to dusty death. Out, out, brief candle!
Life's but a walking shadow; a poor player
That struts and frets his hour upon the stage
And then is heard no more. It is a tale
Told by an idiot, full of sound and fury,
Signifying nothing.[70]

The sense of nothingness is the ultimate essence of evil, and it is toward nothing, through
discord and chaos, that Macbeth is fatally and
helplessly driven. He has nothing to fight for
any longer, and even wishes the estate of the
world undone. But he is filled with the blind
fury of despair, a hatred of the living and a
fear of the doom which has come upon him,

and he fights with the dull rage of an animal at bay. It is the final hopeless, bitter struggle before he vanishes like a dark shadow at the coming of the light. By the power of evil his once noble and resolute soul, vividly conscious of the golden realities of life, has been shattered and disintegrated, drawn farther and farther from the reality of being, till it is lost in the abysm of Absolute Evil—the realm of unreality and nothingness.

But the exact nature of this fatalistic impulse which has led it downward and outward away from Being is difficult to say. It is superficial to inquire whether Shakespeare believed in witches, though this is hardly possible, for what we have in *Macbeth* is much more profound than witchcraft. It is perhaps equally superficial to inquire whether he believed in devils that tempt men spiritually, as Reginald Scott contended, through wicked dreams and suggestions of the flesh. In all probability he did. Macbeth speaks of wicked dreams that abuse the curtained sleep,[71] and Banquo continues to be tempted by them.[72] In many places Shakespeare suggests devilish influences upon the lives of men.[73] But he intimates also that some temptations are only natural impulses of the flesh. Troilus says that in each grace of the Grecian youths there lurks a "dumb-discoursive devil that tempts most cunningly," and that often we are devils to ourselves when we tempt the frailty of our own powers.

But whatever degree of faith Shakespeare may have had in the reality of evil spirits as the media of malignancy in the universe,[74] the fundamental fact in *Macbeth* is that evil seems to be an alien, external thing, an unnatural, formless force, a discord that disrupts the harmony of the soul and of the world, and unchecked leads to chaos. The soul is filled with terror at its inception and pursues it with apparently unwilling fascination. Even when hardened with familiarity, it faces its dissolution with trembling. Metaphysically it is the power of Non-being over Being.

The concept is too abstract for presentation except through such vague, shadowy forms as the Weird Sisters, but its subtle influence is still demonstrated in the degeneration of lives, not only of the nameless thousands who become victims of many vices, but also of those ambitious of high position, like Macbeth, who yield to dreams and opportunities for power which quickly dissolve into Nothing.

But the important fact about this alien force which disrupts the harmony of nature and the soul, as Shakespeare has shown, is that it eventually destroys itself. For it is opposing the Good which the Eternal Law has implanted in the very nature of men, and anything that opposes the universal law, as Aquinas has said, eventually destroys itself in proportion as it succeeds.

FOOTNOTES AND REFERENCES

1. Plutarch (*Morals*, III, 117) says the ancients distinguished between good and evil gods, putting the Dirae, Furies, and Mars in the latter class; and that Empedocles, Plato, Xenocrates, Chryssipus, and Democritus all believed in evil omens. (*Morals* IV, 22).

2. See Frank L. Schoell, *Etudessur l'humanism continental an Angleterre a la fin de la Renaissance* (Paris: 1926), p. 238; Jowett, *op. cit.*, II, 123, 334; Plotinus *Enneads* (London: Philip Lee Warner, 1921-1930), III, 4, 3.

3. *Antony and Cleopatra*, II, iii, 17; IV, iii; *Macbeth*, III, i, 55f.

4. E. C. Knowlton, "The Genius of Spenser," *Studies in Philology*, XXV (1928), 441.

5. Stephen Batman, *Batman uppon Bartholome*, (London: Thomas East, 1582), Bk. II, ch. xix.

6. *Ibid.*, Bk. XI, p. 70.

7. *The Faerie Queene*, Bk. II, canto XII, st. xlvii-xlviii.

8. See note on Bk. I, i, 198, of his translation of the *Georgics of Hesiod*; see Schoell, *op. cit.*, p. 238.

9. *Sonnet* 144. See also *The Tempest*, IV, i, 26-28.

10. *King Lear*, IV, vi, 196.

11. Batman, *op. cit.*, Bk. II, chs. 19-20.

12. *Ibid.*, Bk. II, ch. 14.

13. Hugh Latimer, *Sermons*, ed. for the Parker Society, (Cambridge, England: University Press, 1845), I, 70-81.

14. Evelyn May Albright, "Spenser's Reasons for rejecting the Cantos of Mutability," *Studies in Philology* XXV (1928), p. 106.

15. *Ibid.*, p. 83.

16. *Ibid.*, p. 84f.

17. Hutchinson, *op. cit.*, pp. 134-140.

18. La Primaudaye, *op. cit.*, pp. 167-168.

19. Reginald Scott, *Scot's Discovery of VVitchcraft; proving the common opinions of Witches contracting with DiVels, Spirits, or Familiars . . . to be but imaginary* (London: Adam Islip, 1561), pp. 364ff.

20. *Ibid.*, p. 10.

21. *Macbeth*, I, iii, 41f.

22. *Ibid.*, I, iii, 83ff.

23. *Troilus and Cressida*, I, iii, 109-126.

24. *King Lear*, IV, ii, 46-50.

25. *Timon of Athens*, IV, i, 20f.

26. *Macbeth*, IV, i, 59f.

27. *Macbeth*, IV, iii, 97-100.

28. *Ibid.*, II, iv, 2-4.

29. *Ibid.*, I, i, 10.

30. *Ibid.*, I, v, 1.

31. *Ibid.*, I, iii, 5-22.

32. *Ibid.*, I, iii, 120-133.

33. *Ibid.*, I, iii, 124-126.

34. *Ibid.*, I, iii, 130-137.

35. *Ibid.*, I, iii, 137-142.

36. G. W. Knight, "Macbeth and the Nature of Evil," *Hibbert Journal*, XXVIII (1929-1930), 341.

37. *Macbeth*, I, iv, 50-53.

38. *Ibid.*, I, v, 14-23.

39. *Ibid.*, I, v, 40-45.

40. *Ibid.*

41. *Ibid.*, I, vi, 8-11.

42. *Ibid.*, I, vi, 1-7.

43. *Ibid.*, I, vii, 39-41.

44. *Ibid.*, I, vii, 79f.

45. *Ibid.*, III, v, 28f.

46. La Primaudaye, *op. cit.*, p. 67. The idea is

320   *Shakespeare's Philosophy of Evil*

popular in Stoic thought (See Seneca *Epistles* XCVII, 14, and *De Ira*, II, xxx, 2; III, xxvi, 2) and is found everywhere in the Renaissance.

47. Lipsius, *Sixe Bookes of Politickes and Civil Doctrine*, p. 9.

48. *Richard III*, V, iii, 216-219.

49. *Ibid.*, I, iv, 138-149.

50. *Macbeth*, II, ii, 10f.

51. *Ibid.*, II, ii, 67f.

52. *Ibid.*, II, ii, 33f.

53. *Ibid.*, II, iii, 105.

54. *Ibid.*, III, ii, 4-7.

55. *Ibid.*, V, i, 82f.

56. *Ibid.*, II, ii, 31-33.

57. *Ibid.*, I, ii, 42f.

58. *Ibid.*, II, iii, 117-124.

59. *Ibid.*, III, ii, 16-26.

60. *Ibid.*, III, v, 135f.

61. *Ibid.*, III, iv, 139f.

62. Gilson, *op. cit.*, p. 331f.

63. *Antony and Cleopatra*, III, xiii, 111-115.

64. *Macbeth*, II, ii, 55.

65. *Ibid.*, IV, i, 79-81.

66. *Ibid.*, IV, iii, 165-173.

67. *Ibid.*, IV, iii, 141-159.

68. *Ibid.*, V, ii, 24f.

69. *Ibid.*, V, iii, 22-28.

70. *Ibid.*, V, v, 19-28.

71. *Ibid.*, II, i, 50.

72. *Ibid.*, II, i, 20f.

73. See *Hamlet*, III, iv, 76; *Richard III*, I, ii, 67; I, iii, 293f; *Henry V*, II, ii, 111-125.

74. For a scholarly discussion of the demonology behind the play see Curry, *op. cit.*

Chapter 7

THE TEMPEST GROWS CALM

MANY HAVE wondered why Shakespeare, around 1600, entered the long period of tragic gloom. As stated above,[1] it was hardly the result of deep personal sorrow, for about that time the temper of all England changed. From the earlier enthusiasm, which burst forth in songs, sonnets, and histories exalting the greatness of the past, literature in general took on the somber tone of tragedy and critical satire.

Shakespeare's own mood grew darker through the long period, from his sympathetic treatment of Brutus, the impractical idealist caught in the cross currents of political rivalry, to the blackness of *Macbeth* and the bitterness of *Timon*. The "harsh world" of Hamlet changed to the "tough world" of Kent, and to the agony of Lear, as one tortured on a wheel of fire.

Though Shakespeare must have suffered through the tragedies as he made his audiences suffer, always, with perhaps the exception of Dr. Johnson, the suffering was accompanied by the spiritual uplift which Aristotle called catharsis, the emotional "cleansing" which is characteristic of great tragedy. Black as his world was, Shakespeare never left his audience in despair. Even in the darkness of Macbeth he makes us feel that the powers above are finally putting on their instruments and the slow dawn will bring in a new and happier day.

This is because Shakespeare does not give a distorted picture of the world. Humanity is not all hopelessly evil. Alongside Iago is the innocence of Desdemona and the honesty of Othello, Cassio, and Emilia; alongside the corruption of Claudius and Gertrude is the sweetness of Ophelia and the nobleness of Hamlet and Horatio; alongside Macbeth and Lady Macbeth are Macduff, Malcolm, and the saintly King Edward; and alongside Goneril, Regan, and Edmund are Cordelia, Edgar, Albany, Kent, and the unnamed servant who gave his life for justice and mercy.

The realism, penetration, and sanity with which Shakespeare saw the world have hardly been equalled. Cruelty, corruption, injustice, and suffering were realities which he felt intensely; but he was equally conscious of the unselfishness, loyalty, love, and sacrifice of humanity, on which "the gods themselves throw incense." Though he knew the tragedy and pain, he knew also the humor and laughter of the world. As it has been well said, he "saw life steadily and saw it whole."

Tranquility and Peace

Why Shakespeare, about 1611, turned sud-

denly from tragedy to the charming romances
of his last years we can only guess. Certainly
he had not exhausted all the tragic themes.
Perhaps after his long search into the "mystery of evil," and his conclusion that, in spite
of the suffering which it brings, it eventually
effects its own destruction,[2] he felt that both he
and his audience deserved a change of tone.
Actually the very conclusion he had reached
would suggest a change of emphasis, to the
peace and calm that follows struggle and
storm. Perhaps he also felt that England too
had suffered long enough under the tragic
gloom that had filled the stage, and needed
new faith under the gathering clouds that
would finally bring a second Civil War. At
any rate, *Pericles* struck a happier tone, and
its instant popularity indicated that England
was ready for a change. It set in motion a new
trend to be followed by Beaumont and Fletcher
and later dramatists.

In these closing plays Shakespeare dropped
the realism of tragedy, which demands that
the motivation of every act be adequate and
logical. In *Pericles*, on the contrary, he chose
a highly improbable, almost miraculous, tale,
which was widely loved as it had come down
from the Middle Ages. In all these last plays
he makes little attempt to convince his
audience of the logic of events. Instead he
asks them to fill in the missing links with
their own imagination and accept the story
itself somewhat in the spirit of a parable, in

which the events are unimportant, but the
meaning back of them is vital. Unlike the
motivation of the tragedies he makes no attempt to explain Pericles' long abandonment
of Marina, Leontes' insane jealousy of Her-
mione, Iachimo's unnatural treachery, or the
enchanting magic of *The Tempest*. In all but
the last the action extends over years of time,
in which the impossible might easily seem
possible. Enhanced by the beauty of the verse,
the happy turn of events, the suggestion of
symbolic meanings beyond the fragile tale,
the stories induce in the audience a mood of
happy acceptance and belief.

The Same Tough World

In spite of this change of mood, however,
Shakespeare does not change his view of the
world. In these last plays it is still as corrupt and cruel as it is in the tragedies. He is
fundamentally an idealist, and his very
concept (in *Timon of Athens, Measure for
Measure*, and all the tragedies) of what the
world and humanity ought to be makes sharp-
er and more painful his picture of what they
actually are. As an idealist and a lover of the
romantic, however, he was also a realist. He
could not close his eyes to the realities of the
world.

Pericles opens with the incestuous relations
of Antiochus and his daughter, a sin so ab-
horrent that the Man of Lawe declared that
even Chaucer, who told more than one sala-

cious tale, would never in "none of his sermons" tell of such "unkynde abhomynacions." Upon Pericles' discovery of the repulsive relation he is driven from his kingdom, pursued with relentless vengeance from land to land, shipwrecked, bereaved of his wife and daughter, and driven to the verge of insanity. The woman to whom he had entrusted his daughter attempts to murder her, but she is seized instead by pirates and sold to a brothel for a life of prostitution. The brothel scenes themselves are the most repulsive in Shakespeare, surpassing Doll Tearsheet's petting of Falstaff. Here is vice, corruption, and ruthless cruelty as black as that of the tragedies. The ignorant fishermen comment that fish live as men do on the land,

> . . . The great ones eat up the little ones. I can compare our rich misers to nothing so fitly as to a whale; 'a plays and tumbles, driving the poor fry before him, and at last devours them all at a mouthful. Such whales have I heard on o' the land, who never leave gaping till they swallow'd the whole parish, church steeple, bell, and all.[3]

As in *King Lear* even nature adds unfeelingly to human misery. When Thaisa supposedly dies in childbirth in the fury of the tempest, without light or fire on the ship, Pericles exclaims, "The unfriendly elements forgot thee utterly."[4]

In *Cymbeline*, the Queen, though more cunning, rivals in sheer evil the Gothic Queen Tamora of *Titus Andronicus*, and only the stupidity of her son Cloten prevents him from being even worse. Iachimo is also a pale copy of Iago. In *The Winter's Tale* Leontes' sadistic jealousy and rage bring the tragic death of his son and his trusted servant, with the sailors who carry his daughter away. Even in *The Tempest* there is the overthrow and banishment of the Duke and two attempted murders.

Shakespeare, consequently, shows us in these last plays that the world has not changed. For he is not a romanticist alone, but a realist as well. But in his world, as in ours, extreme crises do not always lead to tragedy. So in these last plays Shakespeare turns near tragedies to happy endings.

But more important than the happy endings is the apparent change in Shakespeare's own attitude toward cruelty and suffering. Perhaps at last the maturity and wisdom attained through the catharsis of his own tragedies, especially *Lear*, have brought to Shakespeare that great compassion for humanity for which Lear prayed, and that patience which Gloucester learned through suffering.

In these last plays a continual repetition and mingling of three prominent themes reflect and explain this change of attitude: First, the emphasis on Destiny or Providence; second, the ultimate triumph of Good over Evil; and third, the spirit of Reconciliation and Forgiveness, which lifts the soul nearer the divine, and can finally give it immortality.

Tempest and storm are symbols of life, time, and eternity from *Pericles* through *The Tempest*. Marina, born in a tempest, rescued from murder only to be sold to a brothel, cries,

> The world to me is like a lasting storm
> Whirring me from my friends.[5]

Pericles calls the baby, born in storm, "this fresh-new sea-farer," and wonders how he can stop the "tempest" of Antiochus' vengeance.

But through all the tempests of life the control of a sympathetic Providence, or Destiny, is clear, and with it the recognition of the need for patience and submission. Old Gower, who is telling the story of Pericles' long suffering and flight, admonishes the audience:

> Be quiet then as men should be
> Till he hath pass'd necessity.
> I'll show those in troubles reign
> Losing a mite, a mountain gain.[6]

Wrecked, and tossed by the sea upon strange shores, Pericles pleads with the stars:

> Yet cease your ire, you angry stars of heaven!
> Wind, rain, and thunder, remember earthly
>   man
> Is but a substance that must yield to you.[7]

Though he knows that yielding to Destiny

is a necessity from which none can escape, yet to yield with patience and a spirit of humility is apparently learned only through experience and suffering. After he seals his wife Thaisa in the coffin and delivers her to the sea, Pericles cries out in anguish:

> We cannot but obey
> The powers above us. Could I rage and roar
> As doth the sea she lies in, yet the end
> Must be as 'tis.[8]

The storm of emotion drives him finally to the verge of insanity; he wears sackcloth, refuses to wash, and will see and speak to no one. Cleon says of him,

> He bears
> A tempest, which his mortal vessel tears,
> And yet he rides it out.[9]

But for Pericles the winds of fate are finally kind. After years of flight from land to land, shipwreck, loss and suffering, he is reunited with his wife and daughter and restored to the security and peace of his kingdom.

Though the emphasis on Providence, or an overruling Destiny, is not so insistent in *The Winter's Tale* and *Cymbeline*, it is present in the abandonment of Perdita on the friendly coast of Bohemia, in Prince Florizel's finding her, and in the ultimate reunion and reconciliation after years of separation.

In *Cymbeline* Shakespeare makes clear

again that a higher than human power plans
and directs the action. Imogen, lost in the
mountains, finds by "accident" her brothers'
cave, and Cloten meets his deserved death at
her brother's hands. As some power surprisingly turns the deception of the faithful
Pisanio into truth, he exclaims, "The heavens
still must work. Wherein I'm false I'm honest."
And in wonder he concludes that "Fortune
brings in some boats that are not steer'd."[10]
The victory of the Britons over the Roman
army is an amazing change of fortune. A lord
in astonishment exclaims:

> This was a strange chance,
> A narrow lane, an old man, and two boys![11]

But Posthumous, who helps to win the
victory, explains that ". . . all was lost, But
that the heavens fought." At the happy conclusion of the victory and the peace with Rome
the Soothsayer says,

> The fingers of the powers above do tune
> The harmony of this peace.[12]

And old Belarius, in restoring the princes
to their father, prays,

> The benediction of these covering heavens
> Fall on their heads like dew.[13]

In these last plays the constant recognition
of a wisdom and a power beyond the human
seems to be more than merely a dramatic
device to explain the plot. It is more reasonable

to conclude with Mr. Knight that these plays reflect to some extent the past progress of Shakespeare's soul,[14] and with Mr. Reese that "the serenity of his final plays emerges from his strengthened conviction in an assured Providence which watches over man."[15]

But the second influence that gave serenity to these last years is the conviction of the ultimate triumph of the Good. This had been tragically demonstrated in *Macbeth*. In the brothel scenes in *Pericles* it is again reflected. The innocence of Marina, with a wisdom beyond her fourteen years, repulses every attempt to prostitute her. The bawd complains that with her "reasons, her master reasons, her prayers, her knees, she would make a puritan of the devil."[16] In sharp contrast with the innocence of Marina was the horrible death of the incestuous Antiochus and his daughter, their bodies so nauseous and "shriveled up even to loathing," that attendants shrank from touching them. In the closing lines the aged Gower evidently gives for Shakespeare the meaning of the "parable" of the story:

> In Antiochus and his daughter you have
>   heard
> Of monstruous lust the due and just reward.
> In Pericles, his queen and daughter, seen,
> Virtue preserved from fell destruction's blast,
> Led on by heaven, and crown'd with joy at
>   last.[17]

The superiority of Virtue, or the Good, is

shown in an even more interesting way, however, by its power of transmission to posterity. Shakespeare is evidently a strong believer in heredity. The King's sons, stolen in childhood and reared in a cave in the wilds of West Britain, nevertheless possessed such princely qualities as continually surprised old Belarius, who exclaims:

> They think they're mine; and, though train'd
> thus meanly,
> I' the cave wherein they bow, their thoughts
> do hit
> The roofs of palaces; and nature prompts them,
> In simple and low things, to prince it much
> Beyond the trick of others.[18]

Both boys fight courageously in the battle, and at Cloten's insult Guiderius strikes as a prince would be expected to do. The qualities of courage, virtue, self-respect, resentment of wrong, and loyalty to their country Belarious can attribute only to Nature, who preserves and transmits them to those who are even unaware of their origins.

> O thou goddess,
> Thou divine Nature, how thyself thou blazon'st
> In these two princely boys! They are as gentle
> As zephyrs, blowing below the violet,
> Not wagging his sweet head; and yet as rough,
> Their royal blood chafed, as the rudest wind,
> That by the top doth take the mountain pine,
> And make him stoop to the vale. 'Tis wonderful
> That an invisible instinct should frame them

> To royalty unlearn'd; honor untaught;
> Civility not seen from other; valour,
> That wildly grows in them, but yields a crop
> As it had been sow'd.[19]

Similarly Perdita in *The Winter's Tale*, reared as a poor shepherd's daughter with no courtly training, amazes King Polixenes with her charm:

> This is the prettiest low-born lass that ever
> Ran on green-sward; nothing she does or
>   seems
> But smacks of something greater than herself,
> Too noble for this place.[20]

She welcomes the guests with the grace and courtesy of a princess, and when she discovers Polixenes to be the king, she faces him unafraid, with a sense of inborn equality.

Shakespeare explains the office of Nature in aiding humanity, as well as flowers, to reach their highest perfection. Perdita, who is a lover of nature and dislikes anything artificial, as she would abhor the painting of her own lips and face, declares she will plant no gillyvors in her garden,

> For I have heard it said
> There is an art which, in their piedness, shares
> With great creating Nature.

Polixenes, without realizing that he is ironically condemning himself in opposing the marriage of his "noble" son to this girl of "baser" stock, replies immediately:

Say there be;
Yet Nature is made better by no mean,
But Nature makes that mean: so, even that art
Which you say adds to Nature, is an art
That Nature makes. You see, sweet maid,
    we marry
A gentler scion to the wildest stock,
And make conceive a bark of baser kind
By bud of nobler race: this is an art
Which does mend Nature—change it rather;
    but
The art itself is Nature.[21]

Shakespeare's statement through Polixenes
should settle forever the long contention between art and nature. As with plants and animals, the highest perfections of humanity are
the results of careful training and culture, the
arts of men. Virtue, the love of the Good, the
longing to share the nature of the Divine—all
are the results of teaching, yet all are possible
only through the Nature which is planted in
us. After all the tragedies with their suffering,
this faith in the Nature of man and its power
to preserve and transmit to posterity the Good
and to bring a higher perfection through the
very arts with which it endows men, becomes
a settled conviction of the poet.

In the third place, through the tragedies
with their clash of wills, their hate, cruelty,
injustice, suffering and disintegration of
human souls, Shakespeare has apparently arrived at the conviction that Virtue, the Good,
alone can survive, and that through forgive-

ness and reconciliation, rather than through hate, men approach the nature of the gods and may eventually attain immortality. Old Cerimon, the physician in *Pericles*, who has studied humanity for many years, comments on the elevating nature of virtue and the wisdom which comes through experience and education, which he calls "cunning,"

> I hold it ever
> Virtue and cunning were endowments greater
> Than nobleness and riches. Careless heirs
> May the two latter darken and expend,
> But immortality attends the former,
> Making a man a god.[22]

After the shocking injustice of Leontes against his wife and his friend, and his long suffering and penitence, the play closes with forgiveness, reconciliation, joy, and love. In *Cymbeline* the battle closes with Iachimo and the Romans as prisoners. Faced by Posthumous, whom he has so deeply wronged, Iachimo kneels in penitence and begs for death, but Posthumous replies,

> Kneel not to me:
> The power that I have on you is to spare you;
> The malice toward you to forgive you: live,
> And deal with others better.[23]

And Cymbeline, who had banished Posthumous for marrying his daughter, says,

> Nobly doom'd!
> We'll learn our freeness of a son-in-law;
> Pardon's the word for all.[24]

Surviving the malice, hate, and treachery of the play, the forgiveness and reconciliation bring a peace whose harmony the "fingers of the heavens" attune, and which lifts men nearer the immortality of the gods.

The Magical Sea Change

The mature and enriched philosophy of Shakespeare, including all the above convictions, reaches its fullest and most beautiful expression in *The Tempest*. Hallet Smith in a compendium of criticism on *The Tempest* quotes T. M. Parrott as calling it "perhaps the best loved of all Shakespeare's plays," and says criticism from Dyrden down "is an uninterrupted chorus of rhapsodic praise."[25]

One could hardly conceive a more perfect play to close his long and varied career and to bid his London audiences and friends farewell.

Because of its rich suggestiveness, however, no play has given rise to so many different interpretations. Sir Arthur Quiller-Couch sees the theme of reconciliation and forgiveness running through all these last plays and culminating in *The Tempest*.[26] Some see in *The Tempest* a kind of allegory involving Art and Nature. Francis Neilson's interpretation of the symbolism is that,

Prospero is thought, and Ariel is the agent of the creative imagination, fulfilling the demands of Art. In Prospero I find: intuition, thought, idea, form. Ariel is the

executor and brings to fruition the desires
of his master. Indeed, he is the one that
gives shape to things. Prospero thinks—
plans, but cannot practice. He needs a working agent to carry out his schemes . . .
Now whether or not Shakespeare ever
gave a thought to the symbolism of his
play is to be doubted. Yet it is there, I ad-
mit, and the student would miss a great
deal if he did not realize it, or if he ignored
it.[27]

But Mr. Neilson also sees a social and political meaning in *The Tempest* as well:

If there be intention in the play, it must
lie in a philosophic interpretation of the
plot. Therein it is possible to glean a
notion of the impotence of man, subject
to a political state, to rule himself; and
that a higher power is essential to set him
free from "a foul and pestilential congre-
gation of vapors."[28]

Many also have identified Prospero with
Shakespeare himself. Others have identified
Prospero with God, directing the affairs of
men through his Providence. Still others,
less definite, like Hallett Smith, "see Ariel
and Caliban as extensions of Prospero, the
former representing an imaginative and spiritual extreme and the latter a physical and
material one."[29] G. W. Knight thinks that
Shakespeare in *The Tempest* put his own
spiritual experience into objective symbols,

and "traces in a compact play the past progress of his own soul. He is now the object of his own search, and no other theme but that of his visionary self is now of power to call forth the riches of his imagination."[30] W. C. Curry, however, thinks the play is an elaborate reflection of Neoplatonic philosophy.

Though these and other interpretations may all be possible, at least in part, Mr. Neilson declares:

> Why it should be necessary to find anything of a symbolical significance in the work, I cannot understand, for the play clearly explains itself, and I cannot imagine a groundling at the Globe, or a man in the gallery of a modern theater, asking for more information about the play when the curtain falls.[31]

Certainly the play tells its own story, a very simple and compact one, for the plot is concisely constructed and the action limited to a very few hours. Prospero's objective as the play opens is to regain his dukedom and punish his enemies. Since Alonzo, the King of Naples, was confederate with Prospero's brother in supplanting him, Prospero plans, as the means of regaining his dukedom, to win the King's aid by a marriage between his daughter and the King's son Ferdinand. As he hopes, Ferdinand and Miranda fall in love immediately. The first obstacle, to his plan, which Ariel easily frustrates, is the plot to kill the King. The second obstacle, which Ariel also frustrates, is the plot of Caliban, Trinculo, and Stephano to kill Prospero. With the banquet scene, however, Prospero has all his enemies completely in his power. He regains his dukedom, but, contrary to his first intention, he *forgives* his enemies.

The story is so slight and inconsequential that readers have almost unanimously concluded that Shakespeare must have some message beyond the plot which he wished to convey. But, as E. E. Stoll has said, the fact "that the story is slight is no proof that therein is another within or behind it."[32]

True, but more important than the story are a world of allusions and suggestions that tantalize the reader with meanings beyond the action. The play is certainly not an allegory in the manner of Spenser or Tennyson; nor is the symbolism like that of Ibsen and the modernists. No symbol is carried out consistently and in detail. Mr. A. D. Nutfall has well said,

> The minutely perceptive scepticism of *The Tempest* defeats the stony allegorist and the rigid cynic equally. The story is never allowed to harden into an ontological dogma to be reduced to symbols or rejected with contempt. Instead we have an extraordinarily delicate and dramatic play, which, until the Last Day makes all clear, will never be anything but immensely suggestive.[33]

This "mystery" of *The Tempest* is achieved through a delicate fusion of the physical world of the passions and greed of men with the world of the spirit, which overshadows, touches, and directs the course of action. In a sense Shakespeare uses a dream technique, in which images and allusions appear for an instant, mingle with reality, then fade and shift into other allusions. They stimulate thought and imagination, and a single incident may suggest simultaneously several different levels of meaning.

Prospero, to be sure, is literally the magician on a Mediterranean island, but as he addresses the "elves of hills, brooks, standing lakes, and groves," and all the rest of the fairy host through whom he has bedimmed the noon-day sun, set roaring war between the green seas and the azure vault, given fire to the dread rattling thunder, and even opened graves and waked their sleepers, who can fail to remember the storms and darkness of *Lear* and *Macbeth* and the host of those long dead from Caesar and Hamlet to Henry VIII who have lived again on Shakespeare's stage? The merging for a moment of Shakespeare the playwright with Prospero the magician does no violence to the story, but rather enriches it.

The theme of Providence, which has grown more pronounced since Hamlet's "divinity that shapes our ends," may also be felt in the magic of Prospero, who foresees events and in-fluences the actions of men, not as helpless puppets, but by creating situations which

lead them voluntarily to reach the decisions
he desires. As Prospero he himself is subject
to influences from above, and in the spirit of
Brutus he can say,

> I find my zenith doth depend upon
> A most auspicious star, whose influence,
> If now I court not, but omit, my fortunes
> Will every after droop.[34]

"By Providence divine" he and Miranda had
been guided to the safety of the island, and now
"bountiful Fortune" is bringing his enemies
within his reach. Though Shakespeare uses
various terms—Providence, Fortune, the Stars,
the gods, Destiny, or Fate—he is clearly a firm
believer in a supernatural Wisdom and Power
which moves in human affairs. As men cooperate with or rebel against this Power, they
succeed or fail. This Destiny, Ariel says,
"hath to instrument this lower world And what
is in it," and even swords cannot successfully
oppose it.

It is also a wisdom which, as Hamlet and
Montaigne both say, often plans for us better
than we know, for

> Our indiscretions sometimes serve us well
> When our deep plots do pall.[35]

Hamlet felt this was true in his discovering
the letters commanding his death and in his
possessing his father's signet ring. It is certainly true in *The Tempest*, and Gonzalo, the
wise old counselor, sums up with astonishment the turn of events which brought them

all far greater happiness than any could have
imagined:

> Look down, you gods,
> And on this couple drop a blessed crown!
> For it is you that have chalked forth the way
> Which brought us hither. . . .

> Was Milan thrust from Milan, that his issue
> Should become Kings of Naples? Oh, rejoice
> Beyond a common joy! And set it down
> With gold on lasting pillars. In one voyage
> Did Claribel her husband find in Tunis
> And Ferdinand, her brother, found a wife
> Where he himself was lost, Prospero his
>   dukedom
> In a poor isle, and all of us ourselves
> When no man was his own.[36]

Though Gonzalo, as well no doubt as all the
rest, attributed the happy conclusion to the
gods, it is clear also that Prospero has been
used so definitely as an instrument of the gods,
that he may well be considered a symbol of the
way Providence works among men.

In *The Tempest* also, more clearly than in
the earlier plays, Shakespeare is emphasizing
the triumph of the Good over injustice and
wrong. As he has shown in *Lear* and in
Pericles, Cymbeline, and *The Winter's Tale*,
the enduring aspect of this triumph is not
in external rewards, but in the growth of the
soul. At the beginning of the play a part of
Prospero's objective is to punish his ene-

mies. He can at times be impatient and
harsh even with the delicate Ariel. But as he
sees his enemies under his control, and hears
Ariel speak of Gonzalo's tears and the penitence of the rest, his fury gives way to a nobler
and higher emotion:

> The rarer action is
> In virtue than in vengeance. They being
>   penitent,
> The sole drift of my purpose doth extend
> Not a frown further.[37]

Some have criticized the strained nature
and the "insincerity" of Prospero's "forgiveness." But for Alonzo, his "inveterate enemy,"
his forgiveness is remarkably generous and
free. When the King finds that Miranda is to
marry his son, he exclaims,

> But oh, how oddly will it sound that I
> Must ask my child's forgiveness.

And Prospero cuts him off at once:

> There, sir, stop.
> Let us not burden our remembrance with
> A heaviness that's gone.[38]

The beauty of real forgiveness is that it
blots out the past as if it had never been, and
Prospero stops his former enemy from even
thinking about it. Such a perfection of relationship, however, depends on genuine repentance, and Prospero's brother Antonio has
expressed no such penitence. Prospero's re-
buke is, therefore, rightly deserved:

For you, most wicked sir, whom to call brother
Would even infect my mouth, I do forgive you
Thy rankest fault—all of them—and require
My dukedom of thee, which perforce I know
Thou must restore.[39]

"Forgive" in this sense means only that he
will exact no punishment for Antonio's crime,
and evidently holds no ill will against him.
Who could expect a better attitude after the
wrong Antonio has done him? But Prospero's
forgiveness of his enemies indicates an enrichment of his soul that lifts him toward the
gods.

Dover Wilson asks, "Is *The Tempest* a
Christian play?" and then answers his own
question:

> . . . It is surely a profoundly religious
> poem, and of a Christ-like spirit in its
> infinite tenderness, its all-embracing
> sense of pity, its conclusion of atonement
> and forgiveness, so general that even
> Caliban begins to talk of "grace." But it is
> not in the least Christian from the theo-
> logical standpoint; there is no word of
> God, nor a hint of immortality. . . .[40]

It is true that Shakespeare uses no theological terms in *The Tempest* and seldom in
any other play. Even the term "grace" is not
used by Caliban in a theological sense. Theological terms would limit Shakespeare's ideas
to comparatively small groups and tend to
antagonize others. Instead his ideas are ex-

pressed in language that gives them almost universal acceptance by believers of all religions and by many Humanists who profess no religion. They are found in pagan philosophies as well as in the Christian faith.

Mr. Neilson's last statement, however, that there is no hint of immortality is surprising. It is true that as Prospero suddenly breaks up the masque, his speech is filled with unutterable pathos and longing:

> Our revels now are ended. These our actors,
> As I fortold you, are all spirits, and
> Are melted into air, into thin air,
> And, like the baseless fabric of this vision,
> The cloud-capped towers, the gorgeous
>   palaces,
> The solemn temples, the great globe itself—
> Yea, all which it inherit—shall dissolve
> And, like this insubstantial pageant faded,
> Leave not a rack behind. We are such stuff
> As dreams are made on, and our little life
> Is rounded with a sleep.[41]

In Prospero's reflection on the brevity of earthly life his mind sweeps across the whole range of human achievement: the "cloud-capped towers" suggesting the power and grandeur of empires; "the gorgeous palaces," the wealth and luxury of earth; "the solemn temples," the great religions and philosophies through which men have reached upward toward the gods; even the great globe itself and all the inheritors of its glory. But the evanescence of all earthly existence and the sleep that rounds our "little life" are not necessarily a denial of the immortality of the soul, which was above the material world and not subject to dissolution.

The Scriptures themselves, which speak constantly of a future life, emphasize repeatedly in equally vivid terms the passing of the material universe, and the dream-like quality of earthly life. James says, "What is your life? For we are a vapor that appeareth for a little time, and then vanisheth away."[42] Peter declares that even "the heavens shall pass away with a great noise, and the elements shall be dissolved with fervent heat, and the earth and the works that are therein shall be burned up."[43] And Jesus spoke continually of death as a sleep: "Our friend Lazarus is fallen asleep, but I go that I may awake him out of sleep."[44]

So the vividness of Prospero's imagery does not necessarily imply a hopelessness of immortality.

Many have wondered about Prospero's extreme emotion as the actors vanish. Francis Neilson thinks it is due to his disappointment over Caliban, whose plot "is a disheartening event, for it really means that the work of twelve years, in trying to civilize Caliban, has been thrown away."[45]

Bradley sees in Prospero's emotion an insight into Shakespeare's own mind in his last years:

That which provoked in Prospero first a

"passion" of anger, and a moment later
that melancholy and mystical thought that
the great world must perish utterly and
that man is but a dream, is the sudden
recollection of gross and apparently incurable evil in the "monster" whom he
had tried in vain to raise and soften, and
in the monster's human confederates. It is
this, which is but the reflection of his
earlier experiences of treachery and ingratitude, that troubles his old brain,
makes his mind "beat," and forces on him
the sense of unreality and evanescence in
the world and the life that are haunted by
such evil. For, though Prospero can spare
and forgive, is there any sign to the end
that he believes the evil curable either in
the monster, the "inborn devil," or in the
more monstrous villains, the "worse
than devils," whom he so sternly dis-
misses? But he has learned patience, has
come to regard his anger and loathing as a
weakness or infirmity and would not have
it disturb the young and innocent. And so
in the ways of King Lear, it was chiefly
the power of the "monstrous" and apparent cureless evil in the "great world"
that filled Shakespeare's soul with horror, and perhaps moved him sometimes to
yield to the infirmity of misanthropy and
despair, to cry "No, no, no life," and to
take refuge in the thought that this fitful
fever is a dream that must soon fade into

a dreamless sleep; until to free himself
from the perilous stuff that so weighed
upon his heart he summoned to his aid
his "so potent art" and wrought this stuff
into the stormy music of his greatest
poem, which seems to cry:

You heavens give me patience, patience
I need, and like *The Tempest*, seems to
preach to us from end to end, "Thou must
be patient," "Bear free and patient
thoughts."[46]

It is hard to believe with Neilson that Caliban, whose incorrigible nature and the impossibility of engrafting any nurture into it
Prospero well knew, and whose present plot he
could so easily frustrate, could move Prospero to such an extreme of "horror." If, however, Caliban's treachery suggests to Prospero the injustice of all his enemies, and to
Shakespeare all the evil of humanity from
Hamlet to the present moment, that might
be sufficient to produce a beating mind and a
wish that the world and all its evil would pass.

But is it not possible that Shakespeare and
Prospero are moved by an altogether different
emotion? Prospero has through the years
drawn intense delight from association with
his fairy friends, through whom he could fill
the air with heavenly music, create storms,
shake promontories, and even raise the dead;
and Shakespeare must certainly have remem-
bered with great satisfaction and joy the years
when the fairy powers of his "so potent art"

had charmed audiences, delighted princes and kings, and brought him praise as the greatest dramatist of his age. Now both he and Prospero are burying their magic wands. Shakespeare had long considered "all the world a stage," and in a parallel passage filled with humorous pathos he had pictured our strange eventful history as ending in "oblivion, Sans teeth, sans eyes, sans taste, sans everything." Now the glory of his Globe, his "little world" in London, is to vanish; and in a brief while the world of Prospero's magic island and the "great globe itself" will alike dissolve and vanish as a dream.

Here is not, as Bradley suggests, a longing for the world with its evil to "fade" but rather a deep pain at the evanescence of earth and a nostalgia for the glory and the grandeur that must pass, which rises to a stateliness and a beauty of expression that here leaves no place for humor.

At the moment when Prospero and his audience are feeling so keenly the pain of earthly dissolution, to mention the immortality of the soul would ruin the emotional effect and be an intolerable blunder. But contrary to Wilson's idea Shakespeare gives us much more than a "hint" of his faith in immortality. Ariel sings to comfort Ferdinand on the death of his father:

> Full fathom five thy father lies,
> Of his bones are coral made.

> Those are pearls that were his eyes.
> Nothing of him that doth fade
> But doth suffer a sea change
> Into something rich and strange.[47]

How could any one express more perfectly
the infinite, eternal transformation, the rich,
strange, permanent beauty, which the magic
sea change can bring? Who would want
Shakespeare to ruin the suggestion with some
theological term which would supposedly
make his meaning clearer to the groundlings?

But what of the symbolism in Ariel and
Caliban? The charm of Ariel and the puzzling
personality of Caliban have led to much
speculation. Ariel and Puck are the most
delightfully enchanting creations of all fairy
lore, but the office of Ariel has a serious aspect
which may imply a meaning beyond the creating of mere puckist confusion.

In Caliban and in Gonzalo's ideal commonwealth, Shakespeare no doubt owes a debt to
Montaigne. Shakespeare, to be sure, is an
idealist, but both he and Gonzalo have too
much common sense to take his commonwealth seriously. Like Montaigne Shakespeare
uses Caliban, as Kermode has pointed out, "to
indicate how much baser the corruption of the
civilized world can be than the bestiality of
the natural." Caliban, the natural man, Kermode says

> . . . exists at the simplest level of sensual
> pain and pleasure, fit for lechery because

love is beyond his nature . . . He hears
music with pleasure, as music can appeal
to the beast who lacks reason, and he
resembles Aristotle's bestial man. He is a
measure of the incredible superiority of
the world of Art, but also of its corruption.
For the courtiers and their servants include the incontinent Stephano and the
malicious Antonio. Caliban scorns the infirmity of the first, and knows better than
Antonio that it is imprudent to resist
grace, for which, he says, he will henceforth seek. Unlike the incontinent man,
whose appetites subdue his will, and the
malicious man, whose will is perverted to
evil ends, "the bestial man has no sense of
right and wrong, and therefore sees no
difference between good and evil. His
state is less guilty but more hopeless than
those of incontinence and malice, since
he cannot be improved." Men can debase
their degree below the bestial; and there is
possibly a hint, for which there is no support in Aristotle, that the bestial Caliban
gains a new spiritual dimension from his
glimpse of the "brave Spirits."[48]

Though Caliban suggests some satire
against civilized society, Mr. Kermode thinks
the real symbolism of Ariel and Caliban is a
contrast between Art and Nature. Robert
Speight, Francis Neilson, and others see the
same symbolism, but Speight also sees in the
servitude of Caliban the right of the civilized

man to enslave the savage, a "right" which Neilson emphatically denies, though he grants it has been the universal practice of nations for the strong to enslave the weak.[49]

The richness of allusion in *The Tempest* may suggest all these and many other meanings, but the striking contrast between Ariel and Caliban and the relation of both to each other and to Prospero seem to imply something more. When we remember the dual nature of humanity, which Shakespeare has presented through all his work, the profound evil of the Macbeths, Iago, Goneril, Regan, and others, and the innocence of Desdemona and Miranda, and the divine pity and love of Cordelia and Kent, the suggestion of G. Wilson Knight is especially apt. Mr. Knight says of Prospero,

> Two creatures serve him: Ariel, the "airy nothing" of poetry; and the snarling Caliban, half-beast, half-man; the embodiment of the hate-theme. These two creatures are yoked in the employ of Prospero, like Plato's two steeds of the soul, the noble and the hideous, twin potentialities of the human spirit.[50]

In view of Shakespeare's wide acquaintance with philosophy, as shown through all his plays, who can doubt his knowledge of Plato's famous allegory. In *The Phaedrus* Plato had likened the soul to a charioteer with two horses: one is white, a lover of glory that needed no whip,

> . . . being driven by the word of command
> alone. The other is crooked of frame, a
> massive jumble of a creature, with thick
> short neck and a snub nose, black skin . . .
> hot blooded, consorting with wanton-
> ness . . . shaggy ears, deaf, and hard to
> control with whip and goad.[51]

When the driver has to pull the black horse
back, he "bursts into angry abuse, railing at
the charioteer and his yokefellow," whose
function is also to check him.

In *The Timaeus* Plato describes the human
personality as having three parts: the Head,
or Reason, which is the Immortal Soul; the
middle soul, or spirit, which is endowed with
courage, and "being obedient to the rule of
reason," it joins with the Immortal Soul in
controlling and restraining the lower soul when
it is not willing "to obey the word of command
issuing from the citadel." Both the white and
the black horse are mortal and both die with the
flesh; only the Reason is immortal.[52]

Whether or not Shakespeare knew of Plato's
allegory is immaterial. Many of his predeces-
sors and contemporaries knew of it, and the
psychology of his time had similar concepts
of the soul. Everybody also knew of the warfare
in the human personality between the spirit
and the flesh, as described by the Apostle
Paul.[53] Rightly controlled, the "flesh" with its
appetites rendered invaluable service to the
soul; it was in fact essential to physical life,

but it had to be constantly "buffeted" and held in subjection.

The implications in *The Tempest* vividly remind us of this complexity of the human personality and its eternal conflict. Prospero first mentions Caliban as a "slave, Who never yields us kind answer,"

> But as 'tis,
> We cannot miss him. He doth make our fire,
> Fetch in our wood and serve us in other offices
> That profit us.[54]

Francis Neilson commends Caliban as the only "chore man," "The most useful member of the small community."[55] He catches the fish, brings in water and wood, knows all the resources of the island—crab-apples, berries, pig-nuts, filberts, jays, marmosets and rock-scamels—and apparently does all the physical labor. Certainly they cannot "miss him," any more than the soul, as long as it is in this life, can do without the "flesh" with its natural appetites and its ability to serve. But they have to keep him under control, just as the soul must keep the flesh in subjection.

Prospero addresses him as "Slave! Caliban! Thou earth, thou! Speak," and Caliban crawls from his sty, grumbling and cursing at his treatment, till Prospero cuts him off:

> Thou most lying slave,
> Whom stripes may move, not kindness! I have
>   used thee

Filth as thou art, with human care, and lodged
   thee
In mine own cell till thou didst seek to violate
The honor of my child.
Cal.   Oh, ho, ho, ho! Would't had been done!
Thou didst prevent me. I had peopled else
This isle with Calibans.
Pro.   Abhorred slave,
Which any print of goodness will not take,
Being capable of all ill! I pitied thee,
Took pains to make thee speak, taught thee
   each hour
One thing or other. When thou didst not, savage,
Know thine own meaning, but wouldst gabble
   like
A thing most brutish, I endowed thy purposes
With words that made them known. But thy
   vile race,
Though thou didst learn, had that in't which
   good natures
Could not abide to be with. Therefore wast thou
Deservedly confined into this rock,
Who hadst deserved more than a prison.[56]

Clearly Caliban has no moral sense. He can
be taught, or trained, as animals are trained to
work and serve. He can by long association
yield to the beauty of music and to dreams that,
while dreaming, seemed to open the clouds and
show him riches ready to drop upon him, that
when he waked he cried to dream again. Such
may be the unutterable longings of the "flesh,"
when, after long association with the spirit, in

moments of dreaming it is freed for an instant from the filth of its "vile race," which permits no permanent improvement, no "print of goodness."

In sharp contrast, Ariel is a spirit too delicate to obey an "earthly and abhorred command." He has been variously interpreted as creative imagination, fancy, art, poetry. Speight thinks he represents "the divine powers lent to his master," "the supernatural force at the service of man for the correction of human nature."[57] Perhaps. But this sounds too much like Calvinist theology to harmonize with the general tone of Shakespeare's thought.

As Tennyson once said of his allegories that he did not want to be pinned down to a single meaning, perhaps Shakespeare has created in his delicate Ariel, qualities that suggest all the above interpretations and more. He is an extremely subtle creation. But like Plato's analogy and the popular concept of the dual nature of man, can he not also represent that part of the human personality, the emotion or will, which, when guided by the intellect, appreciates the beautiful and good and abhors the base and evil—the spirit which the intelligence uses constantly to curb the grossness of the "flesh"?

He can at times by his heavenly music stir intense longings even in the earthy Caliban, but he also has the unpleasant task of racking him with cramps, filling his bones with aches, and making him roar till beasts tremble at the din. For Caliban may serve Prospero in many useful ways, as "the flesh" slaves for the soul, but when opportunity arises he is ready to rebel, as "flesh" also rebels, and can be brought into subjection only by force. Prospero says,

> A devil, a born devil, on whose nature
> Nurture can never stick, on whom my pains,
> Humanely taken, all, all lost, quite lost.
> And as with age his body uglier grows,
> So his mind cankers.[58]

But the time finally comes when the flesh, the "thing of darkness," or "earth," can be left behind on its desert isle, and the delicate Ariel, no longer needed to bring it into subjection, and to fill the isle with his heavenly music, or the London stage with his magic, can be free to fly after the summer merrily. For, as Plato says, both are mortal, and are no longer needed after the great sea change.

That is the moment when Prospero-Shakespeare, not as the magician-dramatist, but the Person, is also set free to receive his "dukedom." Freedom from the London stage is given merely by the applause and acclaim of the audience, but freedom from the "desert isle" is attained only through prayer,

> Which pierces so that it assaults
> Mercy itself, and frees all faults.
> As you from crimes would pardoned by
> Let your indulgence set me free.[59]

As Mr. Curry says, Prospero has gradually

grown in perfection. From the desire to punish those who have wronged him, "He forgives the rankest faults of his enemies—demanding, however, strict justice in restitution—and so finds himself at the close of the play immeasureably nearer than before to the impassivity of the gods . . . He wishes now to take the final step and to consummate the assimilation of his soul to the gods. And this step is to be accomplished through prayer."[60]

Without Mr. Curry's Neoplatonic implications, however, may not Prospero-Shakespeare, like many others, only be asking that through prayer, or reverence for the gods, he may ultimately attain that measure of Virtue, which old Cerimon says will make "a man a god," and set him free from his desert isle?

The Tempest is a delightful story in itself. The humor of Stephano and Trinculo and the ludicrous incidents in which they are involved, the sweetness of Miranda and the love story, the richness of the poetry and music, the sheer magic of the play, and the dramatic and happy outcome are enough within themselves. But if the allusions in the play at times blend Shakespeare with Prospero and Prospero with the Soul, the desert isle with earthly existence, and the dukedom with Stratford, Milan, or eternity, and all give Shakespeare's farewell a threefold meaning, does this rob the play of its magic effect, or enhance its meaning for a varied audience?

In a real sense *The Tempest* marks the conclusion of Shakespeare's long and often agonizing effort to understand the nature of evil. His view of the world did not change. When Miranda sees Ferdinand's father and his friends, she cries,

> Oh, wonder!
> How many goodly creatures are there here!
> How beauteous mankind is! Oh, brave new
> world,
> That has such people in it.[61]

But with infinite pity for what Miranda will ultimately learn, Prospero says, "'Tis new to thee." And both Prospero and Miranda are right. Shakespeare has shown "how beauteous" mankind can be, and also how "tough" the world is. But through long experience, and deep sympathy with his tragic souls, he has learned how to regard it with patience and compassion instead of with bitterness and agony. He has finally developed a faith which triumphs over suffering and doubt.

FOOTNOTES AND REFERENCES

1. *Supra*. pp. 75ff.
2. *Supra*. p. 317.
3. *Pericles*, II, i, 31-39.
4. *Ibid*., III, i, 58f.
5. *Ibid*., IV, i, 50f.
6. *Ibid*., II, prologue, 5-8.
7. *Ibid*., II, i, 1-3.
8. *Ibid*., III, iii, 9-12.
9. *Ibid*., IV, iv, 29-31.

10. *Cymbeline*, LV, 111, 41, 46.

11. *Ibid.*, V, iii, 51f.

12. *Ibid.*, V, v.

13. *Loc. cit.*

14. G. Wilson Knight, *The Crown of Life* (London: Oxford University Press, 1947), pp. 17-18.

15. M. M. Reese, Shakespeare, *His World and His Work,* (London: Edward Arnold & Co., 1953) p. 453.

16. *Pericles*, IV, vi, 8-10.

17. *Ibid.*, V, iii, 85-90.

18. *Cymbeline*, III, iii, 83-87.

19. *Ibid.*, IV, ii, 169-181.

20. *The Winter's Tale*, IV, iii, 154-157.

21. *Ibid.*, IV, iii, 87-96.

22. *Pericles*, III, ii, 26-31.

23. *Cymbeline*, V, v, 414-417.

24. *Loc Cit.*

25. Hallett Smith, *Twentieth Century Interpretations of The Tempest* (Englewood Cliffs, N.J.: Prentice-Hall, 1969). p. 1.

26. Sir Arthur Quiller - Couch, Introduction to *The Tempest*, from *The Works of Shakespeare*, ed. by Sr. Arthur Quiller-Couch and John Dover Wilson (Cambridge, England: University Press, 1921).

27. Francis Neilson, *Shakespeare and The Tempest* (Rindge, N.H.: Richard Smith, Pub., 1956), p. 104.

28. *Ibid.*, p. 180.

29. Smith, *op. cit.*, p. 9.

30. Knight, *op. cit.*, p. 17.

31. Neilson, *op. cit.*, p. 99.

32. Smith, *op. cit.*, p. 9.

33. Ibid., p. 85.

34. *The Tempest*, I, ii, 181-184.

35. *Hamlet*, V, ii, 8f.

36. *The Tempest*, V, i, 201-213.

37. *Ibid.*, V, i, 2730.

38. *Ibid.*, V, i, 198-200.

39. *Ibid.*, V, i, 130-134.

40. Dover Wilson, *The Essential Shakespeare* (Cambridge, England: University Press, 1948), p. 144.

41. *The Tempest*, IV, i, 148-158.

42. James 4:14 (American Revised Version, 1900).

43. 2 Peter 3:10.

44. John 11:11.

45. Neilson, *op. cit.*, p. 166.

46. Bradley, *op. cit.*, pp. 328-330.

47. *The Tempest*, I, ii, 397-402.

48. Frank Kermode, Introduction to *The Tempest* in the Arden ed. *Works of William Shakespeare* (London: Methuen & Co., 1958). pp. xxxviiiff.

49. Neilson, *op. cit.*, pp. 76-78.

50. Knight, *op. cit.*, p. 18.

51. Plato, *The Collected Dialogues of Plato*, ed. by Edith Hamilton and Huntington Cairns (New York: Bollingen Foundation, 1961) p. 499.

52. *Ibid.*, p. 1193.

53. Romans 7.

54. *The Tempest*, I, ii, 310-313.

55. Neilson, *op. cit.*, p. 79.

56. *The Tempest*, V, i, 344-362.

57. Robert Speight, *Nature in Shakespearean Tragedy*, (London: Hollis & Carter, 1955), pp. 156ff.

58. *The Tempest*, IV, i, 188-192.

59. *Ibid.*, V, Epilogue, 17-20.

60. Walter Clyde Curry, *Shakespeare's Philosophical Patterns* (Baton Rouge: Louisiana State University Press, 1937), p. 196.

61. *The Tempest*, V, i, 181-184.

INDEX